THE
ROMANTIC LIFE OF SHELLEY
AND THE SEQUEL

McQueen sc.

Percy Bysshe Shelley
from a Crayon drawing in the Bodleian Library

THE
ROMANTIC LIFE OF SHELLEY
AND THE SEQUEL

BY

FRANCIS GRIBBLE

AUTHOR OF

"GEORGE SAND AND HER LOVERS" ETC.

HASKELL HOUSE PUBLISHERS Ltd.

Publishers of Scarce Scholarly Books

NEW YORK. N. Y. 10012

1972

HASKELL HOUSE PUBLISHERS Ltd.

Publishers of Scarce Scholarly Books

280 LAFAYETTE STREET

NEW YORK. N. Y. 10012

Library of Congress Cataloging in Publication Data

Gribble, Francis Henry, 1862-1946.
  The romantic life of Shelley and the sequel.

  Reprint of the 1911 ed.
  1. Shelley, Percy Bysshe, 1792-1822--Relationship
with women. 2. Shelley, Mary Wollstonecraft (Godwin)
1797-1851. I. Title.
PR5432.G7 **1973**   821'.7 [B]   72-3624
ISBN 0-8383-1566-6

PREFACE

THERE is one charge which every biographer of Shelley must be prepared to face. A certain number—though it may be only a small number —of critics will infallibly arise and reprove him, with solemnity, for indulging in " chatter about Harriet." It is a way, like another, of asserting moral and intellectual superiority; but it may itself be made the object of criticism. For no biographer plunges into " chatter about Harriet " out of sheer wantonness. The purpose of such chatter is to enable, first the writer, and then the reader, to " see Shelley plain."

Any man who chooses may say, of course, that he does not want to see Shelley plain; and that, equally of course, is final. One can no more argue with such a man than one can discuss the intricacies of arithmetic with the man who proclaims that he does not care whether two and two make three or four or five. He is entitled to his indifference, and the road is clear for him to pass by on the other side. But if one does wish to see Shelley plain—if one would

like to know him as one knows the most intimate
of one's friends—then it is imperative that the
chatter about Harriet should be sifted. Sainte-
Beuve said so; and few critics deny the weight
of Sainte-Beuve's authority.

Nor does the repetition of such chatter imply
the least disparagement of Shelley as a man or
a poet. The idea that an interest in Shelley's
relations with Harriet (and with Mary, and
Emily, and the two Janes) is incompatible
with an enthusiastic appreciation of the " Prometheus," the " Cenci," and the " Epipsychidion,"
is the fixed notion of a few pompous people;
but it should be shaken out of them. The men
who knew Shelley best, and loved and admired
him most, did not share it. Hogg speaks of
Shelley as his " incomparable friend "; Medwin
thought him the greatest poet of his time;
Trelawny worshipped him almost as a god. Yet
Hogg chatters about Harriet in the most delightful vein of comedy; and Medwin discusses
Emily without setting any bridle on his tongue;
and Trelawny is very anxious that the world
should see Mary as she really was, in order that
it may judge Shelley justly.

The books of these writers—who, in spite of
their inaccuracies, at least knew their man—
are still the chief sources from which the material
for the picture must be sought; but there are

other sources which have recently been made available,—a good many sources, indeed, which were not opened up until after the publication of Professor Dowden's important work.

Harriet Shelley's Letters to Mrs. Nugent, freely quoted in these pages, are the chief of them. They give us Harriet's own view of the circumstances of her separation from her husband; and another, and very interesting, view of that grave event is contained in a letter, also given in these pages, written by Charles Clairmont to Francis Place, and included in a collection of autographs recently acquired by the manuscript department of the British Museum. On the vexed question of Shelley's relations with Jane Clairmont, fresh light is thrown by the "Talks with Jane Clairmont," published by Mr. William Graham in his *Last Links with Byron, Shelley, and Keats*; by some of the letters from Jane Clairmont to Byron, published in Mr. Prothero's edition of Byron's works; and by some passages in Trelawny's Letters recently published by Mr. Buxton Forman. The queer story of the attempt on Shelley's life at Tanyrallt is elucidated by a recent contributor to the *Century Magazine*; and the *Memoirs of a Highland Lady*, who was on a visit to the Master of University College, Oxford, when Shelley was an undergraduate, supplements Hogg's narrative in some particulars, and invites a revision of our estimate of that catastrophe.

Finally, the Sequel is new. The story there told of the courtship of Mary Shelley by the author of " Home, Sweet Home," and of Mary Shelley's affectionate regard for Washington Irving, is based upon a correspondence only discovered, in circumstances to be related, a few years ago, and, as yet, only privately printed by the Boston Bibliophile Society.

CONTENTS

CONTENTS

THE SEQUEL

LIST OF ILLUSTRATIONS

THF

ROMANTIC LIFE OF SHELLEY

CHAPTER I

THE COUNTY FAMILY

THE genius of Shelley is, as it were, a rare
and radiant flower found blossoming, by some
inexplicable accident, on the genealogical tree
of an obscure but wealthy county family.

There is just one kind of genius which the
head of such a family may be relied upon to
understand and foster : the genius which consists in the possession of ordinary talents raised
to a high power. For the man of genius who
differs from the average man, not in kind, but
only in degree, the path, if he be born into a
county family, is made very smooth. He takes
orders, or is called to the bar, or enters Parliament; he grows up, amid sympathetic applause,.
to be a bishop, or a judge of the High Court,
or a Minister of the Crown.

If Shelley had entertained any one of these
ambitions, he would almost certainly have
achieved it. He was quite clever enough; and
his father and grandfather had £20,000 a year
to spend in pushing his fortunes. His advantages, in that respect, were greater than those

of the most brilliant of the boys whose names one finds grouped with his in an old list of the Upper Fifth at Eton : Bishop Sumner and Sir John Taylor Coleridge. He might have succeeded in life as conspicuously as they did if, like them, he had been satisfied to take the wisdom of his forefathers for granted and walk in the way prescribed for him. " Instead of which," he wrote *The Necessity of Atheism ;* and his county family could not have been more horrified if he had gone about stealing ducks.

One must not blame them overmuch, however, or pretend to think that Shelley's genius would have been appraised more justly in a suburb or a provincial town. There are quite as many prejudices in semi-detached villas as in country houses; and the feeling that everybody ought to be, alike in word and deed, exactly like everybody else, is one of the most deeply-rooted instincts of human nature. Cannibals share that sentiment with County Magistrates; devil-worshippers with dignitaries of the Church. They are at one as to the necessity of conforming, and differ only as to the ideal to which it is proper to conform; the ears of the reformer being nailed to the pump for precisely the same reason for which the bones of the missionary are thrown into the stockpot.

On the whole, therefore, Shelley gained more than he lost by membership of a county family. He gained, at any rate, a good education and good manners,—the power to conciliate and

14

charm. Any society to which he might have belonged would have esteemed him a rebel, and treated him accordingly,—bullied him, and attempted to suppress him. But any society to which he might have belonged would also have set its mark on him in the impressionable years; and the mark of Field Place, Eton, and Oxford is, at any rate, more pleasing than that of the suburb, the Commercial Academy, and the counting-house.

One is sensible of this imprint of the country-house, the public school, and the University, from the beginning to the end of Shelley's career. One is specially sensible of it when one finds him saying and doing the outrageous things which conflict most strikingly with public school and University traditions. Even when he is outrageous he is never uncouth. He never gives the impression, as so many rebels, reformers and original thinkers do, of a strange fowl which has strayed into the wrong farmyard by mistake. He revolts with the air of one who is sure of himself socially as well as intellectually, and also with a certain underlying sweet reasonableness which dissolves rancour and disarms hostility.

Not, of course, all hostility. The savage Cordy Jeaffreson, for one, has written of Shelley in the tone of a ruffled house-wife scolding a maid-of-all-work. The fastidious Matthew Arnold, for another, has written of him as of some obnoxious insect picked up reluctantly with a pair of tongs. But the men who knew him loved him. Byron, who praised few of his contemporaries, praised him without reserve; Trelawny's affection touched the point of hero-worship; and the magic of his personality still, after the lapse of years, makes fresh friends for him across the ages.

Perhaps, however, we may justly say that Shelley's friends and enemies have this in common : that they both tend to take his youthful ebullitions a shade too seriously. The latter give one the impression of brawny blacksmiths smashing a butterfly with sledge-hammers; the former are prone to cut the figure of bearded men sitting, in exaggerated humility, at the feet of a boy-preacher; neither gesture is quite compatible with a true sense of humour or of the fitness of things.

The essential fact which Shelley's biographer must bear in mind is that he has not a complete, but only a truncated life to write about : a life cut short before it could draw its own moral as lives have a way of doing. In the survey of a life extending to the normal span, the things said and done before the age of thirty count, as a rule, for very little,—and Shelley died at twenty-nine. The case is hardly one, therefore, for approval or disapproval,—or even for agreement or disagreement. It will suffice, in the main, to view the fragment of life before us as a spectacle,—a fragment of a tragi-comedy which leaves off instead of ending.

THE COUNTY FAMILY

It is a spectacle of a boy fumbling with life, and making experiments with it,—beginning to play the game of life with deadly earnestness, long before he has any adequate knowledge of the rules. Most boys do that to some extent; but Shelley did it in an exceptionally spectacular and striking way, scornfully refusing to take the rules of the game on trust from his elders, but trying to deduce them from first principles by means of pure reason; resolved to learn what there was to be learnt about the game from his own and not from other people's experience.

His experiments brought him adventures,—not one adventure only, but a vivid series of adventures. He faced the adventures—he went out to look for them, indeed—with the courage of his convictions, and the vitality of his years. He has been charged with a want of humour—an " inhuman want of humour," according to Matthew Arnold; but what of that ? Don Quixote also lacked humour, and so did the Knights of the Round Table; and yet they are among the most treasured figures of romance. Shelley took life pretty much in their temper, inspired by their passion for " riding about " as well as for " redressing human wrong."

Humour would doubtless have come to him later if he had lived; but, in the years of experiment, there was neither room nor time for humour. Experiment spelt mistake; and every mistake suggested a fresh experiment; and each fresh experiment brought a fresh adventure.

THE ROMANTIC LIFE OF SHELLEY

The Human Comedy, after all, is always more visible to the spectator than to the player, who is by no means called upon to be amused by the entertainment which he provides; and that consideration shall assign the limits of the present biographer's task.

He hopes not to be censorious after the manner of the Philistines. He hopes also to put aside the idea that Shelley should be regarded as the founder of the philosophy of all those who agree with his opinions. His quest is rather for Romance, and for the Human Comedy which runs through Romance, giving it sometimes, it may be, a sub-acid flavour; and having thus announced his programme, he may hark back to that genealogical tree, from the shade of which he wandered to make these introductory remarks.

CHAPTER II

ANCESTORS AND PARENTS

SHELLEYS begin to be heard of soon after the Norman conquest, and continue to be heard of from time to time through the Middle Ages. A Sir Thomas Shelley was Ambassador to Spain in the reign of John; and another Shelley was Judge of the Common Pleas in the reign of Henry VIII. Perhaps one may best give the measure of the importance of the Shelleys of those days, by saying that they were just important enough to have to forfeit their heads if they took the losing side in civil strife. Sir William Shelley, the Ambassador's brother, lost his head for " endeavouring to set up Richard II "; and it is from him that Percy Bysshe Shelley's descent is traced in Berry's *County Genealogies : Sussex.*

This younger branch of the house, however, fell upon comparatively evil days. Their sovereigns lost the habit of knighting them, and they were in a fair way to decline from the state of squires to that of yeomen, when first Timothy Shelley (the poet's great-grandfather) and then Bysshe Shelley (his grandfather) restored the fortunes of the family by means of wealthy marriages and political activities.

The case of Timothy Shelley, indeed, was like that of Saul, who sought his father's asses and found a kingdom. He went to America to practise as a doctor—a " quack doctor," according to Medwin, but we need not insist—and married a wealthy widow of the appropriate name of Plum : one of the earliest recorded examples of those transatlantic marriages which have brought American dollars across the ocean to replenish European coffers. Returning to England at an unknown date, he became the squire of Fen Place, Warnham, where he died in 1770, leaving two sons, John and Bysshe. John, who married the daughter of William White of Horsham, lived at Field Place, where he died, childless, in 1790. Of Bysshe there is more to be said.

It had been stated that Bysshe Shelley, like his father, practised medicine, and was, for a time, in partnership with James Graham, the mesmerist in whose establishment Nelson's Lady Hamilton (then Emma Harte) sustained the rôle which her biographers have described. Be that as it may, however, he cannot have practised long; for he was hardly more than thirty when he began his successful matrimonial career. He was a man, apparently, who combined a keen eye for romance with an equally keen eye for the main chance. He married twice; he eloped with each of his two wives; and each of them was a great heiress. The first wife was Mary Catherine Michell, only child and

heiress of the Reverend Theodore Michell of
Horsham; the second was Elizabeth Jane Sidney
Perry, only daughter and heiress of William
Perry of Turvil Park, Bucks, Wormington,
Gloucestershire, and Penshurst, Kent.

Having thus enriched himself, Bysshe Shelley
took an interest in politics on the Whig side.
Political services rendered to the Duke of Norfolk
—the Duke who is chiefly famous as the heaviest
drinker of his age, with the single exception of
the father of Chateaubriand's Charlotte Ives [1]—
were rewarded with a baronetcy by the Whig
Administration of 1806; but his habits were
queer, and his old age was misanthropic. He
was a miser of a rare kind : a miser of a fine
presence and a certain stately grace, who spent
£80,000 in building, but lived, a lonely widower,
in a cottage, with only one servant to wait on
him, and, if we may trust Medwin, " used to
frequent daily the tap-room of one of the low
inns in Horsham, and there drank with some of
the lowest citizens." Another authority states
that he did not drink with the company, but
only argued with them; but that is a minor
detail of little moment even to teetotallers.

By his second marriage Sir Bysshe Shelley
was the ancestor of Baron de Lisle and Dudley;
but the fortunes of his second family are outside
the scope of this work. The children of the

[1] The Duke and Mr. Ives once drank against each other
for a wager. The parson drank The Duke under the table,
and then rang for a tumbler of brandy and water,—"hot
and strong."

21

first marriage were Hellen, who married Robert
Parker of Maidstone, Mary Catherine, who died
unmarried in 1784, and Timothy, born in 1753,
who married in 1791, Elizabeth, daughter of
Charles Pilfold, of Effingham, in Surrey,—a
woman of great beauty, as Romney's portrait
of her attests. Timothy Shelley and his wife
lived at Field Place, and there Percy Bysshe
Shelley was born on August 4, 1792,—the eldest
of a family of seven, of whom two died in infancy, but Elizabeth, Hellen, Mary, and Margaret
survived.

That is enough of genealogy for the present;
but, as the story of Shelley's life begins as the
story of a boy's revolt against his parent's fixed
ideas, Medwin's thumb-nail sketch of Timothy
Shelley must be given. Inaccurate as he is on
many points, Medwin may be trusted here, for
he knew Sir Timothy fairly well. He tells us
how Sir Bysshe, for all his miserliness, gave his
son a good education, sending him to University
College, Oxford, and allowing him to take the
Grand Tour; but he continues :—

" He was one of those travellers who, with so
much waste of time, travel for the sake of saying
they have travelled; and after making the circuit
of Europe, return home, knowing no more of
the countries they have visited than the trunks
attached to their carriages. All, indeed, that
he did bring back with him was a smattering of
French, and a bad picture of an eruption of

Vesuvius, if we except a certain *air*, miscalled that of the old school, which he could put off and on as occasion served.

" He was a disciple of Chesterfield and La Rochefoucauld, reducing all politeness to forms, and moral virtue to expediency; as an instance of which he once told his son, Percy Bysshe, in my presence, that he would provide for as many natural children as he chose to get, but that he would never forgive his making a *mésalliance*."

It is a convincing picture, made more convincing by the further statement that Timothy Shelley " occasionally went to the parish church," but required his servants to do so regularly. One infers from it an empty-headed, muddle-headed man, generally lax in practice but prone to be obstinate in theory; a man who confused his ideals and saw only a blurred line dividing the worship of God from the worship of Mammon; a man who would tolerate a good deal if " taken the right way," but would bring all the intolerance of stupidity to bear upon an attempt to put him in the wrong by defending an unusual course with arguments which he did not see his way to answer. His portrait, it may be added, supports that estimate of him. It is the portrait of a very handsome man, but also of a very silly man, sure to be baffled by new ideas, or even by old ideas if presented to him in a new shape. He might

23

have done well, and gone to his grave universally respected if only he could have passed through life without ever having to cope with a moral or intellectual emergency. Unfortunately for his reputation, the unexpected happened; and he first lost his temper, and then sulked—a ludicrously cantankerous figure.

Nor was his wife much more fit to be the mother than he to be the father of a boy of precocious and eccentric genius. "Mild and tolerant, yet narrow-minded," was her son's ultimate verdict on her. Her fixed ideas were not the same as her husband's; but they were equally fixed, and equally foolish,—the foolish fixed ideas which prevailed in the county society of the period. The noblest work of God, in her opinion, was the successful sportsman. She thought that, in the circles in which she moved, a man's worth should be measured by the contents of his game-bag; and she had a difficulty in applying any more subtle test. She scolded her son and drove him to the pursuit of fish and birds; he bribed the game-keeper to catch the fish and shoot the birds for him, while he lay under a tree with a book.

It would be absurd, however, to base a theory of an unhappy childhood on such an incident as that. The conflict between the boy's view that it was better to dream than to shoot, and the mother's view that dreaming was all nonsense and shooting the one thing needful, may be read as symbolical of graver conflicts to follow; but it meant little at the time. If there was a general

24

ANCESTORS AND PARENTS

lack of sympathy for Shelley at Field Place,
there was no particular oppression. On the
whole he was free to go his own way and dream
his own dreams, if he insisted; the dreams being
of nothing more disturbing to the Philistine
mind than ghosts, fairies, secret chambers, and
haunted ruins. War with the world—the painful
sense of being very different from other people
in a society which held it to be the whole duty
of man to resemble other men—was not to begin
until he was sent to school. But then, to quote
the familiar lines from the Dedication of " Laon
and Cythna " :—

> Thoughts of great deeds were mine, dear
> Friend, when first
> The clouds which wrap this world from youth
> did pass.
> I do remember well the hour which burst
> My spirit's sleep : a fresh May-dawn it was,
> When I walked forth upon the glittering grass,
> And wept, I knew not why ; until there rose
> From the near school-room, voices that alas !
> Were but one echo from a world of woes—
> The harsh and grating strife of tyrants and of foes.
>
> And then I clasped my hands and looked
> around—
> But none was near to mock my streaming
> eyes,
> Which poured their warm drops on the sunny
> ground—

So without shame, I spake :—" I will be wise,
And just, and free, and mild, if in me lies
Such power, for I grow weary to behold
The selfish and the strong still tyrannise
Without reproach or check." I then con-
trouled
My tears, my heart grew calm, and I was meek
and bold.

And from that hour did I with earnest thought
Heap knowledge from forbidden mines of lore,
Yet nothing that my tyrants knew or taught
I cared to learn, but from that secret store
Wrought linked armour for my soul, before
It might walk forth to war among mankind ;
Thus power and hope were strengthened more
and more
Within me, till there came upon my mind
A sense of loneliness, a thirst with which I pined.

That is the poet's memory-picture of his
school-days. He sees the school as the world
in miniature, and himself attacked and persecuted by the world—misunderstood, hunted,
hounded, and mobbed—yet guarding his spirit
unbroken, and resolving, not only to resist, but,
in the end, to overcome the world. One does
not, of course, expect the prose truth to correspond, in every detail, to the poetical fancy;
but the resemblance is nevertheless very close,
as we shall see when we dig up and array the
testimony of school-fellows.

26

CHAPTER III

THE ACADEMY FOR YOUNG GENTLEMEN

SHELLEY'S first school, after he had passed through the hands of a private tutor—a Mr. Edwards of Warnham—was Dr. Greenlaw's Academy for Young Gentlemen, at Sion House, Isleworth. Three of his school-fellows have recorded their recollections of him : his cousin and biographer, Tom Medwin, Sir John Rennie, the engineer who built Waterloo Bridge, and a Mr. Gellibrand, who lived to be ninety-two, and to tell his story to Mr. Birrell, who communicated it to the *Athenaeum* on his informant's death in 1884.

Mr. Gellibrand's principal recollection was that Shelley once wrote a set of Latin verses for him, but inserted a final line—*Hos ego versiculos scripsi, sed non ego feci*—which raised doubts as to their authorship, with the result that Dr. Greenlaw caned Mr. Gellibrand, and Mr. Gellibrand punched Shelley's head. The only further detail is a picture of Shelley as " like a girl in boys' clothes, fighting with open hands, and rolling on the floor when flogged, not from the pain, but from a sense of indignity."

Sir John Rennie's brief note, in his Autobiography, is as follows :—

27

" His imagination was always roving upon
something romantic and extraordinary, such as
spirits, fairies, fighting, etc., and he not un-
frequently astonished his school-fellows by blow-
ing up the boundary palings of the playground
with gunpowder, also the lid of his desk in the
middle of school-time, to the great surprise of
Dr. Greenlaw himself and the whole school. In
fact at times he was considered to be almost
upon the borders of insanity; yet, with all this,
when treated with kindness, he was very amiable,
high-spirited, and generous."

Medwin tells us rather more. He pictures the
head-master as a " choleric man, of a sanguinary
complexion, in a green old age, not wanting in
good qualities, but very capricious in his temper,
which, good or bad, was influenced by the daily
occurrences of a domestic life, not the most
harmonious, and of which his face was the
barometer, and his hand the index." He says
that the boys were " mostly the sons of London
shopkeepers, of rude habits and coarse manners,"
who " made game " of Shelley's " girlishness "
and despised him because he was not " one of
them," and did not care to " enter into their
sports, to wrangle, or fight; " and he thus
pictures the scene of the new boy's arrival :—

" All tormented him with questionings. There
was no end to their mockery, when they found
that he was ignorant of peg-top, or marbles, or
28

leap-frog, or hopscotch, much more of fives and cricket. One wanted him to spar, another to run a race with him. He was a tyro in both these accomplishments, and the only welcome of the Neophyte was a general shout of derision. To all these impertinences he made no reply, but, with a look of disdain written in his countenance, turned his back on his new associates, and, when he was alone, found relief in tears."

A further picture, equally characteristic, is this :—

" He passed among his school-fellows as a strange and unsocial being, for when a holiday relieved us from our tasks, and the other boys were engaged in such sports as the narrow limits of our prison-court allowed, Shelley, who entered into none of them, would pace backwards and forwards—I think I see him now—along the southern wall, indulging in various vague and undefined ideas, the chaotic elements, if I may say so, of what afterwards produced so beautiful a world."

Furious Philistines, of the school of Cordy Jeaffreson, quote statements of that sort, and infer that Shelley was a " muff." Their ideal boy is Tom Brown, the wooden-headed policeman of a young society, rendering invaluable service to his generation by licking the Arthurs of his little world into shape, clapping stoppers on their individualities, and persuading them to model themselves on our admirable average men. They cannot see, any more than Tom Hughes himself could see, that the story of the moulding of Arthur into a sort of refined and etherealized Tom Brown, is one of the most pathetic things in literature,—that Arthur was worthy of better things, just as his prototype, Dean Stanley, was worthy of a better fate than to become a courtier theologian whose occasional bursts of broad-minded tolerance never quite prevented his intellect from letting " I dare not " wait upon " I would."

Shelley, however, though he differed widely from Tom Brown, and hardly less widely from Arthur (whose conversion to cricket is presented to us as an event of hardly less world-shaking significance than Constantine's conversion to Christianity), was very far from a " muff." He lacked neither physical nor moral courage, and he had all the high-spirited vitality which belongs to boyhood. One sees that from the stories just related of his attempts to blow up his desk and blow down the palings; and, in truth, he chiefly differed from other boys in the possession of certain precocious sentiments and curiosities.

His view of flogging—that the pain was nothing to the degradation—is just the view that grown men might be relied upon to express if it were proposed so to punish them for exceeding the speed-limit in their motors. His view of games was approximately Swift's view,—that "games are the recreations of people who do not think." The world, he felt, was so "full of a number of things" that it was absurd to waste time on such trivialities as pegtops and marbles. Elderly gentlemen might appropriately play with marbles or pegtops (just as elderly gentlemen nowadays play golf), in order to divert their minds from anxiety as to the price of stocks and shares; but why should a boy do so when life lay like a fairy land, beginning at his door, and inviting him to explore it? Gunpowder, electricity, burning-glasses, microscopes, and " penny dreadfuls,"—all these things appealed to Shelley's imagination as marbles and pegtops did not; and, if neither burning-glasses nor penny dreadfuls were to hand, he would far rather dream than play.

So he argued with himself; but it would have been idle for him to argue thus with his associates. They had their own standards, and would not judge him by any other. It was everybody's business to be exactly like everybody else; and the new boy must conform or be harried. Shelley did not conform, and was harried, as a cat might be by a pack of hounds, until Sion House became, as Medwin says, " a perfect hell to him." That is practically all that there is to be said about his life at Sion House; and the same thing will have to be said over again, albeit with certain qualifications, when we follow him to Eton, where

31

he was sent in 1804,—Goodall being then head-master, and the more famous Keate the master of the Lower School in which he was placed.

The standards of Eton, of course, differed from those of Sion House. The doctrine that everybody must try to be exactly like every-body else ordained conformity with a somewhat different code; and it was a doctrine which a boy of character could overcome, as he rose in the school, winning applause in the act of over-coming it. The rebel, that is to say, against the tyranny of the mob might ultimately rise to distinction as a rebel against the authority of masters; and that, in so far as one can sum the matter up in a sentence, is what Shelley did. Like Byron at Harrow, he " was a most unpopular boy but *led* latterly; " like Byron, too, he was, at one time, within an ace of being expelled; like Byron, finally, he was called an " atheist," though he did not, like Byron, regard the epithet as offensive.

But this is to anticipate. The story of Shelley's Eton days requires a chapter to itself.

CHAPTER IV

ETON

THE best known of the Eton stories about Shelley is the story of his fight, related by Captain Gronow :—

" It was announced one morning that Shelley, the future poet, had actually accepted wager of battle from Sir Thomas Styles. Whether he had received an insult, and that vast disparity in size gave him confidence, or that, over-full of the war-like descriptions of Homer's heroes, he was fired to imitate their exploits against some one or other, remains a secret. Meet, however, they did, after twelve, in the playing-fields. The usual preliminaries were arranged—a ring was formed, seconds and bottle-holders were all in readiness, and the combatants stood face to face. The tall lank figure of the poet towered above the diminutive thick-set little baronet by nearly a head and shoulders. In the first round no mischief was done; Sir Thomas seemed to be feeling his way, being naturally desirous of ascertaining what his gigantic adversary was made of; and Shelley, though brandishing his long arms, had evidently no idea of their use in a pugilistic point of view. After a certain amount

c

of sparring without effect, the combatants were invited by their seconds to take breath. The baronet did not hesitate to accept the offer to sit upon the knee of his second; but Shelley disdainfully declined to rest, and, calculating upon finishing the fight in a single blow, stalked round the ring, looking defiance at his little adversary.

" Time was called, and the battle was renewed in earnest. The baronet, somewhat cautious, planted his first blow upon the chest of Shelley, who did not appear to relish it. However, though not a proficient in the art of self-defence he nevertheless went in, and knocked the little baronet off his legs, who lay sprawling upon the grass more dead than alive. Shelley's confidence increased; he stalked round the ring as before, and spouted one of the defiant addresses usual with Homer's heroes when about to commence a single combat; the young poet, being a first-rate classical scholar, actually delivered the speech in the original Greek, to the no small amusement of the boys. In the second and last round, Styles went to work like a first-rate artist, and after slighter blows, delivered what is called in the prize-ring " a heavy slogger " on Shelley's bread-basket; this seemed positively to electrify the bard, for, I blush to say, he broke through the ring, and took to his heels with a speed that defied pursuit. His seconds, backers, and all who had witnessed the fight, joined in full cry after him, but he outran them all, and got safe to the house of his tutor, Mr. Bethel."

The story was too dramatic to be left untold; but it is obviously untrue, and illustrates nothing except the mythopœic instinct of schoolboys. If any reader of these pages imagines that the effect of a so-called " slogger " in the so-called " bread-basket " is to increase the velocity and general activity of the recipient, such a one should offer his own bread-basket to a friend (or, better still, to an enemy) for experiment, and make a careful note of the result. That said, we may pass on to better attested stories concerning the bullying of Shelley.

Dr. Hawtrey, who, when Shelley was a small boy, was in one of the higher forms, and who grew up to succeed Keate (who had succeeded Goodall) in the head-mastership of Eton, may be our first, and principal witness.

" I remember his sending for me one evening " (writes Arthur Duke Coleridge in his *Eton in the 'Forties*), " to invoke my authority as a sixth-form boy on behalf of a lad whose notorious oddity and awkwardness seemed to mark him out as a butt for all professional bullies. ' They used to call Shelley *mad Shelley*,' he said. ' My belief is that what he had to endure at Eton made him a perfect devil.' "

A doctrine developed by Hawtrey in a sermon

preached in the chapel, and afterwards privately
printed, wherein he first spoke of the harm
which might be done by "wanton abuse of
authority," and then proceeded to denounce the
errors belonging to "mere strength of body,"
which are "more oppressive, more frequent, and
always more mortifying to the sufferer." "The
objects of such kind of ill-usage," he said, "are
not those over whom there is any lawful or conventional right; they are the weak, the timid,
the eccentric, and the unsociable." The effect
of such treatment, he continued, upon a sensitive mind was often to "waste and devour it,"
until its victims fell into the error "of madly
imagining that Christianity itself is a fable
because those who call themselves Christians
have acted, in pure recklessness, as if they were
heathens." And then followed the instances :—

"Two [1] such I knew in other days—one of
them when I was too young to feel and understand what I *do* understand now. Both of them
are long since gone to their account. The
talents of the first, however abused, earned for
him a reputation which will probably not perish
while one language shall be spoken. But his
life here was miserable from this kind of injustice, and if his mind took a bias leading him
to error—which the Almighty may forgive; for
He is all merciful, and makes allowance for His

[1] The other was T. S. Walker, a brilliant classical scholar,
who died young.

creatures which we in our self-approving severity seldom make—they who remember those days well know how that mind was tortured, and how much the wantonness of persecution contributed to pervert its really noble and amiable qualities."

The details of the persecution thus rhetorically sketched are not very easy to get at, but not very difficult to imagine. The best attested fact is that Shelley refused to fag for Henry Matthews, the subsequent author of *The Diary of an Invalid*; and the fate of rebels of that order, though various, is uniformly painful. For the rest we hear of muddy footballs being kicked at Shelley in the corridors; of his books, or whatever he carried, being knocked out of his hands; of a mob surrounding him, bawling his name, and pointing derisive fingers at him : mere trifles, no doubt, to the harder natures, and not easily represented, in cold print, as serious, but infinitely tormenting to the weak, and sensitive, and self-conscious, giving them the impression that they are alone in a lonely world, and always will be—poor Pariahs in the midst of rough and insolent Brahmins.

" I have seen him " (writes one of the witnesses) " surrounded, hooted, baited like a maddened bull, and, at this distance of time, I seem to hear ringing in my ears the cry which Shelley was wont to utter in his paroxysm of revengeful anger."

The fury to which he was goaded is also said to have "made his eyes flash like a tiger's, his cheeks grow pale as death, his limbs quiver;" and there is a story of his having, in one fit of passion, pinned one of his persecutor's hands to a desk with a fork or a pen-knife. It is quite likely that he tried to do something of the sort, but very unlikely that he actually did it; and the one thing really certain is that, whereas bullying broke the spirit of T. S. Walker, it did not break Shelley's spirit. The ordeal lasted for a year or two; but he lived through it, conquered his right to unmolested eccentricity, and so reached the stage at which Hawtrey describes him as having been " a perfect devil."

Allowance must be made here, however, for clerical rhetoric and the pedagogic point of view. Hawtrey was an excellent man—a sympathetic schoolmaster, and a tolerant divine; but still he was both divine and schoolmaster, and consequently committed to certain fixed opinions with regard alike to theological speculation and the sinfulness of little sins. He, no less than the boys, would have preferred Shelley to be like other people, though he disapproved of the boys' methods of compelling him to be so; and though he was too fair-minded—one may even say too much of a gentleman—to denounce him as an enemy of the human race, he could not help weeping over him as a backslider. Whether the case for tears would have stood the test of cross-examination is another matter; and

Hawtrey certainly could have been confronted with witnesses who gave very different evidence.

" I loved Shelley," says one of them, " for his kindliness and affectionate ways." " I always liked him," says another; " he was such a good, generous, open-hearted fellow; " while Canon Harvey, who fagged for him (or was supposed to do so), spoke of him as a most kind and considerate fag-master. There is clearly no trace of the " perfect devil " in these depositions. The epithet, if founded on fact at all, must be based upon breaches of discipline and defiance of authority; so we will enumerate, and tabulate, as far as the records permit, the incidents which Hawtrey might have cited in support of his allegation :—

1. Shelley hid a savage bull-dog in the desk of Dr. Keate.

2. Shelley pursued the college cook with a roasting spit.

3. Shelley stood up and cursed King George III.

4. Shelley set alight to a tree in the college grounds with a burning-glass.

5. Shelley procured an electric battery, and lured his tutor into laying hands on it unawares, and so receiving an electric shock.

6. Shelley, when summoned to his tutor's rooms to be reprimanded, spilt corrosive acid on the carpet.

That is all that one can rake together from all

the available sources. It amounts, after all, to very little; and there is no reason to doubt that each act received, at the time, the punishment which it seemed to call for. The secretion of the bull-dog in Keate's desk, for instance, strikes one as no worse a misdemeanour (though a more humorous one) than that of Thring, the future head-master of Uppingham, who tied a string to Hawtrey's own bell-rope, and rang it repeatedly and surreptitiously, with the result that the class was interrupted, every five minutes or so, by the arrival of Hawtrey's servant to inquire what was wanted; and if Shelley's offences were no more grave than Thring's, then " perfect devil " is as unfit an epithet for the one offender as for the other.

Nor is there a word of truth in Cordy Jeaffreson's statement that Shelley left Eton in disgrace in consequence of this, or some other, act of insubordination. His own letters show that he was still at Eton in the term immediately preceding that in which he went into residence at Oxford; and though it is doubtless true that his behaviour was of an embarrassing ebullience, it is equally true that he did his work creditably, being specially remarked for his proficiency in Latin verse, and played a proper part on ceremonial occasions, such as speech-day and Montem, while, at the same time, cultivating intellectual interests outside the classical curriculum. There is a fancy picture of him by Moultrie, who came to Eton while his memory was still green there, as " a stripling, pale and lustrous eyed " :—

> *Small sympathy he owned or felt, I ween,*
> *With sports or pastimes of his young compeers,*
> *Nor mingling in their studies oft was seen,*
> *Nor shared their joys or sorrows, hopes or*
> *   fears :*
> *Pensive he was and grave beyond his years,*
> *And happiest seemed when in some shady*
> *   nook*
> *(His wild sad eyes suffused with silent tears),*
> *O'er some mysterious and forbidden book*
> *He pored until his frame with strong emotion shook.*

The " forbidden book," according to Medwin, was generally a handbook of chemistry. He quotes a note to himself from Shelley's father in which he writes : " I have returned the book on chemistry, as it is a forbidden thing at Eton." It may just as well, however, have been Godwin's *Political Justice*, which Shelley is believed to have read at Eton (and which Eton masters would probably have regarded as an improper book for Eton boys to possess); or it may have been one of those " penny dreadfuls," as we should call them, through which Shelley had, already, at Sion House, approached the literature of the imagination. All the lines of thought opened up by all the books that came into his hands seem, at this stage, to have attracted him equally in turn.

He was a scholar, of course,—a clever boy at Eton becomes a scholar as inevitably as a child picks up a foreign language from a foreign nurse. Beyond that, however, it would have been impossible to predict what " particular kind of man," as Alfred de Musset puts it, he was likely to become. There was equal promise in his many-sided precocity of a grave and earnest political philosopher of the style of John Stuart Mill; of a brilliant scientific showman of the calibre of Professor Pepper; of a purveyor of stories of mystery and crime of the school of Messrs. Heath Hosken and William Le Queux. He was destined, in fact, for greater accomplishments than even the greatest of these; but it was in the class of Messrs. Le Queux and Heath Hosken that he first competed by writing and publishing *Zastrozzi*.

One need not trouble to say anything about *Zastrozzi*, except that it was obviously inspired by the writings of " Monk " Lewis and Mrs. Radcliffe; but two of Shelley's letters about it are worth quoting. The first is to Messrs. Longman, to whom he writes :—

" My object in writing it was not pecuniary, as I am independent, being the heir of a gentleman of large fortune in the county of Sussex, and prosecuting my studies as an Oppidan at Eton; from the many leisure hours I have, I have taken an opportunity of indulging my favourite propensity in writing. Should it produce any pecuniary advantages, so much the better for me ; I do not expect it."

The second letter is to Edward Fergus Graham, a *protégé* of Timothy Shelley, then living in London, and studying music at Timothy Shelley's expense. To him Shelley writes :—

" We will all go in a posse to the bookseller's in Mr. Grove's barouche and four.—Show them that we are no Grub Street garetteers. . . .

" We will not be cheated again—let us come over Jock, for if he will not give me a devil of a price for my Poem, and at least £60 for my new Romance in three Volumes, the dog shall not have them.

" *Pouch* the reviewers—£10 will be sufficient I should suppose, and that I can with the greatest ease repay when we meet at Passion Week. Send the reviews in which *Zastrozzi* is mentioned to Field Place, the *British Review* is the hardest, let that be pouched well.—My note of hand if for any larger sum is quite at your service, as it is of consequence in fiction to establish your name as high as you can in the literary lists."

The " Jock " here mentioned is presumably J. Robinson, who, for whatever reason, published *Zastrozzi* instead of Messrs. Longman. His school-fellow, Mr. Packe, says that he received £40 for it, and that " with part of the proceeds he gave a most magnificent banquet to eight of his friends, among whom I was included." On the whole, it is easier to believe that Shelley gave the banquet than that the publisher provided the means of paying for it; for publishers are men of business. That is a detail, however, and does not matter. What does matter sufficiently to arrest the reader is the general tone of the letter : the burst of high spirits which it manifests.

" Pouch," of course, is the slang of the period for " tip." We find Byron, in one of his letters, speaking of the necessity of " pouching " an Eton boy; and the Eton boy's belief that the whole of Fleet Street can be corrupted with a ten-pound note is delightfully boyish if not specifically Etonian. It is a curious coincidence, too, that Byron claimed in jest (in *Don Juan*) to have corrupted the editor of that *British Review* which Shelley speaks of as " the hardest," with precisely the sum which Shelley judged sufficient for the corruption of the entire literary Press. But the main thing notable, after all, is the mental and moral condition in which the letter shows Shelley to have ended his Eton career.

It shows that Hawtrey must have exaggerated, not indeed the persecution inflicted upon him as a small boy, but the effect of that persecution upon his character and opinions. Though his school-days doubtless were, as Packe put it, " more adventurous than happy," he does not write, in his last year, as a boy whose adventures have crushed, or saddened, or embittered him; and the idea that he lost his faith in Christianity because Christians knocked books from under his arm and kicked muddy footballs at him does not carry conviction. Bullies do not, at Eton any more than anywhere else, do that sort of thing in the name of Christianity, or make loud Christian professions while doing it; and Hawtrey's theory of the association of ideas in Shelley's mind requires that missing link, to be complete.

Hawtrey's doctrine, in short, is vitiated by the common clerical assumption that, when a man of genius differs from a clergyman on a point of speculative theology, the clergyman is necessarily in the right and should show the breadth and depth of his sympathy with genius by weeping over the man of genius as a backslider. The general truth is, however, that clergymen have no better title than, say, solicitors or stockbrokers—or dustmen or district visitors —to define the limits within which the human intelligence shall be free to " energize "; and the particular truth is that Shelley's questionings of theological propositions were due to the natural activity of his mind.

It was as natural for him to exercise his mind as it is for some people to exercise their limbs,— as natural for him to think as for other boys to run, or to play leap-frog. He asked questions, and, getting no satisfactory answers to them, thought the more,—trying to perfect himself as an intellectual gladiator in the same spirit in which other boys try to perfect themselves at cricket. There is no reason to look for any more recondite explanation of his heterodoxy, for people who think are always heterodox. Shelley's case in that respect is pretty much like the case of Mr. Bernard Shaw.

If he did not think as wittily as Mr. Bernard Shaw, at least he thought as joyously. Thought was a joyous adventure to him,—the most joyous part of the joyous adventure of life. He went to the adventure in the true spirit of an adventurer; and that temper was probably at its keenest at the time when he left Eton for Oxford.

CHAPTER V

UNIVERSITY COLLEGE, OXFORD

ONE may help oneself to realize the Oxford of Shelley's time by enumerating some of his contemporaries. Arnold of Corpus was the future headmaster of Rugby, and Keble of Corpus was the future author of *The Christian Year*. Whately of Oriel was the future Archbishop, and Milman of B.N.C. was the future Dean. Senior of Magdalen was Nassau Senior the Economist, and Lockhart of Balliol was Scott's son-in-law and biographer.

Those were the great men among the undergraduates of the date,—the men who graduated in high honours, won University prizes, reflected credit on their respective colleges, and proceeded, after graduation, by straight paths, to distinction and success in life. There is no evidence, however, that Shelley knew any one of them; and there are few of them with whom one can picture him associating cordially. He and Whately, perhaps, might have discovered points of sympathy; but Keble's business in life was to be to preach at, and Arnold's to summon to his study and flog, those who, like Shelley, were " tameless, and swift, and proud."

Among out-college men, Shelley's only friends

47

appear to have been a few Etonians. It is said that he was always glad to see them when they called, but equally glad to lose sight of them when they went. The men of his own college, too, saw very little of him,—always excepting his intimate friend, and future biographer, Thomas Jefferson Hogg, who is almost our sole witness for this period of his life.

The romantic Trelawny, whose acquaintance we shall make presently, speaks of Hogg as a hard-headed man of the world who looked upon literature with contempt. It is quite possible that he gave casual acquaintances that impression in later life, when he was a Revising Barrister and a Municipal Corporation Commissioner. One would infer as much from the fact that his wife, Jane Williams (the widow of the Williams who had shared a house with the Shelleys in Italy), only accepted his offer of marriage on condition that he should first " qualify himself " by a long course of continental travel. His acceptance of the condition, however, betokens a character not altogether unromantic. Even in those hard-headed days he said that he regarded the Greek language, equally with the English newspapers, as " a prime necessary of life; " and one imagines that, in 1810, he would have been remarked not only as an ebullient, but also as a romantic and chivalrous young man.

He and Shelley made each other's acquaintance by sitting next to each other in hall, though

Hogg assures us that "such familiarity was unusual"—an interesting precedent for the alleged rule that one Oxford man must not presume even to rescue another from drowning unless he has been introduced to him. They fell into conversation on the comparative value of German and Italian literature, and, after hall, continued the discussion in Hogg's rooms, and sat up nearly all night over it,—each of them ultimately confessing to the other that he had argued for the sake of arguing, and without even a superficial knowledge of the subject. On the following afternoon they met by appointment in Shelley's rooms; and after that, they were inseparable.

Their Oxford, it must be remembered, was the early Oxford in which no games were played. There was no "tubbing" in those days, and no practising at the nets. Unless men haunted the prize-ring and the rat-pit, their one way of amusing themselves was to walk and talk, and no sporting "shop" could cast its monotonous shadow over their conversation. The question whether the college eight was more likely to bump or to be bumped did not arise, and no man burdened his brain with tables of "records" or "averages." The talk was about literature, about philosophy, and, sometimes, about religion; and daring young thinkers hammered out for themselves a good many subjects on which they were not called upon to be examined. That was the case with Arnold and Keble of Corpus

D   49

no less than with Shelley and Hogg of Univ; though the latter pair of friends pursued their speculations with more independence and more courage,—perhaps one should also say with stronger prepossessions in favour of intellectual honesty.

Shelley's activities, indeed, were marvellous and multitudinous. Hogg says that he read (not for "the Schools" but for his pleasure) about sixteen hours a day; also that he was continually making malodorous or sensational chemical and electrical experiments,—so meriting the style of "Stinks Man," elaborated by the wit of a later generation; also that he took long country walks, returning so late and so tired that he "cut hall" and curled himself up to sleep on the hearth-rug. We know, furthermore, that he wrote a great deal in both prose and verse; and there are, finally, indications that he found time to be one of the rowdiest men in a rather rowdy college.

Hogg, it is true, repudiates this last charge. Shelley, he says, had been nicknamed "the Atheist" at Eton, not on account of atheism, but on account of rowdiness,[1] and certain Etonians asked him whether he intended to continue to be that kind of Atheist at Oxford. Whereto he reports Shelley replying : "Certainly not. There is no motive for it; there would be no use in it; they are very civil to us here; they never interfere with us." Even in Hogg's narrative, how-

[1] The veracity of this story is questioned by Etonians.

ever, there appear hints of differences with the
dons, none too deferentially expressed. There
is a story of Shelley walking out of a lecture-
room because the lecture bored him, and up-
setting a chair as he went; and there is the
story of his interview with the tutor who exhorted
him to read Aristotle :—

"'You must begin Aristotle's Ethics, and
then you may go on to his other treatises. It is
of the utmost importance to be well acquainted
with Aristotle.' This he repeated so often that
I was quite tired, and at last I said, 'Must I
care about Aristotle? What if I do not mind
Aristotle?' I then left him, for he seemed to
be in great perplexity."

That is not the manner of a man who likes
dons, or whom dons like; and the practical
importance of the incompatibilities between
Shelley and the dons will soon appear. Meanwhile we may note other evidence which is to
the same effect as Hogg's testimony "only more
so." Ridley, then a junior Fellow, and afterwards Master of University, wrote, at the time,
that "there were but few, if any, who were
not afraid of Shelley's strange and fantastic
pranks;" and this view is confirmed by a
niece of the Master of 1810, who was then on
a visit to her uncle. She was a Miss Grant,
afterwards Mrs. Smith, and her reminiscences,
to which Professor Dowden could not refer, were
edited by Lady Strachey and published by Mr.

Murray, in 1898, under the title of *Memoirs of a Highland Lady*.

Miss Grant, indeed, was equally impressed by the " pranks " of the undergraduates and by the dulness and inadequacy of the dons; and as we are presently to see Shelley and the dons at open war, we may as well have her estimate of both parties to the dispute before us. " Stupidity and frivolity," she says, were the distinguishing characteristics of the latter; and she particularizes :—

" It was not a good style; there was little talent and less polish and no sort of knowledge of the world. Of the lesser clergy there were young witty ones, odious, and young learned ones, bores, and elderly ones, pompous; all, of all grades, kind and hospitable. But the Christian pastor, humble and gentle, and considerate and self-sacrificing, occupied with his duties, and filled with the ' charity ' of his Master, had no representative, as far as I could see, among these dealers in old wines, rich dinners, fine china, and massive plate."

She adds that " the education was suited to the divinity " :—

" A sort of supervision was said to be kept over the young riotous community, and to a certain extent the Proctors of the University and the Deans of the different colleges did see that no very open scandals were committed. There were rules that had in a general way to be obeyed, and there were lectures that must be attended, but as for care to give high aims, provide refining amusements, give a worthy tone to the character of responsible beings, there was none ever even thought of. . . . The only care the Heads appeared to take with regard to the young minds they were supposed to be placed where they were and paid well to help to form, was to keep the persons of the students at the greatest possible distance. They conversed with them never, invited them to their homes never, spoke or thought about them never. A perpetual bowing was their only intercourse; a bow of humble respect acknowledged by one of stiff condescension limited the intercourse of the old heads and the young, generally speaking."

When we come to see Shelley tilting at the champions of orthodoxy, this impartial picture of their manners and customs will be instructive. Meanwhile we will glance at Miss Grant's picture of the manners and customs of the undergraduates. Several of them, it seems (though Shelley was not of the number), tried to get up flirtations with her when she sat under a mulberry tree in the Master's garden. One sought to attract her attention by declaiming poetry from the window; another by tootling on a horn; and more than once Miss Grant found herself, in a corner of the garden, "chatting and laughing merrily with about a dozen commoners."

Next, after relating this pleasant incident, Miss Grant describes how her young friends " ragged " the Dean :—

" Mr. Rowley, having made himself disagreeable to some of his pupils, who found it suit their healths to take long rides in the country, they all turned out one night to hunt the *fox* under his window. A Mr. Fox, in a red waistcoat and some kind of a skin for a cap, was let loose on the grass in the middle of the quadrangle, with the whole pack of his fellow-students barking around him. There were cracking whips, shrill whistles, loud halloos, and louder hark-aways, quite enough to frighten the dignitaries. When those great persons assembled to encounter this confusion, all concerned skipped off up the different staircases, like rats to their holes, and I don't believe any of them were ever regularly discovered. . . . My uncle was very mild in his rule; yet there were circumstances which roused the indignation of the quietest colleges."

The Mr. Rowley against whom the rioters demonstrated was Shelley's tutor, so that the climax follows naturally :—

" The ringleader in every species of mischief within our grave walls was Mr. Shelley, afterwards so celebrated, though I should think to the end half-crazy. He began his career by every kind of wild prank at Eton, and when kindly remonstrated with by his tutor, repaid the well-meant private admonition by spilling an acid over the carpet of that gentleman's study, a new purchase, which he thus completely destroyed. He did no deed so mischievous at University, but he was very insubordinate, always infringing some rule, the breaking of which he knew could not be overlooked. He was slovenly in his dress, and when spoken to about these and other irregularities, he was in the habit of making such extraordinary gestures, expressive of his humility under reproof, as to upset first the gravity, and then the temper, of the lecturing tutor. Of course these scenes reached unpleasant lengths, and when he proceeded so far as to paste up atheistical squibs on the chapel doors, it was considered necessary to expel him."

The hour for expulsion, however, was not yet; but it is significant to find Shelley behaving himself, from the first, in such a way as to make the dons glad of any handle which he might subsequently give them. They probably objected to his addiction to " Stinks," for the Natural Sciences had not yet come into their kingdom at the Universities; and rowdiness is (most naturally) doubly offensive to dons if the offender is rude when they rebuke him. Still there was, for the moment, no handle for the dons to seize; and Shelley was enjoying himself. He would have liked, as, indeed, most of us have at some period felt that we should like, to remain at Oxford for ever.

" It would be a cruel calamity," he once said

55

to Hogg, as if in ominous anticipation of what was to happen, " to be interrupted by some untoward accident, to be compelled to quit our calm and agreeable retreat; " and he continued :—

" I regret only that the period of our residence is limited to four years; I wish they would revive, for our sake, the old term of six or seven years. If we consider how much there is for us to learn, we shall allow that the longer period would still be far too short."

He rejoiced, too, in the privilege of sporting his oak,—" the oak alone goes far towards making this place a paradise; " and the high spirits in which he conducted his metaphysical speculations are evident from Hogg's familiar story of his attempt to test, as it were, by experiment, that Platonic doctrine that all our knowledge is " reminiscence " of things known in a previous existence,—that, as Wordsworth puts it, " Heaven lies about us in our infancy " and " our birth is but a sleep and a forgetting."

He snatched a baby, so Hogg tells us, out of its mother's arms on Magdalen Bridge, and, while the mother clung desperately to its swaddling clothes in an agony of terror lest it should be dropped into the Cherwell, he gravely questioned her :—

" Can your baby tell us anything about preexistence, madam ? " he asked, in a piercing voice, and with a wistful look.

" He cannot speak, sir," answered the mother stolidly.

" Surely he can speak if he will," Shelley insisted, " for he is only a few weeks old. He cannot have entirely forgotten the use of speech in so short a time."

But the mother was as firm as the undergraduate.

" It is not for me to argue with college gentlemen," she rejoined, " but babies of that age never do speak so far as *I* know; " and with that she begged that her infant might be returned to her; and so the incident terminated.

Many similar stories of Shelley's strange sayings and doings in his country walks might be told if space allowed; but those who are curious to read them must be referred to Hogg's undeservedly neglected pages. They all show Shelley as a wild youth,—but of a delightfully fantastic wildness,—long-haired in an age in which it was the fashion for men to wear their hair close-cropped like grooms—standing, or rather, walking, aloof from the conventional studies and normal amusements of Oxford, but rejoicing in his newly-found freedom, and the adventures which it brought. In particular we find him pursuing and rejoicing in literary adventures.

These were at first smiled upon by an unsuspecting father. Timothy Shelley, M.P., when he brought his son to Oxford, took him to the shop of Messrs. Munday and Slatter, booksellers, in the High, and introduced him to one of the partners.

" My boy here," he said, pointing proudly to the long-haired, wild-eyed youth,—" my boy here has a literary turn. He is already an author, and do pray indulge him in his printing freaks."

The member for Shoreham imagined, apparently, that his son, having begun his literary career by writing a penny dreadful, would continue to write penny dreadfuls until he entered Parliament, and settled down. Apparently, too, that was the kind of literature that Timothy Shelley understood and approved of. What he did not understand was that his son was growing up in a sense in which he himself had never grown up, and that certain influences, which he himself had never undergone, were at work on him.

The first influence was that of books—books which, from the point of view of Timothy Shelley, were merely dull and stodgy incumbrances on the shelves. Instead of Aristotle the boy had been reading Locke and Hume. Hume, in particular, had waked him, as it waked Kant, from " dogmatic slumbers "; but he had not Kant's metaphysical narcotic to send him to sleep again. And Hume's scepticism is rather disturbing to intelligent readers who have been reared in orthodoxy, especially if they have not the *Critique of Pure Reason* to check it. That was Shelley's case; and that was the first influence which was tempting him to put pen to paper for other purposes than the composition of those penny dreadfuls which satisfied his father's simple tastes.

The second influence was love; and that obliges us to interrupt our account of Shelley's Oxford career in order to speak of his first love affair.

CHAPTER VI

FIRST LOVE AND NEW THEOLOGY

SHELLEY's very first love appears to have been a young woman in what such young women call " the confectionery." Our authority is Gronow, who reports Shelley as saying to him : " Gronow, do you remember the beautiful Martha, the Hebe of Spiers' ? She was the loveliest girl I ever saw, and I loved her to distraction." On another page Gronow tells us how he and Keate, after Keate's retirement from the headmastership, chuckled together over the memory of a flirtation between this same Martha and Sumner— though whether the Sumner who became Archbishop of Canterbury or only the Sumner who became Bishop of Winchester does not appear. Martha must, indeed, have been a girl who adorned the confectionery to have attracted two admirers of such mark; but unhappily the records of their rivalry are lost. Martha left no mark on either life; and the first feminine influence which Shelley underwent was that of Harriet Grove.

She was Shelley's cousin; and Medwin, who was cousin to both of them, speaks of her as " like one of Shakespeare's women—like some Madonna of Raphael." She came on a visit to

Field Place, and Shelley afterwards stayed at her father's house in London. It is agreed that she was of such an ethereal beauty as was likely to efface all thoughts of the girl in the confectioner's shop; but beyond that fact, one gets no very clear impression of her. Her charms are as elusive as those of Byron's Mary Chaworth; and the effect of them was less enduring, though it was very real for a season, and Shelley dreamt love's young dream in the baseless belief that he had found, in this beautiful girl, an ideal intellectual companion.

Harriet, one gathers, was at first dazzled—it would have been strange if she had not been. She was just clever enough to begin to understand the boy who was different from other people—not clever enough to understand him when he developed beyond the stage which he had reached at the time of their moonlight walks in Timothy Shelley's and the Duke of Norfolk's parks. She heard him gladly when he talked of haunted ruins, spectral apparitions, and the rest of the imaginative stock-in-trade of the writer of penny dreadfuls. She is said to have collaborated with him in *Zastrozzi*. But he grew up faster than she did; and presently he frightened her.

They were too young to be engaged; but there was an " understanding," and a correspondence—and Shelley's communications were no ordinary love-letters. He had been reading Locke and Hume; and the conceptions of those philosophers found their way into his letters. The boy imagined that the girl was, like himself, a seeker after truth; but the girl, though she joined for a moment in the quest, was soon scared by the quarry started. She had " the will to believe," but not the will to know. Ideas made her shudder far more than ghosts and ancestral curses could. She ran in terror to her elders, and sought counsel from them with the result which might have been foreseen. Her father said that the correspondence must cease and the acquaintance be discontinued.

He was obeyed. It would even seem that Harriet obeyed him without much show of reluctance. One gathers, at any rate, from one of Shelley's letters to Hogg, that his sister Elizabeth pleaded his cause with Harriet, but pleaded it in vain. This is what Harriet is reported to have said:—

" Even supposing I take your representation of your brother's qualities and sentiments, which as you coincide in and admire, I may fairly imagine to be exaggerated, although *you* may not be aware of the exaggeration; what right have *I*, admitting that he is so superior, to enter into an intimacy which must end in delusive disappointment, when he finds how really inferior I am to the being which his heated imagination has pictured ? "

Perhaps that paragraph is more helpful to us

61

in picturing Harriet Grove than anything else that we know about her. Her superficiality shines through it, like the sun bursting through a cloud. The common sense of the weak-minded and inadequate is convincingly confused in it with the qualities to which women apply the epithet " cattish." But, of course, Harriet's heart was her own to dispose of; and it was not long before she did dispose of it to a country squire named Heylar. This is how Shelley conveys the news to Hogg:—

" She is gone ! She is lost to me for ever ! She married ! Married to a clod of earth; she will become as insensible herself; all those fine capabilities will moulder. Let us speak no more on the subject."

But if Shelley spoke no more on the subject, that is only because he had already said so much that nothing remained to be said. He had raved at length; but the only examples of his ravings which it is worth while to give are those which show how disappointment in love prepared the way for the incident which led to his expulsion from Oxford. He conceived of himself as the victim, not of woman's fickleness, but of man's bigotry.

He still speaks eloquently of love:—

" Love ! dearest, sweetest power ! how much are we indebted to thee ! How much superior are even thy miseries to the pleasures which arise from other sources ! how much superior to ' fat contented ignorance ' is even the agony which thy votaries experience."

But this invocation of love is sandwiched between two denunciations of bigotry and announcements that the lover is taking, or means to take, the field against it. This, for instance :—

" I shall not read Bishop Pretyman or any more of them, unless I have some particular reason. Bigots will not argue; it destroys the very nature of the thing to argue; it is contrary to *faith*. How, therefore, could you suppose that one of these *liberal* gentlemen would listen to scepticism, on the subject even of St. Athanasius's sweeping anathema."

And then this :—

" On one subject I am cool, toleration; yet that coolness alone possesses me that I may with more certainty guide the spear to the breast of my adversary, with more certainty ensanguine it with the heart's blood of Intolerance—hated name !

" Adieu ! Down with Bigotry ! Down with Intolerance ! In this endeavour your most sincere friend will join his every power, his every feeble resource."

Nor did Shelley make any secret of his opinions

at home. On the contrary he aired them in the bosom of his family, sparing only Elizabeth on the ground that he did not " wish to awaken her intellect too powerfully." He attempted even to " enlighten " his father, but with unsatisfactory results :—

" He for a time listened to my arguments; he allowed the impossibility (considered abstractedly) of any preternatural interferences by Providence. He allowed the utter incredibility of witches, ghosts, legendary miracles. But when I came to *apply* the truths on which we had agreed so harmoniously, he started at the bare idea of some facts generally believed never having existed, and silenced me with a bovine argument, in effect with these words : ' I believe because I do believe.' "

That is characteristic of Mr. Timothy Shelley, of whose theological inadequacy we shall have further proofs. Meanwhile, the effect of the boy's theological outpourings on his mother's mind claims notice :—

" My mother imagines me to be in the high road to Pandemonium, she fancies I want to make a deistical coterie of all my little sisters; how laughable ! "

While as for the collective attitude of the family :

" They attack me for my detestable principles;

I am reckoned an outcast; yet I defy them and laugh at their ineffectual efforts."

These letters were written in the Christmas vacation of 1810–1811. They are important as showing us precisely in what frame of mind Shelley returned to Oxford and catastrophe. Not the least significant fact is that he speaks of his principles, not as " atheistical " but as " deistical "; and this profession of deism is contained in several passages of the letters to Hogg. In one of the letters he goes so far as to speak of " God whose mercy is great." In another we read this:—

" The word ' God,' a vague word, has been, and will continue to be, the source of numberless errors, until it is erased from the nomenclature of philosophy. Does it not imply ' the soul of the universe, the intelligent and *necessarily* beneficent actuating principle ' ? This it is impossible not to believe in; I may not be able to adduce proofs, but I think that the leaf of a tree, the meanest insect on which we trample, are, in themselves, arguments more conclusive than any which can be advanced, that some vast intellect animates infinity."

And then again:—

" Love, love *infinite in extent*, eternal in duration, yet (allowing your theory in that point) perfectible, should be the reward; but can we

E   65 suppose that this reward will arise, spontaneously, as a necessary appendage to our nature, or that our nature itself could be without cause—a first cause—a God ? When do we see effects arise without causes ? "

But, on the other hand :—

" I swear—and as I break my oaths may Infinity, Eternity blast me—here I swear that never will I forgive intolerance. . . . You shall see—you shall hear—how it has injured me. She is no longer mine ! she abhors me as a sceptic, as what *she* was before. Oh, bigotry ! When I pardon this last, this severest, of thy persecutions, may Heaven (if there be wrath in Heaven) blast me. Has vengeance in its armoury of wrath punishment more dreadful ? . . .

" . . . Is suicide wrong ? I slept with a loaded pistol and some poison last night, but did not die."

These excerpts, thus arranged, clear up the situation. Shelley was *not* an atheist, any more than Vincent Crummles was a Prussian. His professions of faith, though rather crudely put, hardly strike one as being more advanced than those of the Rev. R. J. Campbell. But he had been treated as an atheist; and he was in a dangerous mood, and ready for mischief.

CHAPTER VII

"THE NECESSITY OF ATHEISM"—EXPULSION FROM OXFORD

THE facts which must be borne in mind in order that the story of *The Necessity of Atheism* may be intelligible are these :—

Shelley was only eighteen, but was taking to controversy as a duck to water, and saw no reason for keeping his religious opinions in a water-tight compartment. His New Theology, which, in so far as it was coherent, was pretty much the New Theology of the City Temple of to-day—a theology based upon the doctrine of Divine Immanence—had lost him a bride, and had consequently caused him to lose his temper. He had a fluent pen, and was never so happy as when employing it. That to begin with, and further-more :—

Shelley was a rowdy man; and, partly for that reason, and partly because he was a Stinks man —one whose rooms were not only furnished, as Hogg says, with " an electrical machine, an air-pump, a galvanic trough, a solar microscope, and large glass jars and receivers," but were also pervaded with " an unpleasant and penetrating effluvium "—was *persona ingrata* with the dons.

Of his miscellaneous literary activities it would

be superfluous to say much; but there are two points to be noted. He was out-growing penny dreadfuls; and his work was beginning to attract attention in University circles. The last of the penny dreadfuls was *St. Irvyne, or the Rosicrucian,* advertised as " by a Gentleman of Oxford University "; and this romance was not yet out when the author wrote to his publisher, Stockdale of Pall Mall, declaring his determination to produce something more serious and ambitious:—

" I have in preparation a novel; it is principally constructed to convey metaphysical and political opinions by way of conversation; it shall be sent to you as soon as completed, but it shall receive more correction than I trouble myself to give to wild Romance and Poetry."

The novel thus announced was *Leonora,* which may or may not have been begun in collaboration with Hogg, and might or might not, if completed, have turned out to be a romance of New Theology. One likes to imagine it as a sketch of a sort of earlier *Robert Elsmere;* but as it was never printed, or even finished, one cannot make any definite affirmation. The work which interrupted its composition was a volume of poems—*Posthumous Fragments of Mrs. Margaret Nicholson, Widow* —which is said to have been begun in a serious spirit but transformed into a burlesque at Hogg's suggestion and with his help; and this was the production which first caused Shelley to be talked about.

EXPULSION FROM OXFORD

Munday and Slatter, who published the brochure, spoke of it, indeed, as "almost still-born"; but Hogg's statement that the copies which were not given away " were rapidly sold at Oxford at the aristocratical price of half-a-crown for half-a-dozen pages " is made more probable by a letter written by C. Kirkpatrick Sharpe, and printed in Lady C. Bury's *Diary*.

" Talking of books, we have lately had a literary sun shine forth upon us here, before whom our former luminaries must hide their diminished heads—a Mr. Shelley of University College, who lives upon arsenic, aqua-fortis, half-an-hour's sleep in the night, and is desperately in love with the memory of Margaret Nicholson. . . . The author is a great genius, and, if he be not clapped up in Bedlam or hanged, will certainly prove one of the sweetest swans on the tuneful margin of Cher."

A marvellously exact prediction, though there was little to warrant it in the facts before the prophet : a proof, too, that Shelley ceased to be a nonentity while still a freshman.

His zeal for literature, however, paled, at this period, before his zeal for controversy; and that zeal for controversy was found in curious conjunction with a passion for practical joking, and for " pulling the legs " of pompous persons.

69

His favourite device, suggested to him while he was still an Eton boy, by Dr. Lind—a man of science of the town who had encouraged his taste for chemistry—was to write, under an assumed name to strangers—the most grave and reverend strangers whom he thought likely to reply to him—submitting brief abstracts of some heterodox argument, and appealing for assistance in rebutting it. If the person to whom he wrote " took the bait," says Hogg, he would " fall upon the unwary disputant and break his bones." Once, according to Medwin, he lured a bishop into controversy, by pretending to be a woman, and handled him as the impertinent have delighted to handle the pompous from the beginning of the world. On another occasion, it is said, his antagonist, discovering how he had been " got at " by a schoolboy, wrote to the head-master, demanding that he should be flogged for his presumption; and Keate, as we know, was a head-master who snatched at the smallest excuse for the birch.

It was splendid fun, of course—and likely to prove still better fun in a world in which birches were not; and the fun would reach its acme if it were possible to "get a rise " out of the Vice-Chancellor, the Proctors, the Regius Professor of Divinity, and the Heads of Colleges and Halls. These dignitaries being clergymen, atheism was the obvious card to play. The effect of a profession of atheism on clergymen might fairly be expected to be that of a red rag on a bull—the more so if the atheistical conclusions were deduced from works read in the ordinary course of the University curriculum. Shelley, moreover, was the readier to attempt to " draw " them on those lines because his New Theology had been treated as atheism and had, as we have seen, lost him a bride. He was in the mood to say that he would show people what atheism really was.

How Hogg was induced to bear a hand in the campaign one does not know,—most likely for no other reason than because he loved a joke, and admired his friend's skill as a controversialist. At all events he and Shelley did put their heads together; with the result that *The Necessity of Atheism* was produced, and advertised in the *Oxford Herald* of February 9, 1811, and that copies of it were posted to dons and others, " with the compliments of Jeremiah Stukeley."

Nor was that all. There was the off-chance that the dons, scenting a practical joke, might ignore the outrage, and Shelley, avid of publicity, was determined to compel them to take notice. So he came down, with a bundle of his pamphlets under his arm, to Messrs. Munday and Slatter's shop—the very shop in which a lavish and indulgent parent (lavish and indulgent on that occasion at all events) had given out that his " printing freaks " were to be encouraged. He wished those pamphlets, he said, to be offered for sale at sixpence each; he wished them to be well displayed on the counter and in the window; in order that the window might be dressed to his liking, he proposed to dress it himself.

He did so with an obliging readiness which overwhelmed the amiable bookseller's assistant. In a moment of time *The Necessity of Atheism* was displayed in Messrs. Munday and Slatter's shop, much as the first number of a new magazine with a gaudy cover might be displayed on one of the railway bookstalls to-day.

It remained so displayed for about twenty minutes; and then the Rev. John Walker, Fellow of New College—he, apparently, whom Hogg describes as " the pert, meddling fellow of a college of inferior note,[1] a man of an insalubrious and inauspicious aspect "—passed the shop, looked into the window to see what new publications had arrived, read the title of Shelley's pamphlet, and, after being surprised and shocked, was moved to action. He walked into the shop, demanded the proprietors, and gave them peremptory instructions :—

" Mr. Munday, and Mr. Slatter ! What is the meaning of this ? "

" We beg pardon, sir. We really didn't know. We hadn't examined the publication personally. But, of course, now that our attention is drawn to it——"

" Now that your attention is drawn to it, **Mr.** Munday and Mr. Slatter, you will be good enough

---

[1] It is only within comparatively recent years that the reputation of New College has stood high.

to remove all the copies of it that lie on your counter and are exposed in your window, and to take them out into your back kitchen, and there burn them."

Such was the dialogue as one can reconstruct it from Mr. Slatter's recollections contained in a letter to one Montgomery of Lincoln, whom we know as Robert Montgomery, the poet.

Mr. Walker, of course, had no legal right to give those orders. From the strictly legal point of view he was commanding a man over whom he had no jurisdiction to destroy property which did not belong to him; he would never have presumed to give such orders in, say, Mr. Hatchard's shop in Piccadilly. At Oxford, however, his foot was on his native heath, and Messrs. Munday and Slatter knew it. He might speak to the Vice-Chancellor; and the Vice-Chancellor might forbid undergraduates to deal at their establishment. So they were all bows and smiles and obsequious anxiety to oblige.

" By all means, Mr. Walker! An admirable idea, sir! Just what we were ourselves on the point of suggesting. You may rely on us to carry out your wishes."

" You will be good enough to carry them out in my presence. I will accompany you to your back kitchen for that purpose."

" That will be very good of you, Mr. Walker. It will be a great honour to our back kitchen. Will you please walk this way, sir?"

So the holocaust was effected; and Messrs. Munday and Slatter begged Shelley to call on them, and told him what they had been obliged to do.

"We are really very sorry, Mr. Shelley. We really could not help ourselves. Mr. Walker was so very firm in the matter; and even in your own interest, you know——"

Et cetera. The scene can still be reconstructed from the same source. There was to be no further publicity for Shelley through the instrumentality of the booksellers; and as no one was likely to trouble about the authorship of an anonymous brochure which had been reduced to ashes, that might have been the end of the matter if Shelley had not circulated his pamphlet through the post. But then he *had* so circulated it, and the covering "compliments of Jeremiah Stukeley" were very obviously in his handwriting; and the recipients of the presentation copies, who included several bishops, were saying that something really ought to be done; and the dons were not only willing but anxious, and not only anxious but eager, to lay hold of the handle which Shelley had now given them.

Was he not a Stinks Man—a Rowdy Man? Did he not make malodorous chemical experiments, and dress eccentrically, and wear his hair long—and was he not impertinent when "ragged"? Was it likely, then, that the Senior Common-room would stand atheism or any other nonsense from such a man as that ? Of course it would not. Of course Shelley was sent for " with the Dean's compliments "—those compliments of evil omen—and the rest of the story may be best told in the words of the Mr. Ridley already quoted, who is a less prejudiced witness than Hogg :—

" It was announced one morning at a breakfast party, towards the end of the Lent term " (writes Mr. Ridley), " that Percy Bysshe Shelley, who had recently become a member of University College, was to be called before a meeting of the Common-room for being the supposed author of a pamphlet called *The Necessity of Atheism*. This anonymous work, consisting of not many pages, had been studiously sent to most of the dignitaries of the University and to others more or less connected with Oxford. The meeting took place the same day, and it was understood that the pamphlet, together with some notes sent with it, in which the supposed author's handwriting appeared identified with that of P.B.S., was placed before him. He was asked if he could or would deny the obnoxious production as his. No direct reply was given either in the affirmative or negative.

." Shelley having quitted the room, T. J. Hogg immediately appeared, voluntarily on his part, to state that, if Shelley had anything to do with it, he (Hogg) was equally implicated, and desired his share of the penalty, whatever was inflicted. It

75

has always been supposed that Hogg wrote the preface.

" Towards the afternoon a large paper bearing the College seal, and signed by the Master and Dean, was affixed to the hall door, declaring that the two offenders were publicly expelled from the College *for contumacy in refusing to answer certain questions put to them.* The aforesaid two had made themselves as conspicuous as possible by great singularity of dress, and by walking up and down the centre of the quadrangle, as if proud of their anticipated fate."

That is all. There are other versions of the incident; but this is the one which rings truest. Comment is supplied by Robert Montgomery, the pious poet already mentioned—a poet more pious than poetical in the view of persons qualified to judge both departments of endeavour.

" Strange and unnatural as it may appear," Montgomery writes with heavy, not to say hippopotamic, sarcasm, " there are many in Oxford who think that a University, based on the immortal truths of the Gospel, ought not to license or encourage blasphemy, however gilded by genius."

No doubt there are many who would agree with that proposition, not in Oxford only but elsewhere as well. There may even be some who think that Montgomery, rather than Shelley, is the sort of scion that Oxford should be proud of. But Montgomery's principle, whether right or wrong, is hardly applicable to Shelley's case; which was the case, as we have seen, not of a convinced blasphemer, but of a practical joker who had over-reached himself and suffered martyrdom rather than confess that he had been joking.

And that, one concludes, was the view of those later dignitaries of the college who permitted the erection of a Shelley Memorial within the college precincts—albeit in a dark corner of those precincts, only to be reached by way of an obscure passage which looks as if it led to a coal-hole wherein an unwary visitor would run a serious risk of being arrested and charged with intent to commit a felony.

And so to London to face a father, no longer lavish and indulgent, but obstinate and angry.

CHAPTER VIII

SHELLEY and Hogg took lodgings together at
15, Poland Street; and Shelley looked up Medwin
and the Groves while waiting for his father's
arrival.

Harriet Grove is really out of the story by this
time—she was to have no permanent influence on
Shelley's thoughts; but he had not yet forgotten
her,—he can hardly be said to have forgotten her
even when he made up his mind to marry another
Harriet; and therefore it may be worth while to
do what earlier biographers could not do, and
gather up the allusions to his passion for her contained in the volume of verse entitled *Original
Poems* by Victor and Cazire.

The volume was produced by Shelley in conjunction with his sister Elizabeth. Professor
Dowden spoke of it in 1886 as having "wholly
disappeared from human ken," though about a
hundred copies were known to have got into
circulation before Shelley ordered the rest of the
stock to be destroyed, and reviews of it had been
discovered—one of them to the effect that "there
is no original *poetry* in this volume; there is
nothing in it but downright scribble." Twelve

78

years afterwards, however, a copy was found by Charles Grove's grandson, Mr. V. E. G. Hussey, bound up with the third Canto of *Childe Harold* and some others of Byron's poems, and was published by Mr. Lane with an Introduction by Richard Garnett.

The poetry on the whole merits the verdict of the critic quoted; but the personal references may detain us. The names of the persons are, indeed, left blank; but the blanks are easy to fill up. The piece headed " To ——" is obviously addressed " To Harriet," and is as obviously from Shelley's own pen :—

Ah! sweet is the moonbeam that sleeps on yon
fountain,
  And sweet the mild rush of the soft-sighing
  breeze,
And sweet is the glimpse of yon dimly seen moun-
tain,
  'Neath the verdant arcades of yon shadowy trees.

But sweeter than all was thy love and affection
  Which scarce seemed to break on the stillness of
  eve,
Though the time it is passed!—yet the dear recol-
lection
  For aye in the heart of thy (Percy) must live.

And thou, dearest friend, in his bosom for ever
  Must reign unalloyed by the fast-rolling years :
He loves thee, and, dearest one, never oh! never
  Canst thou cease to be loved by a heart so sincere.

79

No less obviously is Harriet addressed in the following :—

> Come, (Harriet), sweet is the hour,
>   Still zephyrs breathe gently around ;
> The anemone's night-boding flower
>   Has sunk its pale head on the ground.
>
> 'Tis thus the world's keenness hath torn
>   Some mild heart that expands to its blast ;
> 'Tis thus that the wretched forlorn
>   Sinks poor and neglected at last.
>
> The world with its keenness and woe
>   Hath no charms or attraction for me ;
> Its unkindness with grief has laid low
>   The heart which is faithful to thee.
>
> The high trees that wave past the moon,
>   As I walk in their umbrage with you,
> All declare I must part with you soon,
>   All bid you a tender adieu.
>
> Then (Harriet), dearest, farewell !
>   You and I, love, may ne'er meet again
> These woods and these meadows can tell
>   How soft and how sweet was the strain.

The lines, it must be allowed, are not on a much higher level of inspiration than those one finds put in evidence in actions for breach of promise of marriage ; but they sparkle with genius when compared with the lines in which Elizabeth Shelley draws a picture of her brother as a love-sick swain :—

POEMS ADDRESSED TO HARRIET GROVE

He neither eats, drinks, nor sleeps, for her sake,
And hopes her hard heart some compassion will take.
A refusal will kill him, so desperate his flame,
But he fears, for he knows she is not common game,
Then praises her sense, wit, discernment and grace,—
He's not one that's caught by a sly-looking face.
Yet that's too divine—such a black sparkling eye,
At the bare glance of which near a thousand will
*   die.*
Thus runs he on, meaning but one word in ten,
More than is meant by most such kind of men ;
For they're all alike, take them one with another,
Begging pardon with the exception of my brother.

Poor stuff, of course, but none the less worth quoting as a document. It belongs, it is pretty clear, to the early days before the New Theology had cast its shadow over the courtship. Elizabeth seems to have been annoyed because her brother published her verses without asking her leave—which, in view of the quality of the verses, is not surprising. That, at all events, is the interpretation which it seems most natural to put on the following entry in Harriet Grove's diary :—

" Received the poetry by Victor and Cazire. C. offended, and with reason. I think they have done very wrong in publishing what they have of her."

Presumably the offence taken by C. was the reason why the volume was so hurriedly suppressed; but that is a small question which need not trouble us. The essential is that the courtship went as merrily (and, one may even say, as conventionally) as any other boy-and-girl courtship until that terrible spectre of the New Theology appeared. How its appearance frightened Harriet into fickleness; how her fickleness excited Shelley to a white heat of passion against bigotry and intolerance; and how this passion determined the lines upon which he would conduct his campaign against the dons—all this we have just seen. It remains to see how Mr. Shelley senior (and Mr. Hogg senior) received the news of their respective sons' joint escapade.

Timothy Shelley, being nearly sixty—and apparently somewhat port-logged—did not hurry. On the contrary he sent for a bottle of port and a copy of Paley's *Evidences*, in order that he might consider the subject leisurely in all its bearings. While sipping the former, he made an abstract of the latter; and then he opened the campaign with a sputtering fire of ungrammatical letters. He wrote to Hogg, cancelling an old-standing invitation to visit Field Place; he wrote to his son commanding him to break off his acquaintance with Hogg, return home, and submit himself to a tutor who should be chosen for him; he wrote to Hogg senior, begging his assistance in the separation of "these youngsters." Then he came to town, and established his headquarters at Miller's Hotel, Westminster.

The phraseology of his letters is eloquent of the

confusion in his mind. To Shelley he spoke of
" the punishment and misery that belongs to the
wicked pursuit of an opinion so diabolical and
wicked as that which you have dared to declare."
The first communication to Hogg senior (of whose
address he was uncertain) concludes with the
delightful postscript : " Sir James Graham tells
me there are several of the name, therefore into
whosever's hands this comes will have the goodness to find out the right person." A later communication shows with what weapons he expected
to be able to confound the boys' New Theology :—

" Paley's Natural Theology I shall recommend
my young man to read, it is extremely applicable.
I shall read it with him. A father so employed
must impress his mind more sensibly than a
stranger. I shall exhort him to divest himself of
all prejudice already imbibed from his false reasoning, and to bring a willing mind to a work so
essential to his own and his family's happiness."

And he really meant what he said—really
believed that the New Theology could be swept
away by Paley's arguments as cobwebs by a
housemaid's broom. He tried the experiment
not only on Shelley, but on Hogg also, inviting
both theologists to dine with him at his hotel,
" doing them well," and priming them with port
before expounding in the manner which Hogg
describes :—

" ' There is certainly a God,' he then said ;

' there can be no doubt of the existence of a Deity; none whatever.'

" Nobody present expressed any doubt.

" ' You have no doubt on the subject, sir, have you ? ' he inquired, addressing himself particularly to me.

" ' None whatever.'

" ' If you have, I can prove it to you in a moment.'

" ' I have no doubt.'

" ' But perhaps you would like to hear my argument ? '

" ' Very much.'

" ' I will read it to you, then.'

" He felt in several pockets, and at last drew out a sheet of letter-paper, and began to read."

What he read was a passage copied from Paley, and was recognized by his listeners as such. They were not convinced by it, as he had hoped they would have been; but the interview—thanks, no doubt, to the excellent port in Miller's cellar— was not so stormy as might have been feared. Hogg voted the member for Shoreham " jolly and hospitable "; and the member for Shoreham congratulated Hogg on being " a nice, moderate, reasonable, pleasant gentleman." He and Timothy Shelley became almost confidential, and, as schoolboys say, " warm," in their speculations as to the causes of Shelley's disconcerting profession of faith. " If he had married his cousin," Hogg thought, " he would have been steadier "; and he suggested that, as he could not marry his cousin, he should be induced to marry some one else :—

" If you were to bring him in contact with some young lady, who, you believed, would make him a suitable wife, without saying anything about marriage, perhaps he would take a fancy to her; and if he did not like her, you could try another."

It may not have been wise advice—Hogg may not have been serious in giving it; but, at least, it contributed to the harmony of the evening— a harmony not perceptibly disturbed even when Shelley was overcome by " a demoniacal burst of laughter " and " slipped from his seat and fell on his back at full length on the floor "; and the scene and the conversation give us an impression of Timothy Shelley not altogether unpleasing. He was port-logged and inadequate; but he meant well. He offered excerpts from Paley, but—*la plus belle fille du monde ne peut donner que ce qu'elle a.*

Evidently he meant to be conciliatory as well as severe; but he had the misfortune not to be on a level with his task. Intellectually, his eighteen-year-old son could dance round him; and he had, or thought he had, grievances which tempted him to do so. Having been compelled to forfeit a bride because of his New Theology, he was now called upon, for the same reason, to resign a friend. That was too much—a last straw—an ultimatum to be treated as a *casus*

85

belli. Chivalry, Shelley felt, forbade him to accept his father's terms. Timothy Shelley, in order to compel their acceptance, stopped his son's allowance.

But not for long, and not with results which perceptibly embarrassed Shelley. His sisters sent him some of their pocket money; his uncle, Captain Pilfold, sent him a present; he borrowed what else he wanted from Hogg; and meanwhile things were happening.

For one thing, Timothy Shelley had found that Hogg was not such an appalling person as he had imagined; for another, Hogg senior had summoned his son to York—which seemed a very long way from London in those days—to begin the dry, but respectable, study of conveyancing. That cleared the air a little; and friends and relatives were, at the same time, at work, trying to patch up a peace. Among the peacemakers were the Groves, Captain Pilfold, and Sir Bysshe Shelley's patron, the Duke of Norfolk. Captain Pilfold— a breezy mariner, who had fought under Nelson in the battles of the Nile and Trafalgar—admired Shelley's spirit more than he disliked his theology, and invited him to his house. The Duke gave a dinner-party at which the pacifying influence of port was once more brought to bear; and it is not unreasonable to suppose that Mrs. Shelley was anxious to see her boy summoned home before he got into further mischief.

Certainly there was some danger. One of Shelley's audacious proceedings at this date was

Shelley's Mother

from a painting in the possession of Sir John Shelley Rolls

to ask Rowland Hill's permission to preach in his chapel; and as one knows pretty well what doctrines he was prepared to preach, one feels sure that the sensation, if Rowland Hill had granted his request, would have been considerably greater than that aroused when Mr. Bernard Shaw preached in the City Temple. And that was only one of the roads by which he was approaching what his mother would have viewed as mischief. It was also at this period that he cultivated the acquaintance of Miss Harriet Westbrook—a most undesirable young person from the county family point of view.

It cannot be said that he was in love with her; for he had not yet ceased pouring out his soul to Hogg on the subject of Harriet Grove:—

" She is *not* lost for ever ! How I hope that may be true; but I fear *I* can never ascertain, I can never influence an amelioration, as she does not any longer permit a *philosopher* to correspond with her. She talks of duty to her *father*. And this is your amiable religion ! "

Harriet Westbrook certainly had not the first place in Shelley's heart when he wrote that; but it by no means followed that she was not a source of danger. There was a danger of which a wise mother, knowing how apt are the hearts of the young to be caught on the rebound, would have been very sensible. Whether Mrs. Shelley had yet heard enough about Miss Westbrook to be aware of the danger is doubtful; but she certainly desired an arrangement which would bring Shelley home; and presently she got her way.

Shelley was offered £200 a year on condition that he would apologize for his New Theology to the Master of his college. He rejected the condition indignantly, and, after an interval, it was withdrawn; so that, presently, we find him writing to Hogg:—

"I have come to terms with my father. *I* call them very good ones. I am to possess £200 per annum. I shall live very well upon it, even after the legal opinion which you inclosed. I am also to do as I please with respect to the choice of abode. I need not mention what it will be.

That was written from Field Place on May 15, 1811; and Shelley remained at Field Place until July. He does not seem to have been worried overmuch about his irreligious opinions. He now speaks of his mother as " quite rational," and as having confessed that " *prayer* and thanksgiving are of no use," and that any good man, whether philosopher or Christian, might fairly hope to " do very well in whatever future state awaits us." Mrs. Shelley's main concern evidently was, not to convert her son, but to keep him out of mischief.

She thought she had done so; but she was mistaken, as we shall soon see when we turn back to Harriet Westbrook.

CHAPTER IX

In order that our appreciation of the second Shelley-Harriet drama may be clear we must bear in mind that the *dramatis personae* were respectively the heir to a baronetcy and great estates and the daughter of a licensed victualler.

A man who is born in a stable is, notoriously, not a horse; a girl who is born behind a bar is not necessarily a barmaid. But she is apt to look like a barmaid when inspected, from a distance, through the eye-glasses and lorgnettes of the heads of county families; and she is also apt, even though her father has made a competence and retired, to think, feel, and proceed after the fashion of a barmaid in the conduct of the affairs of the heart.

And one knows what that means. Barmaids are, at once, romantic and ambitious, regarding romance as a ladder whereby they may climb to success in life. They are no more satisfied to marry licensed victuallers than the modern chorus girl is satisfied to marry a super. If they do marry victuallers, it is a *pis-aller*. They have learnt from novelettes that love levels ranks, and that " nice " girls, of whatever social station, may reasonably expect to marry " gentlemen "

89

in general and baronets in particular. They have also learnt—not so much from novelettes as from other sources—that Heaven helps those who help themselves; and they are consequently prone to show themselves of what philosophers have called a " coming-on " disposition—which disposition their friends and relatives are, on their part, prone to encourage.

That is the situation with which we start in the case of Harriet Westbrook. She impresses one as being somewhat (though not entirely) like one of Mr. Charles Garvice's heroines; resembling such a heroine in her beauty, natural charm, and romantic character, but differing from such a heroine in her greater readiness to help romance to a happy issue by weaving a net, with the help of the members of her family, about the heart of the prospective baronet on whom her affections were fixed. Circumstances favoured her; and two circumstances were particularly favourable. She was at school with Shelley's sisters at Clapham; and Shelley was a conscientious equalitarian whose equalitarianism always reached its zenith when there was an attractive woman in the case.

Almost all the women who played a part in Shelley's life were, as his county family would have said, " not quite "; and there were some of them of whom his county family would have said that they were " not by any means." But that never made any difference to him, as one discovers from the records of his relations with the daughter of another licensed victualler—Miss Elizabeth Hitchener of Hurstpierpoint, whose social standing is defined with rigid precision in a letter written by the Earl of Chichester at a time when a Government Department had reason to desire information about her :—

" Miss Hichener of Hurstpierpoint keeps a school there, and is well spoken of : her Father keeps a Publick House in the neighbourhood : he was originally a smuggler, and changed his name from Yorke to Hichener before he took the Publick House."

Shelley was in correspondence with Miss Hichener at the very time when the Westbrooks were weaving the toils; and the story of his relations with her—such as it is—shall be told in its proper place. Here one need only note that Miss Hichener reminded Shelley of the social gulf between them, and that Shelley replied with a violent expression of scorn for all such artificial distinctions :—

" You remind me thus of a misfortune which I could never have obviated, not that the sturdiest aristocrat could suppose that a *real* difference subsisted between me, who am sprung from a race of rich men, and you whom talents and virtue have lifted from the obscurity of poverty. If there is any difference, surely the balance of real distinction would fall on your side. . . . Have I not forsworn all this ? Am I not a worshipper of

equality ? . . . Where is now *Nature* distinguishing degrees ? or rather do you not see that art has
assumed that office, even in the gifts of the mind.
I see the *impropriety* of dining with you—even
of calling upon you. I shall not willingly, however, give up the friendship and correspondence of
one whom, however superior to me, my arrogance
calls an equal."

If that was Shelley's attitude towards a charming school-mistress who was evidently (at this
stage) careful of the proprieties and very much
afraid of what people would say, it was not to be
supposed that social barriers would impede his
intercourse with a charming schoolgirl who saw
nothing improper or unnatural in his wish to
overcome them, and whose family, far from refusing him facilities for such intercourse, absolutely
showered facilities upon him. And so to the
relation of the romance !

Mr. Westbrook, having retired from his tavern
to take his ease in his house in Chapel Street,
Grosvenor Square, and desiring to give his younger
daughter Harriet a good education, sent her to
the academy for young ladies kept by Mrs.
Fenning (presently to be succeeded by Miss
Hawke) at Church House, on the north side of
Clapham Common, where is now Nelson Terrace.
Mary and Hellen Shelley were also at school there
—little girls at a time when Harriet was a big
girl. Hellen Shelley's impressions, communicated
to Hogg, will be Harriet's best introduction :—

" I remember her well; a very handsome girl with a complexion quite unknown in these days—brilliant in pink and white—with hair quite like a poet's dream, and Bysshe's peculiar admiration. . . . The governesses and teachers used to remark upon her beauty; and once I heard them talking together of a possible Fête Champêtre, and Harriet Westbrook might enact Venus."

Shelley sometimes called at the school to see his sisters. One of the new letters printed in Mr. Roger Ingpen's collection shows him, while still an Eton boy, making an appointment with his friend Graham to meet him there. That was in the penny dreadful days, and he wrote in the penny dreadful style : " At half after twelve do you be walking up and down the avenue of trees near Clapham Church, and when you see a post chaise stop at Mrs. Fenning's door, do you advance towards it, and without observing who are inside of it speak to them—an eventful and terrific mystery hangs over it." *Et cetera;* Elizabeth adding, to avert misunderstanding : " We really expect you to meet us at Clapham in the way described by the *Fiendmonger*."

What happened next—though one does not know whether it happened on this, or some later, occasion—Medwin tells us :—

" It so happened that, as Shelley was walking in the garden of this seminary, Miss Westbrook past them. She was a handsome blonde, not then sixteen. Shelley was so struck with her beauty that, after his habit of writing . . . to ladies who interested him, he contrived, through the intermediation of his sisters, to carry on a correspondence with her. The intimacy was not long in ripening."

It had so far ripened by the time when Shelley returned from Oxford for the Christmas vacation that we find him, on January 11, 1810—in the midst of his trouble over Harriet Grove's fickleness—instructing his publisher to send Miss Westbrook a copy of his penny dreadful *St. Irvyne*. That is the first mention of her name in the correspondence; and it seems that, in the course of the same Christmas vacation, as Charles Grove told Hogg, he called at Mr. Westbrook's house to deliver a present for Harriet on behalf of his sister Mary. The presumption is strong—since Mary was so young—and since the necessity for schoolgirls to exchange presents during their Christmas holidays is not obviously urgent—that Shelley had volunteered to render this service for reasons of his own, and that, even in the hour of his distress because one Harriet had proved untrue, he was drawn to another Harriet by his " peculiar admiration " for her splendid head of hair. That is the way of the young—and sometimes of their elders also.

The correspondence presumably continued (though the letters have disappeared); but the next advances seem to have been made by the

HARRIET WESTBROOK

Westbrooks—first by Harriet herself, then by Harriet's sister Eliza, and finally by Harriet's father, the retired licensed victualler. The time was that of Shelley's residence in Poland Street; and we then find Harriet calling on him in his lodgings as his sister's messenger, bringing him their gifts of money. It seems to some naive biographers " natural " that they should have asked her, and that she should have agreed, to play this part. It was " natural " in a sense, no doubt, but hardly in the sense which they intend. The gifts could easily have been conveyed by other means; but romance is dear to the hearts of schoolgirls; and Harriet, who may fairly be supposed to have been told of Shelley's " peculiar admiration " for her hair, may also fairly be supposed to have jumped at—or perhaps even to have contrived—this opportunity of allowing him to admire it once again.

She gave him not only one opportunity of doing so, but several; the opportunities being contrived with the assistance of her sister Eliza, a maiden lady, thirty years of age—old enough, that is to say, to be regarded as a competent chaperon, but also young enough to discharge the duties of a chaperon in a sympathetic and accommodating spirit. As to what happened one has only scraps of information; but the scraps are sufficient as clues. Eliza, it is clear, brought the wisdom of the serpent to support the harmlessness of the dove. She understood that the heir to a baronetcy and entailed estates (even though temporarily out of favour with his father) was a " catch " for a licensed victualler's daughter, and she saw, more or less, how Shelley's passion for romance could be shaped to a practical end. He was, after Hogg's departure, alone in London; and Harriet's hair was his " peculiar admiration "; so if, not Harriet only, but her family took pity on his loneliness——

That was Eliza's simple idea, and she acted on it. In Shelley's first letter to Hogg from Poland Street we read :—

" Miss Westbrook has this moment called on me with her sister. It certainly was very kind of her."

And, about a week later, after Harriet's return to school—

" I . . . walked about Clapham Common with them for two hours. The youngest is a most amiable girl; the eldest is really conceited, but very condescending. I took the sacrament with her on Sunday. You say I talk philosophically of her kindness in calling on me. She is very charitable and good. I shall always think of it with gratitude, because I certainly did not deserve it, ard she exposed herself to much possible odium. . . .

" . . . I am going to Miss Westbrook's to dinner. Her father is out."

It would be interesting to know what Miss Westbrook talked about at that *tête-à-tête* dinner;

and what she said to her father afterwards; but of these matters there is no record. Presumably she praised Harriet to Shelley, and praised Shelley to Mr. Westbrook. At any rate, our next extract shows that matters have advanced a further stage.

" My poor little friend has been ill, her sister sent for me the other night. I found her on a couch pale; her father is civil to me, very strangely; the sister is too civil by half. She began talking about *l'Amour*. I philosophized, and the youngest said she had such a headache that she could not bear conversation. Her sister then went away, and I stayed till half-past twelve. Her father had a large party below, he invited me; I refused."

Whence various things appear. Eliza was evidently working hard, with a full knowledge of what is likely to happen when " young people " are " thrown together." Shelley, as evidently, was in strange waters, not quite in love with Harriet, though attracted by her, somewhat suspicious of Eliza's motives, and by no means desirous, in spite of his democratic principles, of hobnobbing with the licensed victualler's friends. For some reason he seemed to have convinced himself that the licensed victualler was a tyrant; but the only act of tyranny which he mentions was a very minor one; and he had an opportunity of mitigating it :—

" Yesterday she was better, her father compelled her to go to Clapham, whither I have conducted her, and I am now returned."

But if Harriet was unhappy at home, she was also unhappy at school, as girls are apt to be when the restrictions of discipline impede the free play of the grand passion; and there was a special reason for her unhappiness:—

" I am now called to Miss Westbrook; I was too hasty in telling my first unfavourable impression : she is a very clever girl, though rather affected. No! I do not think that she is. I have been with her to Clapham. I will tell you an anecdote. Harriet Westbrook has returned thither, as I mentioned. They will not speak to her; her schoolfellows will not even reply to her questions; she is called an *abandoned* wretch, and universally hated, which she remunerates with the calmest contempt."

The inwardness of this seems to be that one or more of Shelley's letters to Harriet had fallen into the school-mistress's hands, and that Harriet was, in consequence, in disgrace, and had been held up to the rest of the school as an example of everything that a pupil at a select Academy for Young Ladies ought not to be. A grand passion —that was bad enough; but a grand passion for an avowed atheist—that was indeed, as we moderns say, " the limit." The situation was terrible from the governess's point of view, romantic from Shelley's — and, from Eliza's standpoint, developing pretty much as it should develop.

Eliza, one feels, was, in her own way, a woman of the world. Shelley's atheism seems to have mattered no more to her than if it had been a strawberry mark on the left elbow : a trifle which the daughter of a licensed victualler must on no account allow to stand between her and the chance of marrying into a county family. It would probably wear off; and, if it did not wear off, no matter. Metaphysical speculations were in the clouds; but marriage was a practical enterprise which any woman could understand. The essential thing was to keep on good terms with Shelley; and that is what we find Eliza to have been doing while Harriet endured persecution on his account :—

" I spend most of my time at Miss Westbrook's. I was a great deal too hasty in criticizing her character. How often have we to alter the impressions which first sight, or first anything, produces! I really now consider her as amiable, not perhaps in a high degree, but perhaps she is."

That was written on May 6; and on May 12 we read :—

" I am now at Miss Westbrook's. She is reading Voltaire's *Dictionnaire Philosophique*."

As if Eliza cared twopence for Voltaire's *Dictionnaire Philosophique!* She cared, of course, nothing for it except as a means of humouring Shelley; and we can see that, in that task she was getting on moderately, if not supremely, well.

Probably she also had her work cut out to humour her father, whose attitude towards the courtship, at this stage, is not very clear. Probably he would have been willing enough that Shelley should marry Harriet, but did not believe that he had any intention of doing so. The youth, we can imagine him arguing, who objected to hob-nobbing with a licensed victualler's friends, was likely to think twice before marrying a licensed victualler's daughter—especially as he belonged to a class of society in which licensed victuallers' daughters are regarded as the natural prey of the gallant. There was food for thought there; and, on the whole, it was better that Harriet should remain at school until he saw his way more clearly.

That was the stage which matters had reached when Shelley made terms with his father and returned to Field Place, where his mother doubt-less fondly believed him to be safely " out of mischief " for the present. On May 13, however, we find him writing to Hogg:—

" Misses Westbrook are now very well. I have arranged a correspondence with them, when I will impart of the character of the eldest."

Decidedly there were possibilities in that correspondence.

100

CHAPTER X

THE evidence that Shelley was in love with Harriet Westbrook at this, or at any subsequent, stage of his relations with her, is weak. The references to her in his letters are on a very different plane of emotion from the bitter cry of the outcast suitor of Harriet Grove; and his lamentations over the loss of Harriet Grove continue for some time after Harriet Westbrook has begun to pay her addresses to him. Indeed, this second romance presents itself, at first, as a kind of duel between combatants unequally armed and aiming at different ends: Shelley ready to compass sea and land to make one proselyte, while Harriet watches her chance to entrap an eligible suitor.

The inference is not, of course, that Harriet Westbrook was hard or unromantic. It is quite as romantic to desire a husband as to desire a convert; and Harriet was not to know that Shelley was more eager for a convert than for a wife. How should she even suspect such a thing when he expressed " peculiar admiration " for a head of hair which was like " a poet's dream " ? If she might be his wife, she was quite willing to be his convert too. But she was only sixteen;

101

and she knew that, from the point of view of Shelley's family, she was " not quite "; . . . and she had the practical Eliza to coach her in the arts by which men may be " led on." Manœuvring was bound to follow, and may fairly be assumed to have been part of the programme—of Eliza's programme if not of Harriet's—when the correspondence was " arranged."

That correspondence, unfortunately, has not been published; but Shelley's mind can be read from his letters to other correspondents. We can see from these that his mind was just then far more active than his heart. His opinions were nominally those advertised in *The Necessity of Atheism;* but he was always ready to modify them in a Pantheistic sense; and his real concern was less with religious than with social problems—those problems of the relations between men and women, rich and poor, high-born and humble, of which religion (or at all events religious people) professed to offer cut-and-dried solutions.

Perhaps his own solutions were also cut-and-dried; but at least he cut them and dried them himself, ignoring all authority except that of logic. All men, he said with the revolutionists, were born equal; and therefore he would acknowledge no distinctions between man and man save those which intellect and virtue—the virtue which he himself recognized as such—created. For the same reason, he was on the side of labour as against capital, and of tenants as against landlords, and denounced the institution of marriage as the unwarrantable attempt of society to tyrannize over individuals who knew their own business best. And all this, of course, with the fiery fervour of nineteen—the age which admits neither half-truths nor half-measures, but either believes that kings rule by divine right or else, and more frequently, demands their heads on chargers.

Against marriage in particular Shelley (who was to marry twice), inspired by Godwin (who had already married twice), thundered with his most passionate eloquence. For instance :—

" Marriage, Godwin says, is hateful, detestable. A kind of ineffable sickening disgust seizes my mind when I think of this most despotic, most unrequired fetter which prejudice has forged to confine its energies. Yes! This is the fruit of superstition, and superstition must perish before this can fall."

That is to Hogg. In a letter to Miss Hitchener, the village school-mistress (who may, or may not, at that time, have cherished hopes), he writes in the same strain :—

" *Matrimony*, I know, is a word dear to you; does it vibrate in unison with the hidden strings of rapture—awaken divine anticipation ? Is it not the most horrible of all the means which the world has had recourse to, to bind the noble to itself ? "

Nor was he content to hold his views as pious

opinions, or to confine their applicability to his own case. He wished to impose them on his own family in general, and on his sister Elizabeth in particular, going even so far as to try to arrange a *union libre*—as the French call it—between Elizabeth and Hogg, who had never even seen each other. Convinced that, if they met, a sacred instinct would impel them to fall into each other's arms, he made an amazing proposal. He would smuggle Hogg into the house, which Timothy Shelley had forbidden him to enter, conceal him in his own study, improvize a bed for him on the floor, and point out Elizabeth to him from the window. The sight of her, he said, would amply repay the journey; and " time and opportunity " might be relied upon to do the rest.

But nothing came of that scheme—nothing, of course, was in the least likely to come of it. Shelley might have been capable of accepting such an invitation from Hogg; but there was not the least chance that Hogg would accept such an invitation from Shelley. He had too much common sense, too much regard for his dignity; and he preferred to keep the conduct of his love affairs in his own hands. He addressed complimentary messages to Miss Elizabeth Shelley at Field Place; but he remained at York; and the tone taken in the matter by Miss Shelley herself indicates that, if he had come to Field Place, he would have come on a vain errand. Miss Shelley went so far as to speak scornfully of " you and

your mad friend ; " with the result that, as Shelley
writes, not to Hogg, but to Miss Hitchener :—

" It is in vain that I seek to talk to her.   It is
in vain that I represent, or endeavour to represent, the futility of the world's opinion.
" ' This then is the honourable advice of a
brother ! ' ' It is the disinterested representation
of a friend ! ' To which, unanswered, followed
a sneer, and an affected sportiveness of gaiety
that admitted of no reply."

So that Shelley was disappointed with Elizabeth. He had hoped, but a little while before,
to have her for a disciple as well as a sister; he
had proceeded delicately to that end, trying to
avoid shocking her, preaching only as much of
his revolutionary gospel as he supposed her to be
ready to receive; but now, just as he was hoping
to complete her conversion, he perceived a change
stealing over her.

It was only the change natural to her years.
She was growing up, beginning to wear long
skirts, put up her hair, and think of coming
" out "; and that meant, of course, that, as she
was no genius, but only an ordinary attractive
young woman, new interests effaced the old ones.
Deism was all very well for children; but dancing
was more amusing to grown-up people; and
dancing was not only an end in itself but also
a means to matrimony. The idea of telling a
charming young woman, whom eligible partners

besieged at the county balls, that marriage was
a destiny to be avoided at all costs! That doctrine could not be accepted even from a bearded
philosopher—much less could it be treated with
respect when put forward by a presumptuous
brother of nineteen.

That was Elizabeth Shelley's point of view;
and Shelley could not understand it. He could
only think of her as Browning thought of his
" lost leader "; and he made haste to write of
her as he thought :—

" I will not deceive myself; she is lost, lost
to everything; Intolerance has tainted her—
she talks cant and twaddle. I would not venture
thus to prophesy without being perfectly convinced in my own mind of the truth of what I say.
It *may* not be irretrievable; but yes, it is. A
young female who only once, only for a short
time, asserted her claims to an unfettered use of
reason, bred up with bigots, having before her
eyes examples of the consequences of scepticism,
or even of philosophy, which she must now see
to lead directly to the former. A mother, who
is mild and tolerant, yet narrow-minded; how,
I ask, is *she* to be rescued from its influence ? "

How indeed ? It was apparently as a forlorn
hope to attempt the rescue that Shelley proposed
to smuggle Hogg into his father's house; and as
Hogg did not come, and showed no intention of
coming, it only remained for Shelley to "give

up " Elizabeth as hopeless, and satisfy his sore need of a confidante elsewhere.

He found such a confidante in Miss Elizabeth Hitchener, whom we have already introduced, as a school-mistress, the daughter of a retired smuggler, who had changed his name and taken a public-house. Shelley made her acquaintance —none of his biographers seem to know exactly how—while staying with Captain Pilfold at Cuckfield. She can hardly have been on the captain's visiting list, though one of his daughters was her pupil; but we need not trouble about that. She was about eight-and-twenty,—tall, dark, with black hair, searching eyes, and an illimitable intellectual curiosity—willing, for the sake of an argument, to treat the existence of God, and even the desirability of " matrimonialism," as open questions.

That was what Shelley wanted. He loved argument no less than he loved his own opinions; and he loved toleration better than either, being satisfied that truth was great and had only to be examined in the dry light of reason in order to prevail. So he began by lending books to the school-mistress, and then plunged into a correspondence with her—a correspondence which, he says, " carries its own recommendation both with my feelings and my reason "—a correspondence, too, in which the school-mistress seems to have engaged with an alacrity equal to his own. The first topic discussed was Locke's doctrine of " innate ideas "; but other subjects were quickly introduced: Christianity; the immortality of the soul; the passion of love and the institution of marriage.

It is impossible to know for certain what was in Miss Hitchener's mind. That she was in love is unlikely—a woman verging upon thirty is seldom in love with a boy of nineteen. That she was at first a little abashed by her own temerity in over-stepping social barriers is clear, —a school-mistress, albeit the daughter of a publican, is less temerarious in such matters than a barmaid. Living encompassed by the barriers, she is accustomed to pick her way delicately among them, like a cat avoiding puddles, with an intuitive perception of the things her neighbours will say if she does not. Unquestionably it was Miss Hitchener who pointed out to Shelley—not Shelley who pointed out to her—that there would be "impropriety" in their dining together *tête-à-tête* in a London hotel.

Still, we know from Miss Hitchener's subsequent conduct that propriety was not absolutely a fetish to her; and Shelley was a very charming boy; and his letters were of constantly increasing ardour. He soon began to address his correspondent as "Dear Friend" instead of "Dear Madam"; he soon afterwards assured her that she was the sister of his soul. His soul, in truth, had many sisters, and was always ready for a new one; but Miss Hitchener was not to know that. What she did know—for it was obvious—was that it was a great thing to be the sister of the soul of the heir to a baronetcy and great estates; and if she believed that the Platonic communion of souls was only a stage in the journey of the pilgrim of love towards a goal beyond, and out of sight of, Platonism, she only shared a common opinion for which there is some warrant in the accumulated experience of the race.

On the whole, therefore, it seems probable that Miss Hitchener cherished hopes. On the whole, too, in view of the advantage which a woman of her age has over a boy of Shelley's years, one suspects that those hopes would have been realized if she had had the field to herself, or perhaps even if she had known that there was a rival in the field. But that was the difficulty, real though unperceived. Shelley was allowing himself to be converted from his " anti-matrimonial " doctrine on the ground of " the sacrifice made by the woman so disproportioned to any which the man can give;" but Miss Hitchener was not the only woman who was ready to take advantage of his conversion. While corresponding with her, he had also been corresponding with the Misses Westbrook; and the Misses Westbrook, though less qualified than Miss Hitchener to discuss the subtleties of ethics and metaphysics, had greater skill in the weaving of toils, and better opportunities for weaving them. They could make use of a father who had retired from his public-house. to live on his private means; whereas Miss Hitchener's father, who kept a public-house in

109

her own immediate neighbourhood, was no help, but a hindrance.

So, at the very time of the correspondence with Miss Hitchener, we find the Misses Westbrook continually cropping up in Shelley's letters to Hogg :—

" Pray, which of the Miss Westbrooks do *you* like ? They are both very amiable. I do not know which is favoured with your preference."

" Miss Westbrook, the elder, I have heard from to-day; she improves upon acquaintance. . . . The younger is in prison;[1] there is something in *her* more noble, yet not so cultivated as the elder —a larger diamond, yet not so highly polished. Her indifference to, her contempt of, surrounding prejudice are certainly fine."

" I cannot write except now and then to you— sometimes to Miss Westbrooks."

But the most significant reference is this :—

" I shall be with you in three weeks; possibly less. Take lodgings for me at York; if possible at Mrs. Doughty's. . . . I shall leave Field Place in a fortnight. Old Westbrook has invited me to accompany him and his daughters to a house they have at Aberystwyth, in Wales. I shall stay about a week with him in town: then I shall come to see you and get lodgings."

[1] That is to say, at school.

ELOPEMENT WITH HARRIET

This, when one comes to look at it closely, is like bringing the queen into play in a game of chess against an opponent who is playing without a queen; and one suspects that old Westbrook should not be spoken of as moving in the matter, but as being moved. Within his limitations, he was rather an estimable man. It would be the height of injustice to denounce him as a brutal father, as Shelley seemed inclined to do, merely because he insisted that his daughter should go to school when she desired to stay at home—schools would be but thinly attended if fathers were not firm in such matters. If Mr. Westbrook had really been brutal, he would not have allowed himself to be talked over into sending this invitation, which was obviously sent in his daughter's interest, and not in his.

Personally, he cannot have had the faintest desire for Shelley's society. On the contrary, he must have resented alike Shelley's presumption in lecturing him on his duty towards his daughter, and Shelley's reluctance to drink a friendly glass with his convivial friends in the parlour. Such slights and such effrontery rankle in the bosoms of the best of men. But Harriet was in love, and Eliza had Harriet's interests at heart. Just as Eliza had considerately left Shelley and Harriet alone together in the house in Chapel Street, so now she would contrive to send them for walks together on the beautiful Welsh hills. The sending of the invitation, in short, was a further movement in the weaving of the toils, though it is hard to say whether old Westbrook was a conscious party to the weaving of them.

The invitation, at any rate, found Shelley only moderately keen, and left him comparatively cold. Instead of accepting it, he paid a visit to his cousins, the Groves, in the same neighbourhood. That may, of course, have been partly from fear of further trouble with his father, to whom (as to his mother) the Westbrooks would certainly have appeared "not quite"; . . . but even the prospect of going to see the Westbrooks from the Groves' house does not seem to have quickened his pulse to any perceptible degree. His desire, as the last letter quoted proves, was not to see Harriet, but to see Hogg; and he also had some idea of meeting Miss Hitchener in town, for it was precisely at this time that the question of the "propriety" of a *tête-à-tête* dinner with Miss Hitchener was raised.

That question, as we know, was answered in the negative. Miss Hitchener was presently to modify her attitude towards propriety; but she was a strict stickler for it then. It is clear, however, that Shelley was more interested in her than in Harriet Westbrook; and it is further to be remarked that, whereas there was no one to question him as to his feelings and intentions towards Miss Hitchener, he was quite explicit, in reply to Hogg's chaff, as to his feelings and intentions towards Harriet.

" Your jokes on Harriet Westbrook amuse me :

it is a common error for people to fancy each other
in their own situation, but if I know anything
about love, I am *not* in love. I have heard from
the Westbrooks, both of whom I highly esteem."

That was written, apparently at the end of
July, from the Groves' place at Cwm Elan,
Rhayader, Radnorshire, where Shelley was evidently bored. " All," he writes to Hogg, " is
gloomy and desolate "; and he further protests
that he is living with people " who, strange to
say, never *think*." Letters from Harriet and
Eliza partially relieved this boredom; but there
was no perceptible progress towards the conclusion which Harriet and Eliza desired. It
looked as if Shelley might have been content to
go on for ever, telling the Misses Westbrook
what he thought of the novels which they were
kind enough to send him, but never, as the
practical Eliza would have put it, "coming to
the point."

But then occurred the *coup*, which brought him
to the point. It bursts upon us like a bomb in
the midst of an array of letters mainly devoted
to moral and metaphysical philosophy :—

" I shall certainly come to York, but *Harriet
Westbrook* will decide whether now or in three
weeks. Her father has persecuted her in a most
horrible way, by endeavouring to compel her to
go to school. She asked my advice : resistance
was the answer, at the same time that I essayed

to mollify Mr. W—— in vain! And in consequence of *my* advice she has thrown herself upon *my* protection.

"I set off to London on Monday! How flattering a distinction!—I am thinking of ten million things at once.

"What have I said? I declare quite *ludicrous*. I advised her to resist. She wrote to say that resistance was useless, but that she would fly with me, and threw herself upon my protection."

There we have it; and there is no reason whatever for supposing that Mr. Westbrook played a more subtle part in the proceedings than appears upon the surface. He was not a subtle, but only an obstinate, man, bent solely upon the maintenance of his authority as a father; but he had daughters who were at once subtle and romantic: one daughter who had all an enthusiastic schoolgirl's romantic ideas about grand passions; and another daughter who knew how to adjust means to ends.

We must not be too hard on Harriet. She was only sixteen, and was the daughter of a licensed victualler; she could only know of life what life had taught her; life, as a rule, has taught but little to girls of her age and condition, and has taught that little wrong. No doubt she was as much in love as a girl of sixteen can be; no doubt she had magnified the significance of Shelley's attentions; no doubt she looked upon marriage, like other girls of sixteen, as the end, and not the beginning, of life's drama. No doubt, too, she argued that, as she had endured persecution from her school-fellows for Shelley's sake, Shelley would desire nothing better than to come to the rescue in the fearless fashion of the knights of old; and no doubt, to conclude, there was the underlying confidence that the heir to a baronetcy and great estates could not be " kept out of his rights " for ever.

That, we may take it, was Harriet's point of view : a point sharpened, in some respects, by Eliza's worldly wisdom. She was in love; she thought it would be much nicer to get married than to go back to school; she believed in chivalry, and she appealed to it, and did not appeal in vain. The appeal strained chivalry, but did not break it. Shelley married Harriet from chivalry, and not from love. The fact, indeed, is denied by Cordy Jeaffreson; but it stands out with transparent clearness in the letter in which Shelley announced his marriage to Miss Hitchener :—

" I arrived in London. I was shocked at, observing the alteration of her looks. Little did I divine its cause. She had become violently attached to me, and feared that I should not return her attachment. Prejudice made the confession painful. It was impossible to avoid being much affected; I promised to unite my fate to hers. I stayed in London several days, during which she recovered her spirits. I had promised, at her bidding, to come again to

London. They endeavoured to compel her to return to a school where malice and pride embittered every hour. She wrote to me. I came to London. I proposed marriage, for the reasons which I have given you, and she complied. Blame if thou wilt, dearest friend, for *still* thou art dearest to me; yet pity even this error if thou blamest me. If Harriet be not, at sixteen, all you are at a more advanced age, assist me to mould a really noble soul into all that can make its nobleness useful and lovely."

There, once again, we may claim to have it. No one can read that letter and believe that Shelley, left to himself, with no toils woven around him, would ever have married Harriet Westbrook. Left to himself, he might or might not have married Miss Hitchener—which might or might not have been worse; but Harriet Westbrook he would not have married. To the contrivance of that marriage the weaving of toils was necessary; and the story of it is pretty much the story of the spider and the fly.

The spider was quite a nice spider, as spiders go—an affectionate and well-meaning spider, bent, not upon devouring the fly, but upon living happily with it ever afterwards. But it was a spider nevertheless; and it not merely invited, but manœuvred, the fly into its parlour—not in the fly's interest, but in its own.

CHAPTER XI

BRIDE and bridegroom had thirty-five years
between them—nineteen for Shelley and sixteen
for Harriet. Shelley, that is to say, was of the
age of a modern undergraduate in his first year,
and Harriet a year, or perhaps a couple of years,
too young to leave school. If they were cleverer,
they certainly were not wiser than the generality
of boys and girls of their age; and if they were
more romantic than other children, their conceptions of romance differed widely.

Harriet was romantic after the manner of
a romantic barmaid—helped to be so by Eliza,
who, being fifteen years her senior, was fifteen
years nearer to the bar : cherishing a grand
passion for an engaging youth, but also fully
persuaded that a grand passion for the heir to a
baronetcy and great estates (albeit temporarily
kept out of his rights) has special elements of
grandeur. On Shelley's side the passion for
romance was, rather, the knight-errant's passion
for chivalrous adventure : the passion for redressing human wrong and succouring beauty in
distress.

Succouring, but not marrying; for Godwin's

117

writings had taught him, as we have already seen, that marriage was " detestable." He had not yet made Godwin's personal acquaintance; but Godwin's *Political Justice* was nevertheless his gospel. He accepted its teachings, consenting only to such concessions as Godwin himself had made. But those concessions were important.

The union between a man and a woman, Shelley argued, should last as long as their affection lasted, and no longer. It was awful to think that the contrary doctrine was taught in the name of religion. But religious prejudices were strong; and the religious (and not the religious only) made things uncommonly uncomfortable for women who defied them. Consequently it was not fair for a man to press a woman to defy them; consequently a man might consent to marry for a woman's sake, though he theoretically disapproved of marriage. Godwin had done so; and Shelley would follow his example, feeling that chivalry compelled.

He did so, and got into quite as much trouble by following the call of chivalry as he could possibly have incurred by flaunting an irregular connection in the face of religious relatives. For his relatives, after all, were only moderately religious; and there was a point with them, as there is with most people, at which the principles of religion became subsidiary to the considerations of family pride. The idea of an irregular connection on the part of one of their daughters would, of course, have startled them into
118

violent religious invective; but they would much
rather that their son formed an irregular connection with a barmaid (or any woman whom they
regarded as such) than that he married her.

Timothy Shelley, as we know, not only held
that view, but gloried in it, telling his son
he would cheerfully support his illegitimate
children, but would never tolerate a marriage
with a social inferior; and though his language
may have been less explicit than Medwin, who
reports it, gives us to understand, his point of
view—which was also doubtless that of his
wife—was known. It followed that, if Shelley
was to marry Harriet, the marriage must be contrived and carried out in secrecy. He borrowed
£25, therefore, from Medwin's father, without
telling him for what purpose he wanted it,
quartered himself on the Groves in Lincoln's
Inn Fields, and took Charles Grove, aged seven-
teen, into his confidence. A wedding breakfast
—we may so call it although it preceded the
wedding—was arranged at a tavern; and young
Grove saw the fugitives off by the night coach
to Edinburgh, where marriages could be concluded with more speed and simplicity than in
London. As the coach was passing through
York, Shelley scrawled the following note to
Hogg:—

" My Dearest Friend,
        " Direct to the Edinburgh Post-Office—
my own name. I passed to-night with the mail.

Harriet is with me. We are in a slight pecuniary distress. We shall have seventy-five pounds on Sunday, until when can you send £10 ? Divide it in two.

> " Yours,
> " PERCY SHELLEY."

Hogg, entering into the spirit of the enterprise, set out in pursuit of his friend. What happened before his arrival is described in Peacock's[1] *Memoirs of Shelley :*—

" Their journey had absorbed their stock of money. They took a lodging, and Shelley immediately told the landlord who they were, what they had come for, and the exhaustion of their resources, and asked him if he would take them in, and advance them money to get married and to carry them till they could get a remittance. This the man agreed to do, on condition that Shelley would treat him and his friends to a supper in honour of the occasion."

Necessity compelling, Shelley agreed to this; and Harriet does not seem to have raised any objection. As the daughter of a licensed victualler, she may even have been glad to

---

[1] Thomas Love Peacock, the novelist, afterwards of the East India Company's service. Shelley made his acquaintance in the course of one of his visits to Wales, and the friendship became intimate. He and Mary disliked each other, and some of his statements are, for that reason, open to suspicion.

welcome another licensed victualler as a wedding guest, feeling that his presence would ensure geniality. But there are licensed victuallers *and* licensed victuallers; and this man seems to have been of the baser sort, disposed to provide rather more geniality than was bargained for :—

" In the evening Shelley and his bride were alone together, when the man tapped at their door. Shelley opened it, and the landlord said to him—' It is customary here at weddings for the guests to come up, in the middle of the night, and wash the bride with whisky.' ' I immediately,' said Shelley, ' caught up my brace of pistols, and pointing them both at him, said to him—I have had enough of your impertinence; if you give me any more of it I will blow your brains out; on which he ran or rather tumbled downstairs, and I bolted the doors.' "

That is the story which brings into relief the wildness and the youthfulness of this matrimonial escapade. Shelley and Harriet set out together like adventurous Babes in the Wood; and here was a remarkable adventure to start with. Hardly less characteristic of their tender years was their passionate anxiety that their friends should be the sympathetic spectators of their pastimes. Harriet desired the sympathetic presence of Eliza. Shelley was eager to welcome, with extended arms, not only Hogg, but Miss Hitchener.

His letter to Miss Hitchener on the subject is, indeed, an amazing document. He evidently felt that explanations and apologies were due to her, and he offered them. He apologized, however, not for having preferred another woman's charms to hers, but for having " undergone the ceremony of marriage." She would wonder, he feared, how his " conscience could consent to it "; for he had lately told her that his wish was " to experiment upon morality." Reflection had decided him, however, that it was idle " to attempt by singular examples to renovate the face of society "; but that was no reason why Miss Hitchener should not come and stay with him :—

" Nothing would be transgressed by your even living with us. Could you not pay me a visit ? My dear friend Hogg, that noble being, is with me, and will be always, but my wife will abstract from our intercourse the shadow of impropriety. . . . My happiness is not so great that it becomes a friend to be sparing in that society which constitutes its only charm."

There we have an early exposition of the programme which is characteristic of Shelley's scheme of life and is sometimes presented as his doctrine of " universal love." It is a doctrine on which we shall constantly find him acting— successfully up to a point—but not beyond that point. He loved many women, and many women loved him; but the women who loved him did not always love each other. On the contrary, they were capable of jealousy, and he himself was also capable of that passion (though, having but little cause for it, he took it mildly), as we shall see before we have gone much further.

But we need not anticipate. Miss Hitchener did not receive her invitation to live with the Shelleys until at least six weeks after the wedding day, and it had to be renewed a good many times before she accepted it. The only visitor who actually burst in upon the honeymoon was Hogg, who had not been invited, but whose coming was nevertheless regarded as a glorious addition to the happiness of the party, and to whom we owe our only picture of those extraordinary but radiant weeks.

Timothy Shelley was storming, but Shelley did not mind—he had heard his father storm before. John Westbrook had begun to storm, but had been partially appeased by the sight of Harriet's " marriage lines "—Eliza might be relied upon to see to it that the retired publican ultimately forgave his daughter for eloping with the heir to a baronetcy and great estates. In the meantime, though Shelley's allowance had, once more, been stopped, that open-handed mariner, Captain Pilfold of Cuckfield, had sent him some money to go on with; and, as long as there was money to go on with, Shelley did not allow anxiety to prey on him, but felt that, as all was right for the moment, all would come right in the end.

He wrote innumerable letters; he saw the

sights; he studied; he encouraged Harriet to
study. Not the least distinguishing of his
characteristics was his desire to see women
study. Whenever he loved a woman—whether
he loved her much or little—he always wished
to teach her Latin and Greek, to say nothing
of mental and moral philosophy and the natural
sciences. The necessity of, as it were, saying
her lessons to her husband every morning,
may, in the end, have become somewhat of a
trial to Harriet; but the trouble was not yet
acute. She was not, for the moment, introduced
to any subject more painful than French, but
spent her time in writing out, in a beautiful
Italian hand, a translation of Madame Cottin's
Claire d'Albe—a tearful, sentimental novel of the
sort that she enjoyed. She also, in the evenings,
read aloud to Shelley and Hogg—sometimes from
novels, and sometimes from graver works.

This latter fact has sometimes been cited as a
proof that she was a young woman of great
cultivation, and a most suitable helpmate for
Shelley; but we must not be too sure of that.
Harriet read well, as Hogg testifies, and no doubt
she knew that she read well. No doubt she had
been praised for her reading—she may even have
taken prizes for it—at school; and no doubt she
liked to make a show of her accomplishment—
just as girls who know that they sing well
insist upon being asked to sing. The accomplishment, however, is not a very popular one,
except in the society of the blind; and Hogg tells
124

us that, though he himself was too polite to show
that he was bored, Shelley sometimes was not :—

" The more drowsy Bysshe would sometimes
drop off; his innocent slumbers gave serious
offence, and his neglect was fiercely resented; he
was stigmatized as an inattentive wretch."

And again :—

" Harriet read aloud, in the chaise, almost
incessantly, Holcroft's novels. The rigid, Spar-
tan, iron tone of that stern author was not
encouraging. Bysshe sometimes sighed deeply.

" ' Is it necessary to read all that, Harriet
dear,' he inquired pathetically.

" ' Yes ! absolutely.'

" ' Can you not skip some part ? '

" ' No ! it is impossible.' "

That in the midst of the honeymoon, and on
the way back from it. It must have been very
trying; but we need not make too much of it.
Nor need we dwell upon Hogg's other Edinburgh
stories—the story, for instance, of the rebuke
which a citizen of Edinburgh administered to
Shelley for laughing aloud in the street on the
Sabbath. That story is an antique one, of which
there are many variants; and stranger things
than those which it relates were presently to
happen to Shelley and his party.

The three of them posted back together to
York. Shelley announced his intention of

living at York "for ever," for the sake of Hogg's society, which he believed to be as agreeable to Harriet as to himself. Apparently the idea was that Harriet and he and Hogg should "for ever" share the same lodgings; and they did, at any rate, begin by sharing a sitting-room in the same lodging-house. It was further proposed, as we have seen, that Miss Hitchener should join the community; and Eliza was also to be invited, whether on her merits or as a concession to Harriet; and there was to be a perennial feast of reason and an interminable flow of argument concerning the rights of man, the existence of God, and the immortality of the soul.

It was an amazing dream. None but boys and girls in their teens could have dreamt it; and most boys and girls in their teens would already have been too old to dream it. Moreover, even for these exceptional boys and girls it was easier to dream the dream than to bring the realities into accord with it. The hesitations of Miss Hitchener created one difficulty; the personality of Eliza another; the lack of funds a third. The last-named difficulty was the one with which it was most instantly urgent to cope; and Shelley had hardly settled down in his rooms at 20, Coney Street, York, than he declared that he must set forth alone to Cuckfield to wrestle with it.

He was to pick up Eliza in town, on his return, and bring her to York. Possibly he also hoped

126

to fetch Miss Hitchener from Hurstpierpoint; for he had reached the point of offering to divide his fortune with her, as well as with his sisters and Hogg, when he inherited it, and was protesting against the vagueness of her promise to visit him " at some remote period," saying : " When is this remote period ? When will it arrive ? The term is indefinite, and friendship cannot be satisfied with this." But his main object was to see his father's solicitor, and ask for money; and he thought there would be no harm in leaving Hogg and Harriet alone together in his apartments while he engaged upon the quest.

Perhaps there would have been no harm if all the persons concerned had been philosophers and nothing but philosophers; perhaps, indeed, there actually was no harm. But, whether there was harm or not, there was trouble—such trouble as philosophers should always, if possible, avoid.

While Miss Hitchener was hesitating, Miss Eliza Westbrook was hurrying. Whether Harriet asked her to hurry, or whether she hurried on her own responsibility, one does not know. At all events she did not wait for Shelley to escort her to York, but made the journey alone, and so burst in upon the apartment which Harriet and Hogg were sharing. She did not like Hogg, and Hogg did not like her. Where much is dubious that one fact stands out clearly; and it is as well to state it before proceeding to pose the question : Is it or is it not true that Hogg had been making love to Harriet during Shelley's absence ?

127

CHAPTER XII

HOGG, HARRIET AND ELIZA WESTBROOK—HOW MISCHIEF WAS MADE

LET us review the admitted facts concerning Hogg's intercourse with Harriet, and consider what probabilities they favour.

He was only nineteen, and she was only sixteen. He was a young man of high spirits and vivacity, and she was a remarkably pretty girl. He was a gentleman by birth as well as education, and she, though not exactly a barmaid, was more like a barmaid than a lady.

That was Timothy Shelley's view of her, and it was also Hogg's—no one can read Hogg's narrative and retain any doubt upon the point. The whole tone of his references to her is a tone which a man does not adopt in writing of women whom he regards as his social equals. It may have been an improper tone for him to take; but he took it; and the fact that he took it is a piece of evidence to be noted. He took it, so far as one can judge, without the least intention of being offensive, but simply because obvious facts were too strong for him to do anything else. He liked Harriet; but he allowed himself (and must, indeed, be supposed to have been allowed) an intimacy of manner and address which would

not have been permissible, on the strength of so
brief an acquaintance, with the sort of person
whom he was accustomed to meet in the circles
in which a rising young conveyancer normally
moves in a cathedral city. It comes out, inci-
dentally and as if it were a matter of course, that
he addressed her, not as Mrs. Shelley, but as
Harriet—and not merely as Harriet but as "dear
Harriet."

Being on those terms with her, he was alone
with her in lodgings, shared a sitting-room with
her, and sat with her every evening from tea-time
until bed-time. Conversation had to be made;
and the difficulties which a young man of education finds in making conversation with a young
woman, " *genre* barmaid," are by no means in-
considerable. The stock of commonplaces is
quickly exhausted, and there is no other common
ground. Or, rather, there is no other common
ground except that, if the young woman be
attractive, of gallantry. Hogg, spending the
long evenings alone with Harriet, had practically
only three courses open to him. He might put
a book into her hands and ask her to read aloud;
he might sit in embarrassed silence, boring her
and himself;—or he might pay her compliments.

He tried the first course, but tired of it—let
those who can lay their hands upon their hearts
and avow that they would not have tired of it in
his place. The second course was not in keeping
with what we know of his character. That he
fell back upon the third course, and expressed in

somewhat exaggerated language his admiration of Harriet's eyes and other charming features is, in view of all the circumstances, rather likely. To do so would probably have been to follow the line of least resistance; for a girl of sixteen, *genre* barmaid, does not usually feel that she is receiving more than her due when a young man whom she permits to address her by her Christian name, informs her that he admires her eyes. Most men, it seems safe to assume, would rather spend an evening in paying compliments to a girl of sixteen, if she were beautiful and amiable, than in hearing her read extracts from the historical works of Dr. Robertson. Nor need any trouble be caused by the compliments unless the girl were exceptionally silly—or unless a mischief-maker intervened.

As it happened, however, Harriet was a silly girl, and Eliza was a mischief-making woman—a clever woman, too, and one obviously skilled in the art of making mountains out of molehills when it suited her purpose to do so. She fell upon the curious ménage, as has already been stated, in Shelley's absence. It certainly was a curious ménage; and Eliza, with all her cleverness, was not a woman to take any but a conventional view of it. It was not what she had expected—not what she had been accustomed to —not what friends whose good opinion she valued would approve of; etc., etc. She had not encouraged her sister to elope with the heir to a baronetcy and great estates for the purpose of seeing her compromised—one feels sure that she must have used the word " compromised "— by the articled pupil of a conveyancer. Friction between her and Hogg was therefore inevitable; and Hogg's description of her shows that the memory of the friction still rankled when he wrote :—

" I had ample leisure to contemplate the addition to our domestic circle. She was older than I had expected, and she looked much older than she was. The lovely face was seamed with the small-pox, and of a dead white, as faces so much marked and scarred commonly are; as white, indeed, as a mass of boiled rice, but of a dingy hue, like rice boiled in dirty water. The eyes were dark, but dull, and without meaning; the hair was black and glossy, but coarse; and there was the admired crop—a long crop, much like the tail of a horse—a switch tail. The fine figure was meagre, prim, and constrained. The beauty, the grace, and the elegance existed, no doubt, in their utmost perfection, but only in the imagination of her partial young sister."

That, more or less—for one must allow for prejudice—was what Eliza looked like. She was fifteen years older than Harriet, and therefore fifteen years nearer to the bar—" a barmaid by origin, or at least a daughter of the house," is the way Hogg puts it. She was also about twelve years older than Hogg and Shelley : old enough, that is to say, to tell the latter how she expected her sister to be treated, and to snub the former as an impudent boy of no particular account. She had, Hogg says, " tended, guided, and ruled Harriet from her earliest infancy; " she had " put her up to everything that was to be said or done; " and she had now arrived to " hoist her flag at the masthead, to take the entire command, and for ever to regulate and direct the whole course of her married life." And then, in the twinkling of an eye, we find Hogg and Shelley embroiled.

Eliza, we are told, had found out—Harriet, it is stated, had confessed to her—that Hogg had attempted to " seduce " Harriet during Shelley's absence. Shelley, we further read, taxed Hogg with the crime; and Hogg admitted it. Hogg threatened to blow his brains out unless Harriet forgave him. Hogg suggested a duel; and Shelley replied that nothing would induce him to try to take the life of one who had been his friend. Hogg, of course, ignores the story in his Life; and he could certainly urge, with great plausibility, that, if there had been anything in it, Shelley would not have sought to renew his friendship with him while he and Harriet were still living together. Still, it is in Shelley's own letters to Miss Hitchener that we read of Hogg's alleged " confession "; so that evidently there was something in the story; and the question is : How much ?

Probably very little; almost certainly nothing

which would ever have come to light, or, if it had
come to light, would have caused any serious
trouble, had it not been for the officious interference of Eliza, with her turn for making
mountains out of molehills.

The worst that one is obliged to assume about
Hogg is that, in order to make conversation with
Harriet, and to prevent her from eternally boring
him by reading Robertson's historical works
aloud, he had, as has already been suggested,
paid her such exaggerated compliments as men
pay to pretty barmaids. It is not in the least
necessary to assume that Harriet resented those
compliments, or that she would, if left to herself,
have thought that there was any harm in them.
It is only necessary to assume that she repeated
the compliments to Eliza—the rest explains
itself.

Eliza did not like Hogg; and she was the sort
of woman who gossips with landladies. The landladies in this case did not like Hogg, who describes
them as " dingy milliners " and admits that he
was indiscreet enough to chaff them; and they
would have been very unlike the general run of
landladies if they were unwilling to gossip with
Eliza. In the course of these colloquies between
women who did not like him, Hogg's reputation
would inevitably suffer. Rumour would soon
take tangible shape; and Harriet's report of the
compliments which she had received would be
held to afford confirmation of the rumours. One
can almost see the process at work, the mischief

brewing, and the compliments assuming a new and sinister significance when manipulated by Eliza's fluent and plausible tongue.

"My dear child! He actually said that to you? He actually said that to the wife of the heir to a baronetcy and great estates? And you didn't stop him? You didn't understand? You don't know that men only say that sort of thing to women whom they——? And you haven't told your husband? You didn't think he'd mind? Not mind! My dear silly, innocent Harriet! You must tell him at once. Or better still—leave it to me, and I'll tell him for you."

That is how we must suppose Eliza to have talked. Talk of that sort addressed by a woman of thirty to a girl of sixteen could hardly fail to produce an effect; and one can easily imagine the further speeches which followed when Eliza got hold of Shelley :—

"A nice man, this Mr. Hogg! A pretty sort of friend! You wouldn't call him your friend if you knew as much about him as I do. When the cat's away, you know—Ah! well, I don't mind telling you. In fact I think you ought to be told. I wouldn't tell you if I didn't know it for a fact. If you don't believe me, you can ask Harriet. We'll ask her together. Harriet, my dear, didn't you just tell me that Mr. Hogg——? "

And so forth; a woman of thirty—a clever woman, who knew human nature, and also knew a certain corner of the world—distilling poison into the ear of a boy of nineteen, devoid of the

worldly wisdom which experience gives. The
poison was bound to work. The boy's mind,
dragged down from the regions of abstract
speculation to the unfamiliar level of concrete
calumny, was bound to be perplexed. He might
have doubted Eliza's unsupported word; but
how could he doubt Harriet ? How suspect that
what Harriet said was what Eliza had contrived
that she should say ? What could he do, in
short, except run to Hogg, repeating the charges
and indignantly demanding explanations ?

His letters show that that was what he did;
and it is not difficult to picture Hogg's embarrassment if we imagine him to have had it on his
conscience that his manner with Harriet had been
a shade too free and easy. He could not very
well say, in so many words, that it had seemed
natural to adopt that sort of manner with that
sort of girl—that he had only treated Harriet
as she seemed to expect to be treated. Nor
could he, on the other hand, if he had so treated
her, say bluntly that she was a spiteful little
liar. All that he could do was to try to steer
an embarrassed middle course, protesting somewhat in this style, in the midst of impatient
interruptions :—

"Shelley! Shelley! My dear Shelley!
What an amazing accusation ! Who on earth
has been putting such extraordinary ideas into
your head ? What's that you say ? Harriet
told you herself ? Harriet complained to you
that I chucked her under the chin ? Well I

never—Do I deny it ? you ask.   I've no recollection of doing anything of the kind; but of course
I don't like to contradict a lady; and you may
be quite sure that, if I did, it was done with the
very best intentions.   I'd no idea she minded.
She didn't seem to at the time.   I'm quite willing
to beg her pardon if she did.   I can't say more
than that, can I ?   What !   You're not satisfied ?
You want to pick a quarrel with me about it ?
Well, then, confound it, Shelley, if you insist upon
quarrelling——"

Et cetera.   The   speeches   are,   of   course,
imaginary speeches, suggested in lieu of actual
speeches of which there is no record.   The game
of cross purposes which they illustrate explains
the subsequent course of events far better than
the theory that Hogg was really treacherous and
that Shelley   had   really   acquired   convincing
proofs of his treachery.   It explains alike the
hesitations and fluctuations in Shelley's immediate
wrath, and the completeness of the pardon which
he extended to his friend, after the waning of
Eliza's influence, but before the separation from
Harriet.

In the end Shelley evidently realized that he,
the idealistic philosopher, had been fooled by
the low cunning of the mischief-making daughter
of a licensed victualler.   Even at the moment
he did not permit himself to be fooled quite
without resistance.   The struggle proceeding in
his mind is apparent not only in the letters in
which, with a naiveté partly his own and partly

the characteristic of his tender years, he confided his troubles to Miss Hitchener, but also in the letters to Hogg himself. In one of the letters to Miss Hitchener he writes : " I told him that I pardoned him freely." In another : " I leave him to his fate." That is fairly inconsistent, but the inconsistency in the letters to Hogg is even more remarkable.

Shelley continued to correspond with Hogg for some time after his departure from York. The tone of the earlier letters is such that some biographers have, most naturally, jumped to the conclusion that the misunderstanding had not yet arisen when they were written. The confidences to Miss Hitchener show them to be mistaken. The trouble did, in fact, begin while Shelley was still at York. But we nevertheless find him, after the beginning of the trouble, instructing Hogg to open any letters which may come for him, and even inviting Hogg to visit him. For instance :—

" We all greatly regret that ' your own interests, your own *real* interests ' should compel you to remain at present at York. But pray write often."

And also :—

" Will *you* come ? Will you share my fortunes, enter into my schemes, love me as I love you, be inseparable as once I fondly hoped we were ? . . . Cannot you follow us ?—why not ? "

It is not until some weeks later that we come to the letter which temporarily terminated the intercourse of the two friends. Hogg prints the letter as " a fragment of a novel," suppressing Harriet's name; but there can be no doubt that it is really a fragment of this curious correspondence. These are the essential passages :—

" You talk of female excellence, female perfection. Man is, in your declamation, a being infinitely inferior, whose proudest efforts at virtue are but mockeries of his impotence. (Harriet) is the personification of all this contrast to man, the impassionateness of the most ardent passion that ever burned in human breast could never have dictated a compliment (I will not say a piece of flattery) more excessive. She perceived it (for she has shown me your letter), and remarked with such indignation on the repetition of that continued flattery, which you had made your theme ever since she knew you. I wish you would investigate the sources of this passion, my dear friend; you would find it derived its principal source from sensation.

" Let your ' too, too great susceptibility of beauty,' your own very sincere expression in your letter to (Harriet) suffice to convince you of the true state of your feelings. This caused your error primarily : nor can I wonder. I do not condemn, I pity; nor do I pity with contempt, but with sympathy, real sympathy. I hope I have shown you that I do not regard you as a *smooth-tongued traitor;* could I choose such for a friend; could I still love him with affection unabated, perhaps increased ? Reason, plain reason, would tell you this could not be. How far gone must you have been in sophistry, self-deception, to think sensation in this, in any instance, laudable.

" I am not happy. I tell you so. My last letter was written in the acuteness of feeling; but do you wish that I should be happy ? Re-assure yourself, and then be assured that not a wish of my heart will remain ungratified, as respects you. I have but *one* other wish beside; to that, at present, I will not allude more. (Harriet) will write to you to-morrow. May I require that, as one proof of self-conquest, you will throw the letter into the fire, suppressing all thoughts of *adoration,* which I strongly suspect to arrive from mere sensation, sentiment. But the letter will arrive first : it will be pressed to the lips, folded to the heart, imagination will dwell upon the hand that wrote it; how easy the transition to the wildest reveries of ungratified desire !

" Oh ! how the sophistry of the passions has changed you ! The sport of a woman's whim, the plaything of her inconsistencies, the bauble with which she is angry, the footstool of her exaltation ! Assert yourself, be what you were. Love, adore; it will exalt your nature, bid you, a man, be a God ! Combine it, if you will, with sensation, perhaps they are inseparable; be it so. But do not love one who *cannot* return it,

who, if she *could, ought* to stifle her desire to do
so. Love is not a whirlwind that it is unvanquishable ! "

That is the climax on which the curtain of this
act of the drama falls. The circumstances which
led up to it are left to conjecture; but the difficulties in the way of conjecture are hardly
insuperable. Hogg's letters, and the interpretation put upon them in Shelley's family circle,
are the missing links in the chain which imagination may plausibly supply.

Hogg, we must suppose, was too wise a man
to accept Shelley's invitation to visit him, but
not wise enough to give the right reasons for
his refusal, and was an indiscreet and unpractised
letter-writer, as boys of his age, entangled in
emotional situations of which they have no
experience, are apt to be. He felt, no doubt,
that it would be brutally bad manners for him
to represent himself as insensible to Harriet's
charms—it may even be that he was not insensible to them. Consequently he let himself go
too far in the opposite direction, struck the
attitude of a love-sick swain with a blighted
heart, and once more paid exaggerated compliments—mainly, if not solely, because he supposed it to be the proper thing to do, and
perhaps with the result of working himself up
into a partial belief in his own sincerity.

It was a dangerous thing to do in any case—
doubly dangerous with such a woman as Eliza

in the house. If Eliza got hold of those letters, she could make what she chose out of them—and one knows what she would choose to make. They proved—that is to say, they seemed to prove—that she was right. They proved it easily to Harriet—to whom the idea that a personable young man was pining for love of her need not be supposed to have been repugnant. They proved it, eventually, and by dint of reiteration, to Shelley himself. " I told you so," Eliza was now in a position to say. " His behaviour is, and has been all along, that of the wicked baronet in the novelettes. You really ought to write and tell him so."

And Shelley, who was as young as Hogg, and nearly as young as Harriet, and had an irresistible passion for putting his most sacred feelings on note-paper, sat down and wrote. He may not have written exactly the letter which Eliza would have liked to see him write; but he wrote the letter which has been quoted, and it served as well. Indeed, it served better; for it left the door open for the resumption of friendship at some later date, when Eliza no longer spoke as one having authority, and Hogg and Shelley and Harriet were all old enough to see how silly they had been at her cunning instigation.

But we shall come to that in due course, and shall have to follow Shelley upon many pilgrimages before we come to it.

CHAPTER XIII

AT KESWICK—SHELLEY'S RECONCILIATION WITH HIS
FATHER—HIS RELATIONS WITH SOUTHEY—HIS COR-
RESPONDENCE WITH WILLIAM GODWIN

AT the end of October, or the beginning of
November, Shelley and his party moved from
York to Keswick; his purpose being, apparently,
not so much to see the Lakes as to see the Duke
of Norfolk, who had a place at Greystoke, in that
neighbourhood. As the Duke had made the
peace before between the mutinous son and the
angry father, there was at least a sporting chance
that he might render the same service a second
time; and the need for help was urgent. Shelley
had come to the end of his pocket money. He
had also come to the end of Eliza's pocket money;
and the Duke's response to his appeal found him
in the midst of a desperate correspondence with
the elder Medwin about ways and means.

" *We are now so poor,*" he wrote to Medwin,
underlining the words, " *as to be actually in
danger of every day being deprived of the necessaries
of life.*" Would it not be possible for him, he
asked, in spite of his minority, to borrow on
the security of his expectations ? If so, would
Medwin at once remit a small sum for immediate
expenses ? And the letter proceeds :—

142

AT KESWICK

" Mr. Westbrook *has sent me a small sum, with an intimation that we are to expect no more;* this suffices for the immediate discharge of a few debts, and it is nearly with our very last guinea that we visit the Duke of N. at Greystock, to-morrow. We return to Keswick on Wednesday. I have very few hopes from this visit."

The visit nevertheless marked the turning of the tide. The Duke had already, three weeks before, opened negotiations with Timothy Shelley, as is set forth in an extract from his private Diary first printed in Denis Florence MacCarthy's *Early Life of Shelley* :—

" 1811, Nov. 7.—Wrote to T. Shelley that I would come to Field Place on the 10th, to confer with him on the unhappy difference with his son, from whom I have a letter before me.

" To Mr. B. Shelley in answer that I should be glad to interfere, but fear with little hope of success; fearing that his father, and not he alone, will see his late conduct in a different point of view from what he sees it."

Dukes, however, are not without influence in determining the point of view from which such things shall be seen by country gentlemen. Their arguments count for much, and their examples count for more. When Shelley, Harriet, and Eliza were invited to Greystoke, to join a house party which included Lady

Musgrave, Mrs. Howard of Corby, and James Brougham, the brother of the future Lord Chancellor, Field Place was bound to be impressed, and Mr. Westbrook to be dazzled. To think that he had once kept a tavern, and that his daughters now adorned baronial halls! That was indeed a happy ending to what had seemed a rather doubtful experiment. He must show himself no niggard, but must do " the handsome thing," so as to show himself worthy of the unexpected honour.

He did it, and so made it difficult for Timothy Shelley to do otherwise. It was not agreeable for Timothy Shelley to think that his son had, as he put it, " set off for Scotland with a young female; " but it hardly suited him to see his son dependent upon the charity of the young female's father. He might yield with a good grace, or with a bad grace; but he must yield. Probably, too, he argued that a young female who was thought good enough for a Greystoke house party could not be such a terrible young female after all; and probably that was what the Duke of Norfolk intended him to think when he invited the young female to join the house party.

What the Duke and Duchess really thought of Harriet and Eliza one has no means of knowing. It is not to be supposed that they surveyed them otherwise than from Olympian heights, or judged them by very exigent social standards; but, whatever the test was, they seem to have passed it,—most likely by dint of being careful not to talk too much. One can imagine Harriet's youth, beauty, and shy timidity disarming criticism, and the Duchess working herself up into a state of patronizing enthusiasm over the discovery that she did not drop her h's. The upshot of the visit was, at any rate, that Shelley, at the Duke's instance, wrote his father a letter —two letters, in fact—of dignified apology; and that his father, albeit somewhat grudgingly, renewed his allowance of £200 a year. Mr. Westbrook made his daughter an equal allowance; so that, for the time being, all was well.

Nor were any unpleasant conditions attached to the allowances; for Shelley expressly refused to submit to any :—

" I hope " (he wrote) " you will not consider what I am about to say an insulting want of respect or contempt; but I think it my duty to say that, however great advantages might result from such concessions, I can make no promise of concealing my opinions in political or religious matters. I should consider myself culpable to excite any expectation in your mind which I should be unable to fulfil."

And in the second letter :—

" My principles remain the same as those which caused my expulsion from Oxford. When questions which regard the subject are agitated in society I explain my opinions with coolness and moderation. You will not, I hope, object to my train of thinking. I could disguise it, but this would be falsehood and hypocrisy."

That is important because the time of Shelley's stay at Keswick was the time at which he really began to " find himself," not indeed as a poet— for his poetry was very poor stuff as yet—but as a speculative thinker and a social reformer; and one may properly insert here a picture of him as he appeared to Southey, who was then living at Greta Hall :—

" Here is a man at Keswick " (Southey wrote to Grosvenor C. Bedford) " who acts upon me as my own ghost would do. He is just what I was in 1794. His name is Shelley, son to the member for Shoreham . . . It has surprised him a good deal to meet, for the first time in his life, with a man who perfectly understands him, and does him full justice. I tell him that all the difference between us is that he is nineteen, and I am thirty-seven; and I daresay it will not be very long before I shall succeed in convincing him that he may be a true philosopher and do a great deal of good with £6000 a year, the thought of which troubles him a great deal more at present than ever the want of sixpence (for I have known such a want) did me. God help us ! The world wants mending, though he did not set about it in exactly the right way."

Which shows that Southey, though he observed the surface of things, could not see beneath the surface. He was equally mistaken in expecting that Shelley would ever develop into a man like him, and in supposing that he had ever been a boy like Shelley.

Shelley, as an undergraduate, had been abstemious, whereas Southey had been addicted to negus. Southey had been orderly as an undergraduate, avoiding Walter Savage Landor as a " mad Jacobin," even in the days of his Pantisocratic dreams; whereas Shelley had been wild, a ringleader in mischief, and one who set dons at defiance. It would have been supposed, if they had been college contemporaries, that Southey was the more serious thinker of the two; but there was not only more vivacity in Shelley's revolt against conventional ideas and doings— there was also more intensity, more unselfishness, and more staying-power. Southey, when he soared towards the empyrean, was, in truth, only a captive balloon, secured by cords of common sense, and sure to be drawn back to earth by them after a brief excursion. Shelley's flight suggests, rather, the audacious self-dependence of the aeroplane.

When one looks at him in his Oxford days, indeed, it is a little difficult to disentangle his " message " from his desire to shock and startle serious and self-satisfied persons—people, as he put it to Hogg, " who never think." He was a born preacher as surely as his Oxford contemporary Thomas Arnold, albeit born to preach a very different doctrine; he talked quite as much about Virtue, though he did not always mean by Virtue exactly what other people meant; but he differed from Thomas Arnold in his passion for preaching the sort of sermon which would cause the members of his congregation to jump out of their boots. That is how *The Necessity of Atheism* came to be written by one who was not exactly an atheist; and that is why we have to get Shelley away from Oxford before we can begin to take him seriously. At Keswick, where there were no serious self-satisfied persons to shock (though there was Southey to argue with), one may do so.

The articles of the faith flash out in the letters to Miss Hitchener, in the midst of lamentations over Hogg's excess of gallantry and appeals to his correspondent to come and live with him as the sister of his soul ought to do. The creed varies a little from letter to letter in matters of definition and detail; but the writer remains consistent in essentials. He never seems quite sure whether he is atheist, deist, or pantheist; but he loves Virtue and hates Christianity because he believes Christianity to be opposed to Virtue. In particular he objects to the Christian doctrine of rewards and punishments, maintaining that, unless Virtue be disinterested, it is not virtuous. He also believes in the perfectibility of the human race, the rights of man, and the principles of the French Revolution.

A cloudy doctrine, no doubt; but Shelley took

no unfair advantage of its vagueness. On the contrary he made it definite to his detriment, when he was offered £2000 a year on condition that he would allow certain properties to be included in the entailed estate. " With what face," he then exclaimed, " can they make to me a proposal so insultingly hateful ! Dare *one* of them propose such a condition to my face—to the face of any virtuous man—and not sink into nothing at his disdain ? " The suggestion of such a bargain, he added, would "serve to put in its genuine light the grandeur of aristocratical distinctions and to show that contemptible vanity will gratify its *unnatural* passion at the expense of every just, humane, and philanthropic consideration."

That was the temper of the enthusiasm which Southey thought to damp by the time-honoured device of saying that he had felt it himself when he was young and foolish, but was now old enough to know better. He might as well have tried to extinguish the Fire of London with a garden hose. The most that he could do was to make Shelley lose his patience and his temper; and that he quickly did. He invited Shelley to tea, and offered muffins and good advice; but though Shelley accepted muffin after muffin until there were no muffins left on the plate, he refused the good advice as emphatically as a teetotaller refuses whisky. Southey, he concluded, was not a matured sage but a " lost leader "; and he let him see that he so thought of him :—

" Southey has changed. I shall see him soon and I shall reproach him for his tergiversation. He to whom Bigotry, Tyranny, Law was hateful, has become the votary of these idols in a form the most disgusting."

He suggested, moreover, that Southey has apostatized for fear of poverty :—

" Wordsworth (a *quondam* associate of Southey) yet retains the integrity of his independence; but his poverty is such that he is frequently obliged to beg for a shirt to his back." [1]

The opinion was momentarily revised when Southey was discovered to be " very kind," and manifested his kindness by persuading Shelley's landlord to reduce his rent. Then points of philosophical agreement were found. " Southey is no believer in original sin : he thinks that which appears to be a taint of our nature is in effect the result of unnatural political institutions : there we agree." Moreover, Southey is admitted to be " disinterested so far as respects his family." But Southey's domestic virtues (which all the world allows) are soon overshadowed, in Shelley's eyes, by his comfortable Conservatism. He is presently irritated by Southey's habit of laying down the law. He finds it hard to be polite to him; he writes about him in language which is very far from polite :—

[1] This statement rests, of course, on no authority except Shelley's imagination.

150

" Southey, the poet, whose principles were pure and elevated once, is now the paid champion of every abuse and absurdity. I have had much conversation with him. He says, ' You will think as I do when you are as old.' I do not feel the least disposition to be Mr. S.'s proselyte."

And then again :

" Southey's conversation has lost its charm; except it be the charm of horror at so hateful a prostitution of talents."

The personal relations, indeed, though strained, were not yet strained to breaking-point. Shelley did not openly quarrel with the Tory whose influence had brought about the reduction of a Radical's rent, and who had lent bed and table linen to an ill-provided Radical household. The two men were to correspond courteously before they came to correspond acrimoniously. But Shelley, as he had said, would never be Southey's proselyte; and it was while he was arguing with Southey that he formally seated himself at the feet of William Godwin.

To what an extent Godwin's *Political Justice* had influenced him we have already seen. He had apparently read it at Eton, and he had certainly read it at Oxford. It had long been a fifth gospel to him, if that be a proper expression in the case of a man by whom the four other gospels were rejected. He had supposed—that is to say, he had assumed without inquiring—that the author, like the other evangelists, was dead; but he now learnt that he was alive, and only fifty-six years of age. No sooner had he realized that than he sat down, in his usual impetuous style, and wrote to him, begging for the honour of his acquaintance, and so began relations which were to have momentous consequences. For William Godwin had a daughter, and a step-daughter, and an adopted daughter,—all of whom will presently figure in this narrative.

Presently, but not immediately. For the moment it suffices to introduce William Godwin himself.

Godwin had been a Nonconformist Minister, but had outgrown Nonconformity and become first a Unitarian, and then an atheist, a republican, and an advocate of free love. He earned his living, partly as a man of letters, and partly as a bookseller and publisher. On the whole he was the most effective of the English representatives of the French revolutionary creed, being the sort of man at whose feet disciples naturally take their places. The Government had its eye on him. There exists, at the Record Office, a State Paper—" Domestic, Geo. III., 1813. January to March. No. 217."—in which he is charged with trying to instil poisonous principles into the minds of the young by means of insidious school primers. Nothing came of the charge—apparently because the Secretary

William Godwin
From a painting by J. Northcote R.A.

of State to whom the memorandum was submitted could not be bothered to examine the primers; but their publisher's formal profession of faith was set out in his *Inquiry Concerning Political Justice and its Influence on General Virtue and Happiness*, and also in *Caleb Williams* and other novels; and he had a considerable following among the clever young men of the day. Being a needy teacher, he frequently borrowed money from his disciples; and it is hardly to be doubted that, in his later years, one of his objects in enlarging the circle of his disciples was to extend his possible sources of income.

Shelley, however, knew nothing of that as yet. Godwin, for him, was the one great man who could give him illumination. He confided in Godwin as a woman confides in her confessor,—embroidering the facts a little, as some confessors accuse some women of doing. When Godwin responded encouragingly to his advances, he was as pleased with himself as a Sunday-school scholar who has won a good conduct prize, and began at once to build castles in the air. He would take a mansion in Wales, and Godwin should visit him there. Miss Hitchener, and the pupils into whose minds Miss Hitchener was instilling the principles of true virtue, should also join the party. They and he and Eliza and Harriet would ramble on the hills together by day, and discuss the rights of man and the existence of God by night. Their discussions would be fruitful of enlightenment, not only to themselves but to the world; and, in the meantime, Shelley would do something to prove that he was Godwin's worthy pupil, whether Godwin approved of his proceedings or not. He would go to Ireland and—

But what Shelley really meant to do in Ireland is a thing which his announcement of his intentions does not adequately explain. " We go principally," he wrote to Miss Hitchener, " to *forward as much as we can* the Catholic Emancipation;" and if the idea of the cause of Catholic Emancipation being forwarded by Shelley, at the age of nineteen, is ludicrous, the idea of its being forwarded by Harriet and Eliza is more comic still. Nor do the contemplated means lift the remarkable scheme on to a more serious plane. All that Shelley proposed, apparently, was to issue an address to the Irish People, consisting of " the benevolent and tolerant deductions of philosophy reduced into the simplest language." Later, he conceived that a Debating Society and a Philanthropical Association might be helpful; but the essential notes of the programme are, after all, its vagueness and its earnestness. To Godwin, for instance, Shelley writes :—

" I shall devote myself with unremitting zeal, as far as an uncertain state of health will permit, towards forwarding the great ends of virtue and happiness in Ireland, regarding as I do the present state of that country's affairs as an opportunity

which if I, being thus disengaged, permit to pass
unoccupied, I am unworthy of the character which
I have assumed."

To Miss Hitchener, whom he implores in vain
to join him in his noble undertaking, he exclaims :—

" Oh, my dearest friend, when I think of the
uncertainty and transitoriness of human life
and its occupations, when I consider its fleeting
prospects and its fluctuating principles, how
desirous am I to crowd into its sphere as much
usefulness as possible ! We have but a certain
time allotted to us in which to do its business :
how much does it become us to improve and
multiply this time; and to regard every hour
neglected, misspent, or unimproved, as so much
lost to the cause of virtue, liberty, and happiness."

It is the language of the pulpit—not a parody
of that language, but the thing itself. Not
otherwise do Messrs. Torrey and Alexander talk
when they call upon us to redeem the time.
But the figure which rises before our eyes when
we read the eloquent appeal is not at all like that
of Dr. Torrey, and not very much like that of Mr.
Alexander. There is no modern parallel for it,
but there is an old one. We are reminded of
nothing so much as the blind enthusiasm of the
Knight of La Mancha, so full of chivalry yet so
devoid of humour, so eager to ride about re-

155

dressing human wrong, yet so incapable of realizing the actualities of the life about him. Shelley, in short, must be pictured, if we would picture him truly, as a Quixote of nineteen, steeped in Godwin's political philosophy—steeped in it far more deeply than Godwin himself—instead of picaresque romance, and sweeping his womankind along with him in the headlong welter of an enthusiasm which they could not help trying to simulate, though they were quite incapable of understanding it.

And so, by way of Whitehaven and the Isle of Man, to Dublin.

CHAPTER XIV

THE EXPEDITION TO IRELAND

SHELLEY'S Irish Mission does not seem to have been taken very seriously by any one except Miss Hitchener, who had to be assured, again and again, that the missionary feared no foe, and that the danger of the dagger, the bowl, and even the dungeon, was negligible. Her courage was not screwed up to the point of joining the expedition, even when her attention was directed to the intrepid examples of Harriet and Eliza, who apprehended " no inconveniences but those of a wet night and sea-sickness." Perhaps sea-sickness itself seemed to her too awful a peril to be faced without necessity.

Godwin, at the same time, wrote urging Shelley to go slowly; and in truth he had little opportunity of going at any other pace. Ireland was not then looking out for a Saviour—or, at all events, it did not accept Shelley in that character. The public of Dublin, eager as that of Athens to be entertained by " some new thing," viewed him, rather, as it might have viewed an Infant Prodigy or a Boy Preacher. His Irish servant—one Daniel Healey—entered into the spirit of the thing and gave out, to his intense annoyance, that he was only fifteen years of age.

THE ROMANTIC LIFE OF SHELLEY

There is abundance of credible testimony to the effect that he looked no more.

So nothing happened which need delay any one except the antiquary who burrows after odds and ends of information. Shelley did, indeed, address a public meeting; but it was not a meeting called to hear him. He was merely one of the speakers who responded to a vote of thanks to the Protestants who had attended a Catholic gathering; and none of the papers thought the speech worth reporting at any length, though the *Dublin Journal* printed a letter from a correspondent who wished to bear public witness to his disgust at observing " with what transport the invectives of this renegade Englishman against his native country were *hailed* by the assembly." As for the *Address to the Irish People*, which was distributed in the streets of Dublin, and sent to " sixty public-houses," no reader of the present day—not even Sir Edward Carson—would be likely to regard it as an inflammatory manifesto. It is a document almost as sober as one of Mr. St. Loe Strachey's tracts.

There were indiscretions in it, no doubt; but they were the indiscretions of a youthful philosopher ingeminating peace where there was none. In his desire to be absolutely fair between Protestants and Catholics, Shelley took occasion to remind the latter, not only of the Inquisition and the Massacre of Saint Bartholomew, but also of " the vices of monks and nuns in their con-

158

vents." Mr. St. Loe Strachey, being a good deal older than Shelley when he took to writing tracts, would doubtless have known better than to do that; but much of the rest is thoroughly worthy of Mr. Strachey. For instance :—

" I wish to impress upon your minds that without virtue or wisdom there can be no liberty or happiness; and that temperance, sobriety, charity, and independence of soul will give you virtue, as thinking, inquiring, reading, and talking will give you wisdom. Without the first the last is of little use, and without the last the first is a dreadful curse to yourselves and others."

That, it will be allowed, is more platitudinous than revolutionary; and it reminds one of nothing so much as Mr. Strachey trying to defend the pockets of the well-to-do by assuring the destitute that a new way of life is worth many old age pensions. And of course, Shelley failed, just as Mr. Strachey has failed, to convince the mass of his hearers that abstract virtues would be more helpful to them than concrete reforms.

If Shelley cuts a more romantic figure as a reformer than Mr. Strachey does, that is because he was younger when he plunged into public life than one can easily believe Mr. Strachey to have been even in the nursery. He may have dreamt of the millennium in the spirit of a seer; but he worked for it in the temper of an undergraduate. The announcement of "a plan for proselytizing the young men of Dublin College" is delightful. "Those," Shelley thinks, "who are not entirely given up to the grossness of dissipation are, perhaps, reclaimable": a sentiment which will be specially entertaining to readers familiar with Lever's pictures of undergraduate life in Dublin at this period. Still more delightful is Shelley's description of his method of distributing his tracts: "I stand at the balcony of our window, and watch till I see a man *who looks likely;* I throw a book to him." A description supplemented in one of Harriet's letters thus :—

"I am sure you would laugh were you to see us give the pamphlets. We throw them out of window, and give them to men that we pass in the streets. For myself, I am ready to die of laughter when it is done, and Percy looks so grave. Yesterday he put one into a woman's hood of a cloak; she knew nothing of it, and we passed her. I could hardly get on, my muscles were so irritated."

That was all. Godwin continued to write Shelley letter after letter, imploring him to go slowly and do nothing which might provoke bloodshed; but there was never any danger of that. The masses were not moved, and the authorities were not alarmed. Even when a box of pamphlets, addressed to Miss Hitchener, was opened in the Customs House at Holyhead, the Secretary of State took no steps beyond making a few inquiries about Miss Hitchener; and Shelley himself, like the seconds of French duellists, when they cannot get their principals to fight, decided to regard his mission as terminated.

" I submit," he wrote to Godwin; " I shall address myself no more to the illiterate. I will look to events in which it will be impossible that I can share, and make myself the cause of an effect which shall take place ages after I have mouldered in the dust."

So he packed and departed for Wales; but before we follow him there we may pause to review his personal relations with his wife and the other women who were presently, and for some time, to constitute, as it were, his *smala*, or his caravan.

Though Ireland received him coldly, regarding him as a freak rather than a prophet, he evidently enjoyed, for a season, the rank of a prophet in his own household. He entirely dominated Harriet, and he partially dominated even Eliza— partly, one imagines, in virtue of his higher social origin, but mainly by his intellectual superiority and the communicable contagion of his enthusiasm. The seeds of opposition and revolt were doubtless there. The ideals of the barmaid who does not see what is the use of marrying a gentleman unless she achieves the position of a great

L   161

lady were doubtless at the back of the brains of
both of them, ready to assert themselves when
custom staled Shelley's infinite variety; but
they were, for the time being, dormant.

Eliza occupied the privileged position of Trea-
surer of the party. She " keeps," Shelley writes,
" our common stock of money for safety in some
hole or corner of her dress." He did not yet dis-
like her, but believed himself in a fair way to
convert her from " prejudice " to virtue. Already
at Keswick he had written of her as " a woman
rather superior to the generality," adding : " She
is prejudiced; but her prejudices I do not consider unvanquishable. Indeed, I have already
conquered some of them." Now, at Dublin he
reports progress, representing Eliza's interests as
divided between the useful and the philosophical :—

" You have not seen Tom Paine's works. Eliza
is going to employ herself in collecting the useful
passages, which we shall publish. She is now
making a red cloak, which will be finished before
dinner."

The implication is that Eliza was in a hurry to
finish the red cloak in order that she might be
free to set to work compiling an Anthology of
Rationalism. She may have said so; but it is
more likely that she was biding her time, playing a waiting game, watching for the moment
when it would be proper for her to exhort Harriet

to " stand up for herself," put an end to this wandering Bohemian existence, and insist upon an establishment worthy of her social station.

Harriet, however, was young enough to think it better fun to ramble about in quest of adventures than to settle down to sedate respectability. She seems to have enjoyed herself, and to have been really under that hypnotic influence which Eliza only affected to undergo. She did not merely accept her husband's enthusiasms and eccentricities in the spirit in which the wives of City men accept the fact that their husbands must catch the nine-fifteen every morning, and may sometimes be kept late at the office. She actually adopted his enthusiasms (to the best of her knowledge and belief) and wrote letters about them in a prose style which echoed his even to the point of substituting " hath " for " has " and interlarding " thee's " and " thou's " among the " you's." She became enthusiastic, at his bidding, not only about vegetarianism, which was one of Shelley's hobbies at this time, but also about Miss Hitchener.

Her own particular friend in Ireland was a Miss (or Mrs.) Nugent, first referred to as " sitting in the room now and talking to Percy about virtue." She was an elderly needlewoman employed by a furrier; and it is not clear how Shelley came to know her. If she had simply walked into his apartment and proposed a conversation about virtue he would, at that period of his life, have thought the introduction a sufficient one. Harriet liked her and asked her to dinner (adding a roast fowl to the diet of herbs for the occasion), and waxed eloquent over her qualities and her misfortunes :—

" This excellent woman, with all her notions of Philanthropy and Justice, is obliged to work for her subsistence—to work in a shop which is a furrier's : there she is every day confined to her needle. Is it not a thousand pities that such a woman should be dependent upon others ? . . . The evening is the only time she can get out in the week. . . . She told Percy that her country was her only love when he asked her if she was married. . . ."

Et cetera. One notes the circumstance because Harriet and Mrs. Nugent engaged in a considerable correspondence, first printed in the *New York Nation* in 1889, which throws fresh light upon some of the incidents of Shelley's life; but no story arises out of it for the moment, and the most striking point is that this eulogy of Mrs. Nugent, whom Harriet had only met once, was addressed to Miss Hitchener, whom she had never even seen. Her idea was, apparently, that, just as her marriage had been no ordinary marriage, so her husband was no ordinary husband, but must be regarded, rather, as the founder and managing director of a joint-stock company registered for philosophical and philanthropic purposes, and that Miss Hitchener was a fit and proper person to introduce fresh emotional capital, and join the board. She let her heart overflow and gushed to Miss Hitchener, just as Shelley himself did, addressing her as " My dear Sister," and " My dear Friend."

So the appeal to the Sussex school-mistress to join the party came from the girl wife as well as the boy husband. " In compliance," Shelley writes, " with Harriet's earnest solicitations, I entreat you instantly to come and join our circle; to resign your school—all, everything, for *us* and the Irish cause." He continues : " £400 per an. will be quite enough for us all : our publications would supply the deficiency." As for thoughts of gratitude and obligation— such things may be left to " the grovelling sons of commerce and aristocracy." Evangelists must not entertain them. On the contrary : " Let us mingle our identities inseparably, and burst upon tyrants with the accumulated impetuosity of our acquirements and resolutions." There will be no scandal, for there are no grounds for any : " Who will credit that, when I made a Scotch marriage with a woman who is handsome, any criminality, of the nature of infidelity, can be attached to me ? " As for Miss Hitchener's personal attractions :—

" You have said you are not handsome, but, though the sleekness of your skin, the symmetry of your form, might not attract the courtiers of Dublin Castle, yet that tongue of energy and that

eye of fire would awe them into native insigni-
ficance, and command the conviction of those
whose hearts vibrate in unison with justice and
benevolence."

Thus Shelley; and Harriet simultaneously
exclaims :—

"How good you are thus to busy yourself
about us in this way. Amiable woman ! If I had
known thee before, it would have been delightful :
but I must be content, I know you now."

She goes on to tell Miss Hitchener the story of
her early life and first affections. First she had
doted on soldiers, though she had never wished
to marry one—"not so much on account of
their vices as from the idea of their being killed."
Then she had thought she would like to marry a
clergyman : "Strange idea this, was it not ?
But being brought up in the Christian religion,
'twas this gave rise to it." Then Shelley had
introduced her to atheism, and this had frightened
her because she believed in eternal punishment :
"Now, however, this is entirely done away with,
and my soul is no longer shackled with such idle
fears." And there is another notable respect in
which her views have expanded :—

"You cannot suppose, my dear friend, that I
suspect you of jealousy : 'twould be entertaining
an idea wholly unworthy of you. Jealousy is a
passion known only to the illiberal and selfish
part of mankind, who have been corrupted and

spoilt by the world : but this forms no part of you—'tis utterly impossible."

The utterances are those of a commonplace mind temporarily under a spell. The spell, in time, would lose its potency, and Harriet would revert to type,—helped to do so by the elder sister who was so many years nearer to their father's tavern. Meanwhile she lived in a dream, making what she could of the vision. She echoed Shelley's phrases about vegetarianism and the wrongs of Ireland; she also echoed his invitation to Miss Hitchener: "Do, dear, hasten your departure for us. To Midsummer! That will be such an immense time before it arrives."

Miss Hitchener, of course, was old enough to know better; and probably she did know better. If she did not ultimately act as one would have expected a school-mistress to act, at least she hesitated as one would have expected a school-mistress to hesitate. She had acquired a certain stock of common sense from the practice of her calling, though she was a silly woman by nature. Apparently she was startled into the bold and foolish course by a sudden outbreak of just that scandal which Shelley had told her that she need not fear on account of his position as a respectable married man. She had not sense enough to hold her tongue about her correspondence with the brother of her soul; and when people heard about it, they began to say—what people invariably do say in such cases.

Shelley believed that the slander had been launched by Mrs. Pilfold, who wished Miss Hitchener to remain in Sussex as her daughter's governess; but that is incredible. Women in Mrs. Pilfold's position do not entrust their daughters to governesses, however competent, concerning whom such slanders are afloat. It is far likelier that Miss Hitchener boasted of the invitation, and that her neighbours put an obvious, albeit, as it happened, an erroneous interpretation upon it. They said that she was going to the Shelleys in order to be Shelley's mistress; and then the fat was in the fire to such an extent that even her father saw the blaze.

In a moment of expansiveness Shelley had suggested that he too should join the party in a large house which he proposed to take in Wales. There was a farm attached to the mansion; and Mr. Hitchener might just as well give up his public-house and manage it, while Shelley, his wife, his sister-in-law, and Mr., Mrs., Miss Godwin, and Mrs. Nugent, who had also been invited, were talking about virtue. "It might be a comfort to his declining years," Shelley thought, "to see you independently settled." This at a time when Shelley had not the means either of paying, or of giving security for, the first quarter's rent of the mansion which he talked of taking. It is no wonder, in the circumstances, that Mr. Hitchener attached more importance to the calumnies than to the visionary promise of an independent and secure position. He did so, and Shelley wrote him a letter in the manner of Jupiter Tonans hurling a thunderbolt :—

" I had some difficulty in stifling an indignant surprise in reading the sentence of your letter in which *you* refuse my invitation to your daughter. How are you entitled to do this ? Who made you her governor ? Did you refuse this refusal from her to communicate to me ? No, you have not. . . . Believe me, such an assumption is as impotent as it is immoral. You may cause your daughter much anxiety, many troubles, you may stretch her on a bed of sickness, you may destroy her body, but you are defied to shake her mind. . . . Your ideas of *Propriety* (or to express myself clearer of *morals*) are all founded on considerations of *profit*. . . . Neither the laws of Nature nor of England have made children private property. Adieu, when next I hear from you I hope that time will have liberalized your sentiments."

It is not unamusing to picture the retired smuggler who had become a publican spelling out that communication in the bar parlour; and we will leave him spelling it out while we return to Shelley.

CHAPTER XV

THE next stage of the pilgrimage was Nant-gwillt, in Radnorshire, close to the Groves' place at Cwm Elan—" an old family house," wrote Harriet to Mrs. Nugent, " with a farm of 200 acres meadow land." That is the farm which Shelley invited Mr. Hitchener to manage, instead of his public-house, while the rest of the party were talking about virtue. There was only one obstacle to be overcome—the payment of the rent; but that difficulty proved insuperable.

Shelley had hoped that the elder Medwin would enable him to raise the money; but Medwin either could not, or would not, do so. Consequently the virtue party had to be postponed, and Shelley had to vacate the premises in a hurry, and ask the Groves to put him up while he made other arrangements. There seems to be a beginning of discontent, if not of peevishness, in Harriet's complaint to Mrs. Nugent : " We are to begin travelling again soon, and where to bend our steps I know not; " and there are also certain inferences to be drawn from her remarks about the Groves :—

" Percy is related to Mr. Grove, and his wife is

170

a very pleasant woman, tho' too formal to be
agreeable. He is a very proud man. Therefore,
you may guess how we pass our time."

It is the characteristic note of the bride who
feels that her husband's relatives regard her
as " not quite," . . . though they receive her
with courtesy for her husband's sake. " Stuck
up " and " stand-offish " are the epithets which
Harriet would probably have applied to the
Groves if she had spoken in her vernacular. " We
must remain here," she says, " until we receive
remittances from London "; and there is pathos
in that " must." There was talk of going to
Italy, but : " We think of going to the seaside
until our passports come." Whence one infers
that neither Harriet nor Mrs. Grove desired the
visit to Cwm Elan to be a long one; and very
likely Shelley and his host were at one with the
ladies in this matter. It was at Cwm Elan that
Shelley wrote, though he did not then print, a
certain Letter to Lord Ellenborough which might
be expected to make trouble; and one can
imagine Mr. Grove preferring that the trouble
should be made elsewhere than at his house.

The Italian project, however, was abandoned,
probably for lack of funds; and Shelley set out
for Chepstow. Godwin had given him an address
there; but the quarters, when inspected, proved
disappointing. The fact appears in a letter in
which Harriet expresses her regret that Mrs.
Nugent cannot visit her :—

" Continue, oh ! amiable woman, the path marked out to thee by virtue and humanity, and let not the whisperings of selfishness in us take thee from so laudable an undertaking. We may yet meet ere this world shall close our eyes, and that we both desire it our hearts are the best judge. . . . When we arrived at Chepstow we found the house not half built and by no means large enough for our family."

Godwin seems to have considered that it ought to have been large enough for a man of Shelley's age and income; and he made remarks on the subject which Shelley would have resented if they had been offered by any one for whose character and philosophy he had had less regard. As it was, he politely explained his objections to " pigging it " in a rickety labourer's cottage, and passed on. He started for Ilfracombe, but got no farther than Lynmouth, whence Harriet reports progress to Mrs. Nugent in a more contented letter than that written from Cwm Elan :—

" We have taken the only cottage there was, which is most beautifully situated, commanding a fine view of the sea, with mountains at the side and behind us. Vegetation is more luxurious here than in any part of England. We have roses and myrtle creeping up the sides of the house, which is thatched at the top. It is such a little place that it seems more like a fairy scene than anything in reality. All the houses are built in the cottage style, and I suppose there are not more than thirty in all. We send to Barnstaple for everything, and our letters come but twice a week. . . . It seems as if nature had intended this place should be so romantic, and shut out from all other intercourse with the neighbouring villages and towns."

That letter is dated June 30—a time of the year when it is not difficult to live happily at Lynmouth, even in a cottage which, as Shelley writes to Godwin, " exceeds not in its accommodations the dwellings of the peasantry which surround it." Harriet insisted, indeed, that it was not a good enough place to invite Godwin to; but it was quite good enough for her and her husband; and there is evidence that she and Shelley were still fairly well pleased with each other. Shelley read, while at Lynmouth, *The Empire of the Nairs; or, the Rights of Woman*, by Chevalier Lawrence; and he wrote to the author, expressing his admiration and defining his own attitude towards the marriage question :—

" I am a young man, not yet of age, and married to a woman younger than myself. Love seems inclined to stay in the prison, and my only reason for putting him in chains, whilst convinced of the unholiness of the act, was a knowledge that, in the present state of society, if love is not thus villainously treated, she, who is most loved, will be treated worse by a misjudging world.

In short, seduction, which term could have no meaning in a rational society, has now a most tremendous one."

It was understood, however, that love was not to be kept in solitary confinement. There were to be as many visitors as possible to keep the ball rolling in the conversations about virtue. Godwin's adopted daughter Fanny was invited; but Godwin would not let her come, feeling that he ought to make his disciple's personal acquaintance before trusting him so far. Miss Hitchener came, however, having at last given up her school and promised to remain " for ever "; and Harriet's opinion of the guest thus quartered on her is, of course, the opinion which we are most anxious to hear. We get it in a letter to Mrs. Nugent; and it is favourable, and even enthusiastic, though there are points in the enumeration of her merits at which it seems possible to read between the lines :—

" Our friend, Miss Hitchener, is come to us. She is very busy writing for the good of mankind. She is very dark in complexion, with a great quantity of long, black hair. She talks a great deal. If you like great talkers she will suit you. She is taller than me or my sister, and as thin as it is possible to be. . . .

" . . . Miss Hitchener has read your letter, and loves you in good earnest—her own expression. I know you would love her did you know

174

her. Her age is thirty. She looks like as if she was only twenty-four, and her spirits are excellent. She laughs and talks and writes all day."

Miss Hitchener was to prove to be shallow; but Harriet, who wrote " like as if," was not to be expected to foresee that. She was, at any rate, disposed to make the best of Miss Hitchener, and does not seem to have doubted that her writings contained an instructive message to her age. One would give a good deal to see them. Medwin quotes, or professes to quote, one line from them —the first line of a Feminist Ode, running : " All are men—*women* and all " ! But it seems fairer to judge her by her published works, even though these belong to a later period of her development, and appeared long after her departure from the Shelleys' roof. There are copies of two such works in the Library of the British Museum.

One of them is a long poem of no importance on " The Weald of Sussex," noticeable only for a reference to those lakes and mountains of Wales which the author had seen in Shelley's company, and of which she says that " language is inadequate to give a just idea of their beauty." The other is " The Fireside Bagatelle containing Enigmas on the Chief Towns of England and Wales "—composed, according to the Preface, in " the hope that it may be found useful " and because the author considers " everything, however insignificant in itself, yet acceptable, if in the slightest degree calculated to excite in young minds a spirit of inquiry and a taste for literature," and launched under the auspices of a " Dedicatory Ode affectionately addressed to some Amiable Young Friends " :

> *Domestic pleasures will insure*
> *Contentment, health, and ease ;*
> *They all of earthly bliss secure,*
> *And never fail to please.*

> *For Home's the empire of the heart ;*
> *Its circle Nature's trace ;*
> *Then, faithful to her wish, impart*
> *Affection's winning grace.*

> *It soothes, refines, it softens man,*
> *It solaces his care ;*
> *In Paradise its source began,*
> *And, followed, leads us there.*
> *Then let us still its course pursue,*
> *Agreeable to Nature true.*

That, when we get down to bed-rock, seems to be the essence of Miss Hitchener's message to her age. It is an admirable message, lacking nothing except originality : a most suitable message for the head-mistress of a Seminary for Young Ladies to deliver. That the author of it should have been urgently, insistently, and repeatedly summoned from her Seminary to converse about virtue and God and " innate passions " with the author of *Epipsychidion* is one of the most

curious facts in the history of English Literature—only less curious, indeed, than her own
willingness to engage in that queer enterprise,
and to sacrifice to it a lucrative and reputable
means of livelihood. There is nothing to be said
except that she was a silly woman, and that
Shelley was too young to understand how silly
she was, being only nineteen when he summoned
her to his side, and only twenty when she obeyed
the summons.

Though only twenty, however, he seems already to have been shaping a scheme and theory
of life. His idea, almost though not quite formu-
lated, was to be in the world but not of it, standing
aside from life that he might criticize it, holding
a watching brief for humanity at large, aiming
the shafts of right reason and hot indignation at
tyrants and unjust judges as often as he saw his
opportunity. Though he was beginning to write
poetry—the first draft of " Queen Mab " belongs
to this period—he was very modest about it. He
saw himself chiefly as a prophet denouncing
priests—a friend of man declaring war against
oppressors. He pictured Miss Hitchener helping
all his causes by " writing for the good of mankind." He believed—and he had even persuaded
Harriet to believe—that the delightful crusade
might last for ever.

It lasted, in fact, for about four months. At
the end of the four months the crusaders were in
London, negotiating for the dissolution of their
partnership. Exactly what had happened in the

M   177

meantime one cannot say, for all the available statements on the subject are *ex parte* statements. The only impartial witness is Hogg, who saw in the proceedings a trial of strength between Miss Hitchener and Eliza, and regarded both ladies as equally objectionable; but Hogg's evidence only bears upon the last scenes in the struggle.

Shelley had burst in upon Hogg in his chambers in the Temple, and made up his quarrel with him. Time, distance, and experience of Miss Eliza Westbrook's conversational habits had evidently taught him to take a truer view of Hogg's supposed gallantries. Perhaps Harriet had herself confessed to having misunderstood, and therefore exaggerated, Hogg's attentions. She and Hogg had both been young enough to be permitted to be silly. At all events, it was once more glad confident morning between the two friends; and Hogg dined with the Shelleys on the day of Miss Hitchener's departure, and allowed himself to be made useful in keeping up appearances at the hour of strained relations. Shelley said he had an engagement; Harriet said she had a headache; Hogg was told off to take Eliza and Miss Hitchener for a walk, keeping the peace between them.

" With the Brown Demon on my right arm," he writes, " and the Black Diamond on my left, we went forth into St. James's Park, and walked there, and in the neighbouring parks, for a long time, a very long time. ' These were my jewels,' as Cornelia proudly exclaimed."

The ladies snapped at each other, firing their shots across their cavalier as well as their opportunities allowed. Miss Westbrook, not being a match for Miss Hitchener in dialectics, presently relapsed into silence and sulks. Miss Hitchener then monopolized her escort. Miss Westbrook was annoyed; and when she got Hogg alone, she let him know it.

" How could you talk to that nasty creature so much ? " she asked. " How could you permit her to prate so long to you? Why did you encourage her ? Harriet will be seriously displeased with you, I assure you; she will be very angry."

But then dinner was served; and immediately after dinner Miss Hitchener was handed into her coach; and that is all that Hogg has to tell us. The rest is best related in Harriet's communication to Mrs. Nugent :—

" The lady I have so often mentioned to you, of the name of Hitchener, has to our very great happiness left us. We were entirely deceived in her character as to her republicanism, and in short everything else which she pretended to be. We were not long in finding out our great disappointment in her. As to any noble disinterested views, it is utterly impossible for a selfish character to feel them. She built all her hopes on being able to separate me from my dearly loved

M 2

Percy, and had the artfulness to say that Percy
was really in love with her, and it was only his
being married that could keep her within bounds.
Now, Percy had seen her twice before his marriage. He thought her sensible, but nothing
more. She wrote continually, and at last I wrote
to her, and was very much charmed with her
letters. We thought it a thousand pities that
such a mind as hers appeared to be should be left
in a place like that she inhabited. We were,
therefore, very urgent for her to come and live
with us; which was no sooner done than we found
out our mistake. It was a long time ere we could
possibly get her away, till at last Percy said he
would give her £100 per annum. And now, thank
God, she has left us, never more to return. We
are much happier now than all the time she was
with us."

Shelley's testimony is to the same effect. He
writes to Hogg :—

" The Brown Demon, as we call our late tor-
mentor and school-mistress, must receive her sti-
pend. I pay it with a heavy heart and unwilling
hand; but it must be so. She was deprived by
our misjudging haste of a situation, where she
was going on smoothly : and now she says that
her reputation is gone, her health ruined, her
peace of mind destroyed by my barbarity; a
complete victim to all the woes, mental and
bodily, that heroine ever suffered. This is not all
fact; but certainly she is embarrassed and poor,

and we being in some degree the cause, we ought to obviate it. She is an artful, superficial, ugly, hermaphroditical beast of a woman, and my astonishment at my fatuity, inconsistency, and bad taste was never so great as after living four months with her as an inmate. What would Hell be, were such a woman in Heaven ? "

So that Miss Hitchener must at least be acquitted of the charge of having made trouble between Shelley and Harriet. Whether she failed to do so because she was too silly or because she was too ugly does not matter. She did afterwards try to make trouble by embroiling them with their neighbours; but that effort also was unsuccessful, though it did cause Shelley to write a letter in which he spoke of " the wiles of a soured and disappointed woman." Captain Pilfold, who was somehow or other dragged into the matter, declared that her calumnies were inconsistent with Mr. and Mrs. Shelley's " known moral and virtuous good characters."

How long Shelley continued to pay Miss Hitchener her £100 a year is uncertain. She was, at any rate, too wise to rely upon it as her sole resource; and she and her sister started a girls' school at Edmonton, which prospered. Her pupils spoke of her with respect and affection; and, as a middle-aged woman, she captured the heart of an Austrian officer, who married her and took her abroad. Let us bid farewell to her, and turn back to Shelley.

181

CHAPTER XVI

WE left Shelley at Lynmouth, where he was long remembered, not as a man of genius, but as a man who blew soap-bubbles on the doorstep of his cottage. None the less he was engaged in queer attempts to drive his thoughts over the universe "like winged seeds to quicken a new birth." He had with him several boxes full of pamphlets, setting forth, among other things, that "government has no rights"; and he corked them up in empty bottles, and pitched the bottles into the Bristol Channel, in the same spirit of evangelistic zeal in which missionaries of another school of thought scatter tracts in cabs and railway station waiting-rooms. Other copies of the document were dispersed over Exmoor by means of toy balloons on the chance that a copy here or there might stir the stagnant pool of a bucolic mind.

At the same time Shelley engaged Mr. Syle of Barnstaple to print his Letter to Lord Ellenborough, protesting against the imprisonment of Daniel Isaac Eaton for publishing " a blasphemous libel on the Holy Scriptures." [1] His

---

[1] From the pen of Tom Paine.

punishment, it seemed to Shelley, though a less grave matter than the crucifixion of Christ, was equally unjustifiable ; and we need not waste words in supporting so obvious a contention. The holier the Holy Scriptures the less their need of a testimonial from the Old Bailey. But those were the days in which Keate told the Eton boys that he should enforce purity of heart with the birch; and Keate's point of view was fairly representative of that of the governing classes. It was not merely an offence in their eyes to speak evil of dignitaries; it was even an offence to dispute with dignitaries. So there was trouble. Shelley's servant was arrested for distributing the tracts in Barnstaple, and was sentenced in the Mayor's Court to six months' imprisonment, or a fine of £200.

No doubt Shelley would have paid the fine for him, if he had had the money; but he could no more, at that time, lay his hand on £200 than on £200,000. He decided—urged, as one imagines, by the unanimous entreaties of his womankind—to leave the neighbourhood before worse befell him; so he drove to Ilfracombe and crossed to Wales, where, at Tanyrallt, he found a landlord who promised to wait for the rent until he came of age. Thence, early in October, he proceeded to London, where he got rid of Miss Hitchener, in the circumstances already described. And that, of course, was his opportunity of calling on Godwin.

Godwin, who spent his summer holiday that

year at Bristol, had set out down the channel
to pay his young admirer a surprise visit, but
had not arrived at Lynmouth until about three
weeks after his departure. He found his lodging, however, and reported that the landlady
" quite loved the Shelleys,"—loved them so well
that she did not exercise her lien on their luggage,
though they left without paying their bill. They
paid it afterwards, however, in instalments;
so that the fact is only mentioned as a proof of
Shelley's power of fascinating women of all
ages and classes. He was presently to exercise
that power in Godwin's house ; so we will now
note Harriet's first impressions of the Godwin
household.

" We have seen the Godwins. Need I tell
you how I love them all ? . . . There is one of
the daughters of that dear Mary Wolstoncroft
living with him. She is nineteen years of age,
very plain, but very sensible. The beauty of her
mind fully overbalances the plainness of her
countenance. There is another daughter of hers
who is now in Scotland. She is very much like
her mother, whose picture hangs up in his study.
She must have been a most lovely woman. Her
countenance speaks her a woman who would dare
to think and act for herself."

The daughter would also dare to think and act
for herself in ways concerning which Harriet
would, in due course, have a good deal to say; but
coming events cast no shadows before as yet.
184

Another fact which Harriet remarked was that the Godwins were " sometimes very much pressed for enough ready money; " but she was not to foresee that that circumstance also would affect her. On the whole she was pleased with everybody and everything, voting the second Mrs. Godwin " a woman of very great magnanimity," and finding " very great sweetness marked in her countenance." Of Godwin she says :—

" G. is very much taken with Percy. He seems to delight so much in his society. It gives me so much pleasure to sit and look at him. Have you ever seen a bust of Socrates, for his head is very much like that ? "

A little later, in November, she met Mary Godwin, who had returned from a visit to Scotland, accompanied by her Scotch friend Christy Baxter. Mary, however, was only fifteen, and made no particular impression on Harriet, who, on her part, made no particular impression on Mary. The only recollection preserved of that interesting meeting is Christy's; and Christy was chiefly struck by Harriet. Even in her old age Christy spoke of " her beauty, her brilliant complexion and lovely hair, and the elegance of her purple satin dress; " so that Harriet enjoyed her hour of social triumph while sitting at table with the girl who was to deprive her of her husband.

Progress towards intimacy with the Godwins,

however, was slow. Godwin was no longer the enthusiast he had been when he wrote *Political Justice*. He kept a shop, and was very much married, sometimes inclining to the view of widows which one associates with the elder Mr. Weller. As for his disciples, he besought them not to take his doctrines too seriously, but to lend him money instead. That was a strain upon Shelley's, as it would have been upon any man's, enthusiasm; and he does not seem to have found Godwin's wife congenial. Godwin's friends, indeed, seldom did find Mrs. Godwin congenial, and Charles Lamb's sketch of her as a disgusting woman who wore green spectacles seems to have expressed a widespread prejudice. So Shelley, on this occasion, left London without saying good-bye to Godwin; and Harriet changed her mind about his merits :—

" Godwin, he too is changed, and filled with prejudices, and besides, too, he expects such universal homage from all persons younger than himself, that it is very disagreeable to be in company with him on that account, and he wanted Mr. Shelley to join the Wig party and do just as they pleased, which made me very angry, as we know what men the Wigs are just now. He is grown old and unimpassioned, therefore is not in the least calculated for such enthusiasts as we are."

Such, with its characteristic faults of orthography and syntax, is Harriet's reconsidered verdict, delivered from the midst of the Welsh mountains, where she and Shelley remained rather more than three months,—which was rather a long time for Shelley to remain anywhere. His criticisms of life at the time were certainly not those of a Whig. The average Whig is a person who is only prevented from being a Tory by the exigencies of the party system. He prides himself on being rather more aristocratic than the Tories, whom he is always ready to join when the populace comes between the wind and his nobility. Aristocracy, for Shelley, though he was an aristocrat by birth, remained the accursed thing. There was too much aristocracy in Wales to please him; and he poured out his soul on the subject to Hookham the Bond Street bookseller :—

" There is more philosophy in one square inch of any tradesman's counter than in the whole of Cambria. It is the last stronghold of the most vulgar and commonplace prejudices of the aristocracy. Lawyers of unexampled villainy rule and grind the poor, whilst they cheat the rich. The peasants are mere serfs, and are fed and lodged worse than pigs. The gentry have all the ferocity and despotism of the ancient barons, without their dignity and chivalric disdain of shame and danger. The poor are as abject as samoyads, and the rich as tyrannical as bashaws."

187

All that because an aristocratic old lady of Wales had said that atheists were worse than murderers. It pained Shelley to linger where that view prevailed; and Harriet seems to have been as little enamoured of her mountain home. Her husband required her to learn Latin, and tried to drag her through the *Odes of Horace.* A lady whose English grammar was as bad as we have seen Harriet's to be was not likely to make much of those Odes or to desire to do so. Horace is too cynical a poet to appeal to young married women,—especially if they have to look most of the words out in the dictionary; so we may reasonably picture Harriet getting bored—wondering when the county would call—desiring opportunities of frequenting bonnet shops.

Doubtless, however, she was consoled by the thought that her deprivations were unlikely to be permanent : that Shelley would soon come of age, and if he did not exactly " come into his rights," would at least be in a position to raise money on his expectations. Then she might hope to keep her carriage, to wear purple and fine linen, to adorn her dinner table with costly silver plate, and to have delicate dishes handed to her by magnificent footmen in plush breeches, with padded calves and powdered hair. She and Eliza must often have anticipated such glories in their confidential talks. Meanwhile, she could accept her adventures in a tolerably good temper; and some of the adventures were certainly strange and startling :—

LIFE AT TANYRALLT

" Dear Sir,

" I have just escaped an atrocious assassination. Oh, send £20 if you have it. You will perhaps hear of me no more !

" Your friend,
" Percy Shelley."

" Mr. Shelley is so dreadfully nervous to-day, from being up all night, that I am afraid what he has written will alarm you very much. We intend to leave this place as soon as possible, as our lives are not safe as long as we remain. It is no common robber we dread, but a person who is actuated by revenge, and who threatens my life and my sister's as well. If you can send us the money, it will greatly add to our comfort.

" Sir, I remain your sincere friend,
" H. Shelley."

Thus Shelley and Harriet, on the same sheet of paper, to Hookham of Bond Street; and all the biographers have been profoundly exercised by the question : What was the trouble about ?

What Shelley said was that a mysterious stranger had broken into his house at the dead of night, exclaiming, " By God, I will be revenged ! " threatening, not only to murder him and his wife but also to ravish Eliza. There was, at any rate, no doubt that Shelley fired a pistol, and raised the household, declaring that his assailant had first fired at him, and that the ladies, coming

189

downstairs in their night-dresses saw evidences of a scuffle. But what had happened ? That is a mystery about which biographers have argued at great length, propounding many theories.

There is the theory that the intruder was an ordinary burglar; the theory that Shelley invented the whole story, and arranged the *mise-en-scène*, in order to give himself an excuse for leaving the neighbourhood without paying the tradespeople; the theory that Shelley's Irish servant was paying his master out for his imprisonment at Barnstaple; the theory that Miss Hitchener had stirred up evil feeling by denouncing Shelley to his neighbours as a monster of sedition; the theory that Shelley had taken too much laudanum—a drug to which he was addicted—and that the whole story was the hallucination of an opium-eater. No one of these theories is very convincing; and another, based upon local tradition, was put forward by Miss Margaret L. Crofts in the *Century Magazine* for October, 1905 :—

" Shelley was in the habit of climbing up the Roman steps near Tanyrallt to the rocky height which was a grazing place for sheep. Here Shelley had more than once put an end to the life of a sheep affected with scab or some other lingering disease. It was his habit to carry pistols, and in his pity for the helpless creatures, he would put an end to them by a kindly shot. This habit of Shelley's had so exasperated a rough specimen of the rough mountain sheep farmer, named Robin Pant Evan, that he and his friends came down to Tanyrallt on that wild February night, and Evan fired a shot through the window, not meaning to murder any one, but to give the inconvenient meddler a good fright. Shelley's pistol flashed in the pan. Robin entered the room, wrestled with him, knocked him down, and then escaped through the window. It was his rough face and form that Shelley afterwards saw standing near the beech-tree; and when Shelley gazed out, all bewildered with the night alarm and the shaking, he thought he saw the devil. Robin gained his end, for Shelley and Harriet and her sister left the place next day, never to return."

That version of the assault is said to rest upon the assailant's own confession, made to members of the Greaves family who lived at Tanyrallt from 1847 to 1865. On the whole it is more credible than any of the other versions; though we may still invoke the laudanum to account for Shelley's extraordinary access of terror, and his consciousness that his opinions had made him unpopular, and his inability to pay his debts, to explain the precipitation of his departure.

There is evidence, at any rate, that this last difficulty was just then acute; and the £20 which Hookham sent him in order that he might " go to Dublin to dissipate the unpleasant impressions

associated with the scene of our alarm " was not
sufficient to remove it. " Could you," he wrote
to John Williams, *en route*, " borrow twenty-five
pounds in my name to pay my little debts ? "
" You would oblige me," he wrote to the same
correspondent, on his arrival at Dublin, " by
asking your brother to lend me £25." And then,
a few days later, as proof at once of the urgency
of his needs and the value of his security :
" Bedwell has written to tell me that all my bills
are returned protested. I know not what to
do."

What he did is not quite clear; but he
evidently got a loan from some one; and, on the
proceeds of it, he dashed off to Killarney, where
he was staying when Hogg came to pay him a
surprise visit at Dublin. Why he went to
Killarney, and what he did when he got there,
are equally mysterious matters. All that is
certain is that he did not, this time, entangle
himself in Irish politics or trouble his head about
Catholic Emancipation. Thoughts of these
things seem to have vanished from his mind
as a dream vanishes when the sleeper wakes.
No doubt he had other things to think of;
and the nature of some of his reflections may be
inferred from the fact that, when he quitted
Killarney as precipitately as he had quitted Dublin
—and Tanyrallt—he managed to leave Eliza
behind.

Ostensibly Eliza seems to have remained as a
hostage for the payment of the rent; but Shelley

nevertheless was full of triumph at the thought that he had got rid of her by a trick. Or so Hogg says.

As a rule, Hogg tells us, Shelley was not much addicted to laughter. " I am convinced," he quotes Shelley as once saying to him, " that there can be no entire regeneration of mankind until laughter is put down." But, on this occasion, he did laugh, feeling that the regeneration of mankind was not at stake, and that the joke was really a good one.

" He was evidently weary," Hogg writes, " of angelic guardianship, and exulted with a malicious pleasure that he had fairly planted her at last. He made no secret of his satisfaction, but often gave vent to his feelings with his accustomed frankness and energy. The good Harriet smiled in silence and looked very sly."

That is our first hint of feelings which were to culminate in Shelley's description of Eliza as " this miserable wretch " and " a blind and loathsome worm." Things, however, were not yet quite as bad as that; and Eliza, on her part, was a woman on whom hints were wasted. How she got clear of Killarney is not stated, but it probably would not have been beyond her power to give the landlord his due out of her own pocket. Whatever her methods, she soon followed Shelley and Harriet back to London, where, as Hogg writes, she " resumed her sovereign functions."

CHAPTER XVII

ESTRANGEMENT FROM HARRIET

WE are approaching the moment of Shelley's estrangement from Harriet; and we must, as in all such cases, distinguish between the immediate occasion of the trouble and its underlying causes.

Those underlying causes lurked in the problem from the first, as they always lurk in the problem created when a gentleman, who is also a man of intelligence and taste, marries a young woman *genre* barmaid. The barmaid in such circumstances discovers that marriage to a gentleman does not suffice to make her a lady, acceptable to other ladies; while the husband, going into society without his wife, is pained to observe how other ladies differ from barmaids. The lofty doctrine, however sincerely held, that all men (and women) are born equal is inadequate to deliver him from his discomfort; and various pin-pricks prejudice him in favour of what George Meredith called " leasehold marriages."

Shelley had always entertained that prejudice. He had taken it from Godwin, long after Godwin himself had repudiated it; and he was always polygamous in theory even when he was monogamous in practice. He talked of virtue and of free love in the same breath, regarding them,
194

it would seem, as two facets of the same precious jewel. He believed that Harriet shared his views, but did not foresee a time when either of them would be tempted to translate theory into action. " Love," we have seen him writing from Lynmouth to a perfect stranger, " seems inclined to stay in the prison; " but the time was even then approaching when Harriet's luxurious tastes and social ambitions would disconcert him.

Our first clue to that is in a letter written from Wales to Fanny Godwin. Exactly what Fanny had said one does not know; but she had evidently observed a certain pretentiousness in Harriet— a certain affectation of " style," alarming to simpler-minded persons; and Shelley wrote in Harriet's defence :—

" How is Harriet a fine lady ? You indirectly accuse her in your letter of this offence—to me the most unpardonable of all. The ease and simplicity of her habits, the unassuming plainness of her address, the uncalculated connection of her thought and speech, have ever formed in my eyes her greatest charms; and none of these are compatible with fashionable life, or the attempted assumption of its vulgar and noisy *éclat.*"

Perhaps—when the spell was fresh, and there was Mrs. Nugent to talk to. Harriet had certainly begun by behaving rather well in trying

N 2   195

circumstances, learning Latin with docility, if not with success, and waiting patiently for her husband to come into his rights. But she did not mean that sort of thing to go on for ever,—nor did Eliza. Underneath the apparent Harriet, so simple and studious, there was a real Harriet with aspirations after grandeur and gorgeous apparel: a Harriet who looked forward to treating the Latin Grammar as Becky Sharp treated the English dictionary, and riding in the Park, arrayed like Solomon in all his glory. Fanny Godwin had divined that, and Shelley was to discover it.

Already, indeed, Harriet was trying to fortify her dubious social position by replenishing her wardrobe in costly style, and clamouring for a carriage and silver plate. The state of her health —she was then expecting her first child—may be a partial explanation of the sudden and inopportune whim; but she may also have argued, not unreasonably, that if Shelley could rush about raising money for the payment of Godwin's debts and the reclamation of Welsh morasses,[1] he might as well raise some more while he was about it for the purpose of enabling his wife to live as a lady.

At all events she did prefer such demands,— unnecessarily and inopportunely. Hogg declares that no one ever saw her ride in her carriage, and

---

[1] Shelley had rushed from Tanyrallt to London with a view to organizing a subscription to complete an embankment begun in the neighbourhood by a local landowner.

that Shelley was so little in a position to pay for it that the creditor referred the matter to the bailiffs, who, not knowing Shelley by sight, tried to arrest Hogg in mistake for him. Though Hogg laughed the incident off, it must none the less have been a cause of friction between Shelley and his wife; and, if Shelley had been like most other men, there would have been a further cause of friction in Harriet's gross incompetence as a housekeeper.

Hogg draws a vivid picture of the dinners which she set before him:

" Some considerable time after the appointed hour a roasted shoulder of mutton of the coarsest, toughest grain, graced or disgraced the ill-supplied table; watery gravy that issued from the perverse joint when it was cut, a duty commonly assigned to me, seemed the most apt of all things to embody the conception of penury and utter destitution. There were potatoes in every respect worthy of the mutton; and the cheese, which was either forgotten or uneatable, closed the ungenial repast. Sometimes there was a huge boiled leg of mutton, boiled till the bone was ready to drop out of the meat, which shrank and started from it on all sides, without any sauce, but with turnips raw, and manifestly unworthy to be boiled any longer. Sometimes there were impregnable beef-steaks—soles for shooting-shoes."

One suspects with Hogg, that, even though

Shelley was not like other men, such meals must sometimes have set him sighing for other flesh-pots, and that the horrible handiwork of Harriet and the lodging-house landladies partially explains his vegetarianism, and his habit of rushing into bakers' shops, buying loaves of bread, and eating them ravenously as he walked down the street. It does not follow that there was no cause for friction because Shelley was barely conscious of it at the time; and still more dangerous possibilities lurked in the enlarging of his circle of acquaintances.

It was at about this time that *Queen Mab* was privately printed; and its appearance made its author something of a personage, albeit only in a small coterie. Through Godwin, too, he came to know a good many people, mainly cranks, who introduced him to other people, also mainly cranks. They were disposed to make much of him—a good deal more than they were disposed to make of Harriet. The women, in particular, were disposed to make a good deal more of him than of Harriet.

They did not belong to the society which is now-a-days called "smart." One would look for their modern analogues in Bedford Park rather than in Berkeley Square, or even Harley Street,—at the Sesame Club or the Pioneer Club rather than at the Carlton, the Marlborough, the Travellers', or the Bachelors'. Hogg, who was not in sympathy with "movements," writes of them somewhat contemptuously, finding among them,

as he says, " two or three sentimental young
butchers, an eminently philosophical thinker, and
several very unsophistical medical practitioners
or medical students," remarkable for their
" higgledy-piggledy ways " ; but that description
is evidently an after-thought,—applicable, perhaps, to some of the company, but by no means
to all of them. Certainly it cannot have been
applicable to the ladies of the party ; for, if it
had been, Hogg would not have accepted their
hospitality and corresponded with them.

Those of them whose names are worth remembering are Mrs. Boinville, her sister Mrs. Newton,
and her daughter Cornelia Turner,—the others
form merely the chorus of the play. Mrs. Boinville—whom we may call Madame de Boinville
if we like—was the daughter of a wealthy West
Indian planter, and had made a Gretna Green
marriage with a fascinating French *émigré :* an
important *émigré* who had shared with Lafayette
the honour of guarding Marie-Antoinette's
carriage on that day, in October 1789, when
the women of Paris marched to Versailles to
fetch the royal family. She was to live to see
her son an important Protestant pastor, and
to disapprove of Shelley, who, however, never
disapproved of her, but wrote, as late as 1819,
that " nothing earthly ever appeared to me
more perfect than her character and manners."
Some biographers have boldly declared that, in
1813, though she was fifty, Shelley was in love
with her ; but love is a word with many grades

199

of meaning, and it suffices to suppose that he was in love with the atmosphere of charm, sympathy, intelligence and enthusiasm, which he breathed in her house.

He had latterly, we must remember, had no one to talk to except Harriet, who did not understand, and Eliza, who did not try to understand; and he had begun to discover that purple and fine linen were more to Harriet than either dead languages or living ideas. Now he had fallen among people to whom ideas were the most important things in the world, who had the Athenian enthusiasm for discussion, who did not move in the realms of thought like schoolgirls learning lessons, but took their exercise there for their enjoyment; people, too, whom thought had not saddened, but who rejoiced in their youth as the young should.

It was an impossible society for Harriet—a society to which Harriet must have seemed an impossible person. She must have felt as much out of her element in it as one would imagine the average commercial traveller to feel if one could picture him missing his way to the commercial room and taking his place, in error, at a Royal Academy banquet. As Shelley obtained his introduction to it about the time of the birth of his daughter Ianthe, his wife's health may have been his excuse for generally leaving her at home. It is, at any rate, clear that his friends were only her acquaintances; and it is not less clear that he found keen pleasure in his new social opportunities.

There were dances, and visits—one visit, at all events—to Vauxhall Gardens. There was pleasant *badinage* of the light French sort, and the pleasant homage which beauty pays to genius when it presents itself in an attractive shape. It is to one of the new friends of those days that we owe the description of Shelley as " a moss-rose still dripping with the dew." We know from Hogg that, at this time, women—and more particularly young women—liked to sit up all night with Shelley, in order to hear him talk, so that he literally and truly did not go home till morning : that it was not an unknown thing for a young woman to sit up all night alone with him.

It seems all to have happened, as the French phrase is, *en tout bien et tout honneur;* but still, in view of the fact that Shelley had a wife— and also a sister-in-law, zealous for his wife's dignity, the seeds of discord were rather obviously being sown. It generally is so when a husband's intellectual life expands while his wife's intellectual life is shrinking. It is sure to be so when the wife is not the only pretty woman in the case—even if she be the prettiest—and the husband is young enough to feel capable of a fresh sentimental start. The only question then is : What occasion will make the causes operative ?

They did not become operative immediately.

A dash for the North—first for Keswick and then for Edinburgh—with Thomas Love Peacock for travelling companion, took place first. Hogg says that that was the only occasion on which he knew Harriet to make use of her carriage. Peacock bears witness that there were no visible dissensions during the journey, though the *Shelley Memorials* state the contrary. It is Peacock's testimony that Harriet's letters confirm; these indicating—what Peacock also asserts—that the birth of Ianthe served, for the time being, as a link between her parents. " I wish," Harriet wrote, " you could see my sweet babe. She is so fair, with such blue eyes, that the more I see her, the more beautiful she looks." And Shelley, as we know from Peacock, took great pleasure in nursing the baby, and, in particular, in singing it to sleep, with a tune of his own composition, which lulled the infant, though it exasperated other listeners. And Harriet wrote further :—

" A little more than two years has passed since I made my first visit here to be united to Mr. Shelley. To me they have been the happiest and longest years of my life. The rapid succession of events since that time make the two years appear unusually long. I think the regular method of measuring time is by the number of different ideas which a rapid succession of events naturally give rise to. When I look back to the time before I was married I seem to feel

A SECOND VISIT TO IRELAND

I have lived a long time. Tho' my age is but eighteen, yet I feel as if I was much older. . . . Mr. Shelley joins me and Eliza in kind regards. . ."

Perhaps the reference to " Mr. Shelley "—instead of " Percy," as of old—indicates a new stiffness in the conjugal relations; but it may merely render Harriet's aspirations after what she conceived to be " good form." One discovers, at any rate, no other symptoms of estrangement unless it be in the allusions to finance :—

" Mr. S. is of age, but no longer heir to the immense property of his sires. They are trying to take it away, and will I am afraid succeed, as it appears there is a flaw in the drawing up of the settlement, by which they can deprive him of everything. . . . They have put it into Chancery, though I fancy it can and will be kept an entire secret. . . . Our friends the Newtons are trying to do everything in their power to serve us; but our doom is decided. You who know us may well judge of our feelings. To have all our plans set aside in this matter is a miserable thing."

It is not a very coherent account of the financial situation, but there sounds in it the bitter cry of a woman whose high financial hopes have been blighted, through no fault of her own; and it seems true that the dash to the North was inspired by the necessity of avoiding creditors.

A scrap of a letter to an unknown correspondent shows Shelley once more in urgent need of ready money, begging that his bill for £30 may be honoured, as he is in danger of being driven out of his lodgings. One can believe that Harriet was displeased and " said things." One has still less difficulty in believing that Eliza " said things."

Apparently the difficulties were cleared, either by the help of Medwin of Horsham or by the sale of *post-obit* bonds; but the letters just quoted, from Harriet to Mrs. Nugent, are our very last tokens of harmony between husband and wife. They returned to London, and from London went to Bracknell, to be near the Boinvilles. Hogg, meeting Harriet in London, found her an altered woman—and altered by no means for the better. She no longer studied, and Shelley no longer urged her to do so. Her invariable objective, when she went out, was the bonnet-shop. She insisted, to Hogg's great annoyance, upon taking him to the bonnet-shop with her. It bored him equally to watch her trying on the bonnets, and to hang about on the pavement waiting for her. So he lost sight of her, and for a time, and to some extent, lost sight of Shelley also. One gathers that Shelley was often at Bracknell while Harriet was in London, and *vice versa*.

There is no record of the proceedings at Bracknell—presumably there was nothing to record. The story that Shelley went punting in a washerwoman's tubs, and persevered until he had knocked the bottom out of every tub, is hardly worth reviving. We find him, in spite of this recreation, plunged in the despondency to which a well-known letter to Hogg bears witness :—

" My friend, you are happier than I. You have the pleasures as well as the pains of sensibility. I have sunk into a premature old age of exhaustion, which renders me dead to everything but the unenviable capacity of indulging the vanity of hope, and a terrible susceptibility to objects of disgust and hatred. . . . I am here like the insect that sports in a transient sunbeam, which the next cloud shall obscure for ever. I am much changed from what I was."

Then follows the inevitable reference to Eliza :—

" I certainly hate her with all my heart and soul. It is a sight which awakens an inexpressible sensation of disgust and horror, to see her caress my poor little Ianthe, in whom I may hereafter find the consolation of sympathy. I sometimes feel faint with the fatigue of checking the over-flowings of my unbounded abhorrence for this miserable wretch. But she is no more than a blind and loathsome worm that cannot see to sting."

But the most significant sentence is this ; the letter being, it is to be observed, written from Mrs. Boinville's house at Bracknell :—

THE ROMANTIC LIFE OF SHELLEY

" I have sometimes forgotten that I am not an inmate of this delightful house—that a time will come which will cast me again into the boundless ocean of abhorred society."

A time will come, that is to say, when Shelley will have to go back to Harriet—and perhaps also to Eliza; and the prospect chills and appals him.

That was the emotional situation into which he and Harriet had blundered; and their choice now lay between blundering out and muddling through. Being what they were, they were bound to be disappointed with each other, —bound, therefore, to be unhappy. Harriet, to give her her due, would have made a pleasing wife for a licensed victualler; but Shelley's ideal of womanhood differed from that of licensed victuallers, and could not be satisfied by a licensed victualler's daughter. There is nothing for the moralist to say (if he would avoid platitude) except that both the girl-wife and the boy-husband had begun the game of life too young, with too little knowledge of the rules; nor can one see that there was anything to be done except to sweep the pieces off the board and start afresh. The trouble was that, while Shelley was eager for the fresh start, Harriet was not.

Not that she was any longer passionately in love with him. There is no evidence of that, but much evidence to the contrary—notably the evidence of certain poems from Shelley's pen, written in complaint of her unaccustomed coldness. Though the poems prove nothing as to the causes of the coldness, they may be taken as proving the fact. But a woman's coldness to her husband does not necessarily imply a desire to get rid of him, and is compatible with vehement indignation at the idea that he should wish to get rid of her. It proved, as we shall see, to be quite compatible with it in Harriet's case. She seems to have argued—if one may express her feelings in terms of reason—that, if she could no longer love Shelley herself, then he must be content to go unloved; and there is no doubt whatever, as her letters prove, that she was very angry with Mary Godwin for loving him.

CHAPTER XVIII

SEPARATION FROM HARRIET AND ELOPEMENT WITH
MARY GODWIN

In the spring of 1814, Shelley saw a good deal
of Mary Godwin. Her father's financial affairs
were then passing through one of their periodical
crises; and Shelley was trying to help him to
raise the money he wanted—no less a sum, it is
said, than £3,000. It was not a matter, of course,
merely of drawing a cheque. Before the money
could be lent, it must be borrowed. Godwin is
said to have suggested *post-obit* bonds, and there
were, at any rate, elaborate negotiations with
lawyers. Shelley was in town attending to the
matter, while Harriet remained in the country.
Attending to the matter meant calling constantly at Godwin's house. Calling at Godwin's
house entailed many incidental meetings with the
various members of Godwin's complicated family.
It will be as well to enumerate them before going
further.

The eldest was Fanny—the natural daughter
of the first Mrs. Godwin, whom we have already
discovered in correspondence with Shelley. It has
been said that she was in love with him; but it is
quite certain that he was not in love with her.

Mary Wollstonecraft Shelley

From a portrait by Reginald Easton

A plain girl, but amiable and sensible, is the verdict of those who knew her. Next we may notice Jane and Charles Clairmont—the children of the second Mrs. Godwin by her first husband. Jane was both beautiful and enterprising; she and Charles were alike addicted to dashing, romantic, unpractical courses—wild and extravagant freaks of which they boasted as Clairmont characteristics. William Godwin—the son of Godwin by his second wife—who had a career of no particular interest as a newspaper reporter, was a child at this time, and does not concern us. There was also Mary—as beautiful as Jane and cleverer—sixteen years of age.

All the world knows Hogg's story of his visit with Shelley to Godwin's shop and of Mary's sudden appearance in the background :—

" The door was partially and softly opened. A thrilling voice called ' Shelley ! ' A thrilling voice answered ' Mary ! ' And he darted out of the room, like an arrow from the bow of the far-shooting king. A very young female, fair and fair-haired, pale indeed, and with a piercing look, wearing a frock of tartan, an unusual dress in London at that time, had called him out of the room." . . .

. . . " ' Who was that, pray ? ' I asked; ' a daughter ? '

" ' Yes.'

" ' A daughter of William Godwin ? '

" ' The daughter of Godwin and Mary.' "

o209

THE ROMANTIC LIFE OF SHELLEY

All the world knows, again, how Shelley gave Mary a copy of *Queen Mab*, and how, underneath the printed dedication to Harriet, he wrote the enigmatic words : " Count Slobendorf was about to marry a woman who, attracted solely by his fortune, proved her selfishness by deserting him in prison." What Mary wrote on the fly leaves at the end of the volume has also been printed. The most significant sentences are these :—

" This book is sacred to me, and as no other creature shall ever look into it, I may write what I please. Yet what shall I write ? That I love the author beyond all powers of expression, and that I am parted from him. Dearest and only love, by that love we have promised to each other, although I may not be yours, I can never be another's."

It must have been at about the time of that inscription and of the hesitations which it chronicles, that Peacock called on Shelley and found him with tumbled hair, disordered dress, blood-shot eyes, and a bottle of laudanum beside him, saying, " I never part from this," and quoting from Sophocles :—

> " *Man's happiest lot is not to be :*
> *And when we tread life's thorny steep,*
> *Most blest are they who, earliest free,*
> *Descend to death's eternal sleep.*"

And he added, Peacock says : " Every one who knows me must know that the partner of my life should be one who can feel poetry and understand philosophy. Harriet is a noble animal, but she can do neither." The date of that incident is uncertain; but it must have been very near the end. On July 14, 1814, Shelley saw Harriet, and told her that he could not live with her any longer. A fortnight later, he had overcome Mary's hesitations, and persuaded her to leave her home and travel with him.

The rights and wrongs of this have often been argued; but they can never be determined. Different moralists judge them from different standpoints; and some of the facts which might influence their judgment are unascertainable. If the present writer joins in the discussion of a point so doubtful, his purpose is not so much to adjudicate as to put fresh statements in evidence and print new documents.

Up to the present the only point of view fully and fairly presented has been that of Field Place. We get it alike in Professor Dowden's *Life of Shelley*, and in Mrs. Marshall's *Life of Mrs. Shelley*. The source, in both these cases, is *The Shelley Memorials*: a work nominally compiled by Lady Shelley, but actually put together, if we may accept a statement in Trelawny's recently published letters, by Richard Garnett, of the British Museum. This is the statement :—

" He (Shelley) was still extremely young. His

anguish, his isolation, his difference from other men, his gifts of genius and eloquent enthusiasm made a deep impression on Godwin's daughter Mary, now a girl of sixteen, who had been accustomed to hear Shelley spoken of as something rare and strange. To her, as they met one eventful day in St. Pancras' churchyard, by her mother's grave, Bysshe, in burning words, poured forth the tale of his wild past—how he had suffered, how he had been misled; and how, if supported by her love, he hoped in future years to enrol his name with the wise and good who had done battle for their fellow-men, and been true through all adverse storms to the cause of humanity. Unhesitatingly she placed her hand in his, and linked her fortune with his own."

Side by side with this should be read Mrs. Shelley's remarks in her edition of Shelley's *Poems* :—

" This is not the time to relate the truth, and I should reject any colouring of the truth. No account of these events has ever been given at all approaching reality in their details, either as regards himself or others; nor shall I further allude to them than to remark that the errors of action committed by a man as noble and generous as Shelley was, as far as he only is concerned, may be fearlessly avowed by those who loved him, in the firm conviction that, were they judged impartially, his character would stand in brighter and fairer light than that of any contemporary."

212

There is obviously some veiled meaning here—a suggestion of extenuating circumstances which the writer declines, out of consideration for the feelings of others, to disclose. There could be only one extenuating circumstance of which the average reader of the plea would admit the force —misconduct on the part of Harriet. That that was, in fact, the extenuating circumstance which Mrs. Shelley meant to urge appears from a note appended by Jane Clairmont to a copy of some letters addressed by her mother to Lady Mountcashell :—

" He (Shelley) succeeded in persuading her (Mary) by declaring that Harriet did not really care for him; that she was in love with Major Ryan; and the child she would have was certainly not his. This Mary told me herself, adding that this justified his having another attachment."

That is precise. Harriet a guilty wife, and Major Ryan the accomplice of her guilt—such, when the dots are put on the i's, is the Field Place case. But Jane Clairmont, though she reported the charge, did not believe it. Hogg and Peacock do not seem even to have heard of it. " I feel it my duty," writes the latter, " to state my most decided conviction that her conduct as a wife was as pure, as true, as absolutely faultless, as that of any who for such conduct are held most in honour." And to Mrs. Boinville, and Mrs.

Godwin, the very name of Major Ryan was unknown.

That he was a real man is proved, indeed, by mention of his name alike in Mary Shelley's Diary and in Harriet Shelley's letters; and it is credible enough that Harriet had not been too careful of appearances. None of the allusions to Major Ryan, however, are such as to warrant an unfavourable inference; and it cannot be said that the general tone of Harriet's letters is that of a woman who has preferred a lover to her husband. Those letters can be quoted now, though they could not when either Professor Dowden or Mrs. Marshall wrote. It will be seen that they gradually run up the scale of indignation; the first letter, dated August 25, being quite vague :—

" Mr. Shelley is in France. You will be surprised to find I am not with him; but times are altered, my dear friend, though I will not tell you what has passed, still do not think that you cloud my mind with your sorrows. Every age has its cares. God knows, I have mine. Dear Ianthe is quite well. She is fourteen months old, and has six teeth. What I should have done without this dear babe and my sister I know not. This world is a scene of heavy trials to us all. I little expected ever to go through what I have. But time heals the deepest wounds, and for the sake of that sweet infant I hope to live many years."

Mrs. Nugent seems to have replied to that that she had always feared and suspected that Mr. Shelley, etc., etc., etc.; and Harriet's next letter assured Mrs. Nugent that her suspicions had indeed been warranted :—

" Your fears are verified. Mr. Shelley has become profligate and sensual, owing entirely to Godwin's *Political Justice.* The very great evil that book has done is not to be told. The false doctrines there contained have poisoned many a young and virtuous mind. Mr. Shelley is living with Godwin's two daughters. . . . Mary was determined to seduce him. She is to blame."

Then circumstantial details of Mary's culpability are heaped up :—

" She heated his imagination by talking of her mother, and going to her grave with him every day, till at last she told him she was dying in love for him, accompanied with the most violent gestures and vehement expostulations. He thought of me and my sufferings, and begged her to get the better of a passion as degrading to him as to herself. She then told him she would die—he had rejected her, and what appeared to her as the sublimest virtue was to him a crime. Why could we not all live together ? I as his sister, she as his wife ? He had the folly to believe this possible, and sent for me, then residing at Bath."

That, though couched in the language of the

penny dreadful, is specific. It is, as one would have expected, in flagrant contradiction with the Field Place version of the story. One's first impulse is to dismiss it as incredible and ridiculous; but there nevertheless is almost certainly a grain of truth in it. It explains, as Lady Shelley's narrative does not, the amazing letter which Shelley presently addressed to Harriet when he was with Mary at Troyes—the letter, derided as " a *bête* letter " by Matthew Arnold, in which he urged Harriet to " come to Switzerland, where you will find at last one firm and constant friend, to whom your interests will always be dear, by whom your feelings will never wilfully be injured." It is, of course, more probable that Harriet trifled with the truth than that this proposal for a joint ménage emanated from Mary; but it is quite clear that Harriet did not invent it; and her indignation at it is intelligible. She continued :—

" You may suppose how I felt at the disclosure. I was laid up for a fortnight after. I could do nothing for myself. He begged me to live. The doctors gave me over. They said 'twas impossible. I saw his despair, the agony of my beloved sister; and owing to the great strength of my constitution I lived; and here I am, my dear friend, waiting to bring another infant into this woful world. Next month I shall be confined. He will not be near me. No, he cares not for me now. He never asks after me or sends me word

how he is going on. In short, the man I once
loved is dead. This is a vampire. His character
is blasted for ever. Nothing can save him now.
Oh, if you knew what I have suffered, your heart
would drop blood for my miseries."

After her confinement she resumes :—

" Ianthe has a brother. He is an eight months'
child, and very like his unfortunate father, who
is more depraved than ever. Oh, my dear friend,
what a dreadful trial it is to bring children into
the world so utterly helpless as he is, with no
kind father's care to heal the wounded frame.
After so much suffering, my labour was a very
good one, from nine in the morning till nine at
night. He is a very fine, healthy child for the
time. I have seen his father; he came to see me
as soon as he knew of the event; but as to his
tenderness to me, none remains. He said he was
glad it was a boy, because he would make money
cheaper. Money now, not philosophy, is the
grand spring of his actions. Indeed, the pure and
enlightened philosophy he once delighted in has
flown. He is no longer that pure and good being
he once was, nor can he ever retrieve himself."

There is more; but that may suffice. Harriet's
defence, it will have been observed, is that
offensive defence which military tacticians recommend. She had not been educated to pick
her words, or to endure injustice with com-

posure. There is no reason to assume that she was careful to tell the exact truth when her case could be made to look stronger by a little divergence from it. Perhaps women with grievances seldom are. Harriet's wild assertions, in short, inspire as little confidence as Mary's insidious hints; and one has to end as one began by admitting that the rights and wrongs of the case are too confused to be unravelled. At least, however, it will be possible to show that Harriet's picture of Shelley allowing money to become "the grand spring of his actions" is misleading; and to that end we may call a fresh witness and print an unpublished document.

Let Charles Clairmont speak.

CHAPTER XIX

CHARLES CLAIRMONT ON THE SEPARATION

CHARLES CLAIRMONT, already introduced as the son of the second Mrs. Godwin and her first husband, was a bright, though rather unpractical, youth, who had received a good education at the Charterhouse : not the sort of education that was likely to suggest an eccentric or unconventional attitude towards sexual and social problems. By way of a good, and not at all unconventional, start in life, he proposed to set up in business as a distiller. He hoped to be financed in his distillery by Francis Place, the well-known tailor-reformer; and he was afraid that Francis Place might be prejudiced against him by the news of Mary Godwin's elopement with a married man. So he wrote Francis Place a long letter, which may be read in the Manuscript Room at the British Museum, enlarging upon the rosy prospects of the distilling industry, and, at the same time, justifying Shelley's separation from his wife :—

" Here," he wrote, " is a young man of the greatest refinement and learning, and the most uncommon talent, by a puerile inexperience thoughtlessly married to a pretty, trifling girl of the most slender capacity, whose only pleasures and occupations are balls, theatres, and such frivolous amusements."

Perhaps that was what Fanny Godwin meant when she spoke of Harriet as " a fine lady "; but, of course, the Charterhouse boy was not to be dazzled so easily as the homely girl. He referred to the circumstances of Shelley's first acquaintance with Harriet, and continued :—

" He never had for her any strong attachment; he thought her certainly a pretty woman, and was married to her when quite a boy, under circumstances so very peculiar as could never have happened to any one but of so very strange a turn of mind as himself. Her love towards him was precisely of the same cold nature; this she most fully proved at the time of their separation. Her love for Shelley was absolutely none ! So long as he was the minister of her pleasures and her respectability, she pretended a sympathy with his principles and an admiration of his character; but so soon as her interest became unconnected with his, she became his secret enemy, and the enemy of all his friends."

She became the enemy even of Godwin, though Godwin wrote to her, and called on her, and went out of his way to assure her that he disapproved of Shelley's proceedings. Moreover, in money matters she had behaved most reprehensibly :—

CLAIRMONT ON THE SEPARATION

" She associated (I do not mean what the world calls criminally) with an Irish adventurer, whom she commissioned to take all possible advantage of Shelley. She knew his embarrassed circumstances at the time, and yet glutted her revenge by running up the most extravagant and needless bills against him, amongst tradesmen, where she knew she could obtain credit. In short, it was only her impotence to injure that rendered her innocent of the most wide-spreading, blasting mischief."

Charles Clairmont, that is to say, acquits Harriet of the graver charges involving Major Ryan, but also contradicts, in a very circumstantial manner, her assertions regarding Shelley's grasping greed. " I would not require of her," he continues, " that she should become a crouching, puling, begging suppliant; she has certainly every right to feel her pride injured; yet still I cannot think that a woman who sincerely loved could descend to the low revenge of abuse and scurrility." And then follows a contrast between Harriet's and Mary's qualities, and something of the nature of a philosophical disquisition :—

" But now, even suppose Mrs. Shelley's passión for her husband had been as intense as that which Shelley felt for my sister; still I cannot see that this would have been sufficient to entitle her to the preference when it was a question with whom Shelley should associate and domesticate for life.

A certain portion of unhappiness necessarily falls to her whose love is unreturned; would cohabitation have remedied this evil? Shelley felt he could not esteem her; would a generous hypocrisy have produced the effect of passion? and, if it could, how would the wretched victim of such a melancholy farce, a man of sensibility and virtue, have deserved this hopeless solitude of the heart? Because he is exquisitely framed to perceive and adore true excellence, must he be everlastingly chained to dulness and sickening folly? And who is she for whom his happiness and (so far as depends on his life and reason) his usefulness is bartered? She is totally unlike his companion. She delights in frivolous amusements, and despises from her heart all literature or learned employments. Her fondness for her husband induces her to adopt principles and approve conduct which she has neither the understanding nor the courage to prefer for their intrinsic worthiness. Their intercourse must be full of irritating discomfiture. Their natures are distinguished by antipathies which no despotism but that of marriage could ever attempt to coalesce. I am persuaded that he who leaves such a woman for another in every respect more suited to his intellectual nature, acts neither selfishly nor sensually. If it be true that a person is justified in terminating a connection thus unsatisfactory when the other party has feelings in some degree inimical to the proceeding, surely the justice is much more evident when the

222

reluctance to the separation clearly arises out of the most vicious and ignoble motives that can disgrace the human heart.

" What love can the person who enjoys frivolity and parade bear to the solitary student ? Love is produced by a real or supposed sympathy of tastes and dispositions. Subtract these causes : what remains but avarice or sensuality ? Perhaps you may think my sentiments too wild and undigested for a maturer age; yet, if so, I hope you will agree with them in their bulk and main tenor. I believe you to be a thoroughly unprejudiced man, and I think I must have been wrong in supposing you would allow your judgment to be shackled on this subject. This long account is no doubt troublesome and tedious to you, yet I am afraid it was necessary."

Necessary, that is to say, for the purpose of persuading Francis Place to finance the writer in the distilling trade—yet failing to serve its purpose, for Francis Place's reply was " in the negative." He would be reluctant, he said, to invest money in a distillery, even for his own advantage; still less did he care to do so for the advantage of another. Nor did he wish, he added, passing to another branch of the subject, to " take the chance of being involved in any transactions between you and Shelley " : a wise refusal, doubtless, though expressed in the needlessly unpleasant language of a needlessly unpleasant man.

That, however, is a side issue, and irrelevant.

223

One gives the letter as the deposition of a witness who, if not impartial, was at any rate behind the scenes, and watched the proceedings from closer quarters than either Hogg or Peacock : a witness, too, who had learnt what a public school education teaches of propriety and morals. For Charles Clairmont, as for Hogg, Harriet was a barmaidenly maiden who had " caught " the heir to a baronetcy and great estates. He had no sympathy with such; and, indeed, it is difficult, even with all the precepts of all the churches before one, to blame the men who tire of barmaidenly maidens and, tiring of them, leave them. Even a bishop, one supposes, would not easily wax enthusiastic over the spectacle of a sublime poet enduring a superannuated barmaid in the spirit in which the saint submits to his hair shirt.

It is not true, at any rate, that Shelley left Harriet alone in a lonely world—as calumniators have said that he did—with only fourteen shillings in her pocket. She was far richer, when they parted, than he was, having liberty to draw on him, as long as there was a balance to his credit, and having also a father who was willing to receive her, and could perfectly well continue his allowance to her of £200 a year. She went to his house, and might have remained in it but for circumstances of which it is enough to say, for the moment, that they were well within her own control. We will leave her, and follow Shelley.

Whether Shelley had persuaded Mary, or Mary

(as Harriet said) had persuaded him, they were off together to the Continent, posting with four horses, to be sure of eluding pursuit. No one was in their confidence except Jane Clairmont; and Jane went with them, though why they took her with them no man knows. The suggested explanation that they thought her knowledge of French might be useful to them does not inspire confidence. The view that Shelley was (already) in love with Jane as well as Mary is equally unconvincing. Perhaps the clue to the mystery lies in Mary's sense of the impropriety of her proceedings. One can (without too great effort) picture her fancying that the impropriety would be halved if Jane would share it; while Shelley may have humoured the belief from the fear lest her courage should break down if he did not.

Be that as it may, however, the three fugitives got into their chaise at the corner of Hatton Garden, and galloped off along the Dover road; and Mrs. Godwin, missing her daughter and stepdaughter, and guessing what had become of them, got into another chaise and galloped in their train. She was not far behind them; but they got to Calais first, after a stormy passage, and Shelley said: "Mary, look; the sun rises over France."

CHAPTER XX

MRS. GODWIN overtook the fugitives at Calais, but did not capture them. She found Jane as defiant as Mary; she could only scold and depart.

Perhaps Jane had been unhappy at home; perhaps only dull. She was, at any rate, the sort of girl who describes herself as " a girl of spirit," and hankers after the adventures for which the common round affords no scope. She surpassed Mary in enterprise as much as Mary surpassed her in intellect, and took life in the spirit of a girl who has been brought up on boys' books and sighs for a boy's liberty of action. Her character attracts and repels alternately : attracts by its recklessness of revolt, but repels through a certain lack of tenderness. That, intellect apart, was the main difference between Jane and Mary.

Mary, though needing help to screw her courage to the sticking-point, could count the world well lost for love. Jane, being bolder, could count the world well lost for excitement—for a part in a thrilling drama which would give her the centre of the stage. That was how, as their lives diverged, she came to despise Mary as a slave, ready to

226

abase herself in the hope that the light of Mrs. Grundy's countenance might once more shine on her. That was why her own life resolved itself into a series of *frasques* for which she had to pay the price. And this was her first *frasque*. She was out for adventure in the holiday spirit, and in the scorn of consequence, just as Shelley had been when he ran away with Harriet, and Hogg when he hurried to join them on their honeymoon.

But so, for that matter, were they all. In each of the three lives the adventure was to mark an epoch. All three of them had taken the first step on a road the end of which they did not know, but from which there could be no turning back to walk in the old paths as before. Shelley had shouldered a far heavier responsibility in abducting the woman whom he loved than in marrying the woman to whom he was indifferent. Mary, in crossing the channel, had also crossed that Rubicon which the careful women who remain on the near side of it forbid any female traveller to recross. Jane had placed herself under influences by which her whole life— and she was to live to be eighty—would be deflected. Yet they all rushed off, without either money in their pockets or the certainty of obtaining any, with what looks like the irresponsibility of school children breaking bounds.

It would be too long a business to follow them through all the stages of their journey. The narrative is contained in the *History of a Six Weeks' Tour,* published in 1817, and based on the Diary which Shelley and Mary jointly kept. Professor Dowden supplements it with some extracts from Jane's Diary. The route was from Paris, via Neuchâtel, to the Lake of Lucerne, and home by way of the Reuss, the Rhine, and Rotterdam. The story is fascinating; but the secret of its fascination lies less in the adventures than in the temper of the adventurers.

Adventures, indeed, they had none worth speaking of, though they took a certain risk by crossing France on foot, at a time when the country was infested with disbanded soldiers, and the conduct of Cossacks had created a prejudice against foreigners. But they were young and snapped their fingers at care, as long as they could pay their way, convinced, if one may judge from their behaviour, that it was the business of Providence to provide, and that manna would fall if they clamoured for it.

They did clamour for it, and for a while it fell. For the first supply, indeed, Shelley's watch and chain had to be sacrificed—the proceeds of the sacrifice being exactly £6 12s.; but then he found bankers to honour his signature. A Parisian banker dealt out £60. A Neuchâtel banker handed over a heavy bag packed with gold and silver coins. Whether they were transmitting Shelley his own money or lending him some of theirs is not clear; but it is certain that he suddenly woke up to the fact that he had not enough to go on with and must not expect any more. With what celerity he then changed his plans may best be shown by an abbreviated extract from the Diary.

The Lake of Lucerne was the goal. The reader follows the travellers thither, expecting to hear of a long stay; and this, if we only transcribe the record of the movements of the party, is what he reads :—

" *Tuesday, August* 23 :—Arrive at Lucerne about ten. After breakfast we hire a boat to take us down the lake. . . . We sleep at Brunnen.

" *Wednesday, August* 24 :—We consult on our situation. We cannot procure a house; we are in despair. . . . At last we find a lodging in an ugly house they call the Château for one louis a month, which we take; it consists of two rooms.

" *Thursday, August* 25 :—We pack up our things and take possession of our house, which we have engaged for six months.

" *Friday, August* 26 :—Determine at last to return to England; only wait to set off till the washerwoman brings home our linen. . . . The linen is not dry; we are compelled to wait until to-morrow. We engage a boat to take us to Lucerne at six the following morning.

" *Saturday, August* 27 :—We depart at seven. We conjecture the astonishment of the good people at Brunnen."

Their astonishment must indeed have been great; for the age of the leisurely grand tour was hardly over. Even Jane seems to have

229

been a little astonished at the suddenness of the command to pack. This is how she notes the occurrence :—

"Get up at five. Bustle, toil, and trouble; most laughable to think of our going to England the second day after we entered a new house for six months; all because the stove don't suit. As we left Dover and England's white cliffs were retiring, I said to myself, 'I shall never see these more,' and now I am going to England again—dear England. After having travelled and viewed the follies of other nations, my own country appears the most reasonable and the most enlightened."

Truly it is amazing; and what is still more amazing is that Shelley had, only a few days before, written to Harriet—inviting her to join the party. He hoped, he wrote, " soon to have the pleasure of communicating to you in person, and of welcoming you to some sweet retreat I will procure for you among the mountains; " and he enjoined Harriet to bring with her certain legal documents. That certainly looks as if he had really expected her to come; and what would have happened to her if she had come is an interesting matter of conjecture. Shelley, at any rate, started for home without waiting for her answer to his letter; and one is reduced to wondering whether he had forgotten that he had written it.

Very likely he had; for his active mind was ranging over so wide an area that he may easily have lost track of some of its movements. He and Mary and Jane were no ordinary tourists, engaged in ordinary sight-seeing. They were nearly always reading; and when they were not reading, they were writing. We have records of their reading *King Lear* and *As You Like It*, and *Mary, a Fiction*, by Mary Wollstonecraft, and Byron's latest Poems, and the description of the siege of Jerusalem in Tacitus. Shelley had no sooner read the last-named narrative than he decided to base a novel on it. He had no sooner conceived the idea than he proceeded to dictate the novel to Mary. She wrote from his dictation during the two days' sojourn at Brunnen, in the interval between packing and unpacking, and also in the inns on the way home. In the scanty leisure which still remained she tried to write a novel of her own.

And so back to England, dropping literature, at intervals, to fight the battle of life in an unfamiliar tongue with innkeepers and other extortioners; fighting it in such a way as just to hold their own—enduring discomfort and sea-sickness, yet resisting sea-sickness sufficiently to " dispute with one man about the slave trade " —landing, at last, at Gravesend, without even a cab-fare in their pockets, obliged to drive from place to place until they could borrow the fare, and to engage lodgings without any certainty as to where the rent would come from.

231

It was their darkest hour; and nearly four months were to elapse before the dawn. The trials of that time mark the end of Shelley's boyhood and Mary's girlhood. They found out then what life was really like—what were the rules of the game, what penalties enforced those rules. Even Jane had to face disagreeable realities, and listen to home truths couched in homely language, about " birds of a feather," and the necessity of lying on the bed which one had made. It was pointed out to Jane that she was no longer a fit companion for Fanny, who was destined to be a teacher in a select Seminary for Young Ladies, kept by her aunts at Dublin. It would be so bad for Fanny. If the parents of the pupils came to know. . . .

But Jane was not much troubled. On the whole, she was pleased with her new way of life. If her position lacked stability, she could at least reflect that Godwin's house also had no appearance of being founded on a rock. There, too, the atmosphere had been one of the acceptance and discounting of bills, and of borrowing in a hurry from Peter to pay Paul, who had put in the bailiffs. It had not been amusing; for Godwin, whatever his value as a philosopher, was a dull dog who retained the manners, though he had shed the prejudices, of the Nonconformist Ministry. A Nonconformist Minister in trouble about his bank account is not a cheerful spectacle; and one can picture Jane deciding that, if she had to choose, she would rather be renounced by Godwin than obliged to see too much of him.

So she fastened herself on Shelley and Mary, and lived with them in lodgings. Possibly she saw more of Shelley than was well for her peace of mind—certainly she saw more of him than was well for Mary's peace of mind. The time was to come when Mary would speak of Jane as " the bane of my life." The day was also to come when Jane, with the Byron story (of which more in its place) behind her, was to speak of Shelley as the only man she had ever loved. The foundations for those feelings may well have been laid during those days of Bohemian distress, and that may be one of the reasons why Jane did not find them distressing. Shelley, at any rate, was never to be as anxious to get rid of her as he had been to get rid of Miss Hitchener, though Mary was to refer to one of her departures as " our regeneration." That was not yet, however; and in the meantime, though the distresses were severe, the elasticity of youth triumphed over them.

The story is in Mary's Diary, which is too long to be reproduced. It is a curious and rather tangled story of spirits too effervescent to be repressed—a literary Mark Tapleyism maintained in · the midst of a hand-to-mouth existence—a hold on life and its varied interests kept up through study at times when financial embarrassments came very near to entailing actual hunger. The central figure of the picture is Shelley—*à la*

recherche de la pièce de cent sous. The chase takes
him to Insurance Offices, and Banks, and the
offices of lawyers and money-lenders, and the
houses and lodgings of his friends. It takes him
even, from time to time, to Harriet.

Not the least amazing fact in the amazing
story is that, when Shelley brought Mary home
from the Continent, Harriet paid the cabman.
The discovery of it certainly follows strangely
upon the perusal of Shelley's proposal to procure
Harriet " a sweet retreat among the mountains."
The explanation lies in the use which Harriet had
made of Shelley's instructions to his bankers to
honour her signature. He had believed—perhaps
it was a part of his general belief in the perfectibility of human nature—that she would only
draw sufficient for her modest needs. She had,
in fact, drawn the very last penny; and, as cab-
men do not give credit without public and
sonorous remonstrance, Shelley had to knock at
Harriet's door, leaving Mary and Jane in the
cab while he called on her.

He stayed two hours, and received £20. He
bought a suit of clothes—one infers from the
wording of the Diary that they were ready-made
clothes—and then resumed the quest on which
we have to picture him engaged for a period of
about four months. Godwin has to be pictured,
at the same time, refusing to communicate with
Shelley except through his solicitor, yet watching
the chance of borrowing from him, also through
the medium of his solicitor. Finally we have to

picture creditors—principally tradespeople with whom Harriet had pledged his credit—hampering his quest; pursuing him while he pursues the coins—setting the bailiffs after him, and trying to lodge him in a sponging-house.

Things happened, in consequence, pretty much as in the second act of a farcical comedy: a very farcical comedy, played by very serious young people, but played with more sentiment than is usual in farce. The law being what Mr. Bumble called it, they took advantage of its limitations. Shelley disappeared from his lodgings, and then reappeared in them, with something of the mysterious suddenness of a comedian making exits and entrances through trap-doors. He and Mary had stolen meetings in the Alsatias in which writs did not run, and snatched kisses at hours at which arrests could not be made. At other times they wrote each other furtive love letters like schoolboys and schoolgirls evading the watchful eyes of tutors and governesses. Charles Clairmont supplemented Jane in the rôle of messenger, communicating with Fanny, who communicated with the Godwins. Mrs. Godwin, distraught by conflicting sentiments of indignation and curiosity, peeped in surreptitiously on the party through the window, but tossed her head and turned away when any of them came out to speak to her. Altogether, it was a very queer game of cross purposes.

One cannot follow all its vicissitudes—there are far too many of them. One reads, in the

Diary, of frequent visits to the lawyers, and
" nothing done "; of the flight from bailiffs, and
the need for bail; of attempts to speak to Fanny,
whom Jane chased unsuccessfully up the street;
of negotiations with Harriet, who, at one moment,
sends " a good-humoured letter," and is " very
civil," but, at another, " sends her creditors
here," and " threatens Shelley with her lawyer."
One even reads of an occasion on which there
was neither money nor food in the house, and it
was necessary to appeal to Peacock for " eatables." Being nearly as poor as the applicants,
Peacock could only provide cakes; but, fortu-
nately, they were all young enough to be very
fond of cakes.

This at a time when Mary was expecting the
birth of her first child. The circumstances truly
were sad ones to surround such expectations.
Yet youth, as has been said, triumphed, and refused to be oppressed. Shelley and Mary only
thought of their troubles at the hours when the
troubles were actually upon them. They felt—
they did not need to prove—that happiness was
in the mind, and that externals, however embarrassing, cannot destroy it. They walked with
Peacock on Hampstead Heath, discussed " the
possibility of converting and liberating two
heiresses," and sailed paper boats on the ponds.
They entertained Hogg, and were vexed with
" his attachment to sporting," but amused by
his mental confusion when the time came to talk
about virtue.

236

Above all, they studied. "Learn Greek all morning," is one of the notes in Mary's part of the Diary. It appears on the same date as the entry: "People want their money; won't send up dinner, and we are all very hungry." Other similar entries are: "Read Greek grammar." . . . "Read a little of *Petronius*, a most detestable book." . . . "*Suetonius* is finished, and Shelley begins the *Historia Augustana*." . . . "In the evening read *Emilia Galotti*." On the whole, there could be no better proof of the innocence of their minds—their intuitive perception of their right to live their lives as they chose, instead of sacrificing their inclinations to Society —than this eagerness to snatch quiet hours with the classics at the time when they were most harried by moral remonstrances and material cares.

And so the time passed until, early in January, 1815, Sir Bysshe Shelley died, and Sir Timothy Shelley presently came to terms, agreeing to pay his son's debts,[1] and allow him £1,000 a year.

---

[1] His promise to help Godwin was treated as a debt, and duly fulfilled.

CHAPTER XXI

THE DEATH OF HARRIET—THE CHANCERY SUIT

SHELLEY's increased allowance was conditional upon his overcoming his reluctance to entail certain properties. His poverty, but not his will, consented. The demand for his *post-obit* bonds at this period was far from brisk; and he was practically compelled to tie his hands for the future in order to free them in the present, and obtain the wherewithal to live.

There was no shirking of his pecuniary responsibilities to Harriet, nor any intentional unkindness to her. It was not he, but Mary, who spoke of Harriet as " nasty " and " selfish." A readiness to speak kindly of other women was not included among Mary's virtues—it seldom is included among the virtues of women whose position in society is equivocal. They feel that they must defend themselves with such weapons as they have; and Mary, in this respect, was distinctly feline. Shelley's affections were more widely dispersed, and his impulses more indiscriminately generous. His impulse now—on which he lost no time in acting—was to clear Harriet of debt and make her an allowance of £200 a year: also to continue to show an active interest in her welfare.

THE DEATH OF HARRIET

Apparently both women misunderstood him, as wives and mistresses are apt to misunderstand the man on whom they both have claims. Mary probably feared, and Harriet certainly hoped, that the lover's passion would prove to be only a temporary aberration, and that conjugal affection would emerge triumphant in the end. The mistress, that is to say, was not quite sure that she had won Shelley, and the wife was not quite sure that she had lost him; while Shelley himself, desiring to do even-handed justice to both of them, failed to give full satisfaction to either. One imagines that a man in his position rarely can, however hard he tries.

Harriet probably could not see that Mary was " any better " than herself. The daughter of a retired licensed victualler is not likely to consider herself socially inferior to the daughter of a bookseller in active service. Least of all can she be expected to take that view when the licensed victualler pays his way, whereas the bookseller is always on the look-out for a kind friend to back a bill. But that reasoning, whether sound or unsound, was irrelevant. Between Shelley and Harriet there was a gulf not merely of incompatibilities, but of incongruities. He had outgrown her; her presence was a perpetual irritation to him. At the same time, he felt that she was not to blame for being what she was; and he tried to make things as pleasant as he could for her without knowing exactly how to set about it.

At her earnest entreaty, he left the children in her charge. Most likely—though there is a gap in the evidence here—it was Mary's wish as well as Harriet's that he should yield to that entreaty. He also continued to communicate with Harriet from time to time; and the communications were not unfriendly. What hopes they inspired in her we can only guess. It certainly was not with the intention of inspiring hopes that they were made; and any hopes which they did inspire soon flickered out. Then there was silence, and then the news, from what source derived one does not know, that Harriet had disappeared from her home; and the rest of the story is told in this paragraph which appeared in a corner of the *Times* on December 12, 1816 :—

" On Tuesday a respectable female, far advanced in pregnancy, was taken out of the Serpentine River and brought to her residence in Queen Street, Brompton, having been missing nearly six weeks. She had a valuable ring on her finger. A want of honour in her own conduct is supposed to have led to this fatal catastrophe, her husband being abroad."

Harriet, that is to say, after abandoning hope, had asserted her right to live her own life as Shelley was living his; and she was not, like Shelley, one of the exceptional people who may do exceptional things with impunity. That is the comment which her conduct suggests; and there is no need to supplement it with platitudes. Living one's own life in preference to the life prescribed by custom and convention needs a certain courage; and Harriet lacked that courage. There was no question of destitution, or even the fear of it; there can hardly be said to be any question of a new lover who had ceased to love—but only of a new protector who had ceased to protect. His protection cannot have amounted to very much if, as is said, he was a groom. But when he failed her, Harriet's nerve failed her too. She feared scandal as she might have feared the Devil, and ran along the line of least resistance, which led her to the Coroner's Court.

Those are the facts, in so far as they can be ascertained. The only essential fact to be added is that Harriet's later conduct had estranged her father and her sister, and that Shelley considered them, and them only, accountable for her fate. "There is but one voice," he wrote, " in condemnation of the detestable Westbrooks. If they should dare to bring it before Chancery, a scene of such fearful horror would be unfolded as would cover them with scorn and shame."

On the other hand, of course, there were those who said that all the blame for what had happened was his. Southey, in particular, said so in a correspondence which broke out between them in 1820; the immediate occasion of the exchange of letters being a review of *The Revolt of Islam* in the *Quarterly* which Shelley sus-

Q   241

pected Southey of having written. He described
the author of it, whoever he might be, as " an
unprincipled hireling " who had so far forgotten
himself as to " insult over the domestic calamities
of a writer of the adverse party." Southey
disclaimed the authorship, but made severe remarks about Shelley's speculative opinions and
their practical consequences, and concluded by
praying : " God in His infinite mercy bring you
to this better mind." Whereupon Shelley saluted
Southey as "such a pure one as Jesus Christ
found not in all Judæa to throw the first stone
against the woman taken in adultery," and
rejoined indignantly :—

" I take God to witness, if such a Being is now
regarding both you and me, and I pledge myself,
if we meet, as perhaps you expect, before Him
after death, to repeat the same in His presence
—that you accuse me wrongfully. I am innocent of ill, either done or intended ; the consequences you allude to flowed in no respect
from me. If you were my friend, I could tell you
a history that would make you open your eyes ;
but I shall certainly never make the public my
familiar confidant."

In response whereto, Southey launched his
thunderbolt. He recalled the days of their friendship at Keswick, the speculative opinions which
Shelley had then expressed, and his own interest
in Shelley's welfare ; and he proceeded to state

THE DEATH OF HARRIET

Shelley's case as he saw it—" in no uncharitable spirit," he said, " and with no unfriendly purpose " :—

" You forsook your wife because you were tired of her, and had found another woman more suited to your taste. You could tell me a history, you say, which would make me open my eyes; perhaps they are already open. It is a matter of public notoriety that your wife destroyed herself. Knowing in what manner she bore your desertion, I never attributed this to her sensibility on that score. I have heard it otherwise explained : I have heard that she followed your example as faithfully as your lessons, and that the catastrophe was produced by shame. Be this as it may, ask your own heart whether you have not been the whole, sole, and direct cause of her destruction. You corrupted her opinions; you robbed her of her moral and religious principles; you debauched her mind. But for you and your lessons, she might have gone through the world innocently and happily."

The words are strong; but the argument, which, after all, is the main thing, is weak. The desertion of a wife by a husband whose departure leaves his wife unaffected alike in her pocket and in her " sensibility " is hardly distinguishable in thought from a separation by agreement for the mutual advantage of the parties. Certainly it cannot be held to make the husband responsible for any follies which the wife may afterwards commit. There remains the allegation that the husband's anti-matrimonial arguments had undermined the wife's pious principles; but that charge breaks down under the weight of the facts. As we have seen, it was not Shelley who proposed to run away with Harriet, but Harriet who insisted upon running away with Shelley. He made her his wife, to the detriment of his worldly prospects, because he wished to do the right thing, in spite of her offer to live with him as his mistress. Before that evidence, Southey's indictment collapses.

That Shelley's conscience pricked him is nevertheless certain. " It was a heavy blow to him, and he never forgot it. For a time it tore his being to pieces," is Leigh Hunt's testimony; and Peacock, who, unlike Leigh Hunt, was Harriet's friend, said much the same: " Harriet's untimely fate occasioned him deep agony of mind, which he felt the more because for a long time he kept the feeling to himself." Peacock also tells us of Shelley's determination to " take a great glass of ale every night," reporting him as adding : " I shall do it to deaden my feelings : for I see that those who drink ale have none." It was his great discovery that life is a more complicated matter than we know when we make our youthful plans for " arranging " it; that it is easier to design a romance than to live it; easier to set forces in motion than to control them; impossible always to avoid remorse even for the least intended consequences of actions which seem, at the time, to be the most rational open to us.

His pain was doubled by the judgment of Lord Eldon in the Court of Chancery, depriving him, at the instance of the Westbrooks, of the custody of his and Harriet's children. It is hard to say whether he lost his case because he was badly represented, and had Sir Samuel Romilly against him, or whether he was bound to lose it at a time when the Christian religion was a part of the law of the land. He succeeded, at all events, in persuading the Court that Mr. Westbrook and Eliza were improper guardians to appoint : the grandfather because the fragrance of licensed victualling might be supposed still to cling to him ; the aunt because it was by her that the runaway match had been contrived. Instead of them, Shelley's own nominees, Dr. and Mrs. Hume, of Hanwell, were appointed ; but their father was only to be allowed to see his children once a month, and then only in their guardians' presence. In his will, dated February 18, 1817, he bequeathed them £6,000 apiece : exactly the sum which he left to Mary's children.

That, perhaps, is all that need be said on this very sad branch of the subject. Shelley's opinions as expressed in *Queen Mab*—though *Queen Mab* was only privately printed—and his conduct in living conjugally with Mary were jointly responsible for the judgment. The two things taken in conjunction proved, according to the Court,

that Shelley recommended immoral conduct as
" worthy of approbation." Whether they did
prove it or not depends, of course, upon our
definition of immorality; and that is a point
upon which opinions differ even more widely
now than in the reign of George III. Lord
Eldon's lights assuredly are not ours, but he
seems, according to his lights, to have done his
conscientious best.

That said, we will hark back and resume our
story where we quitted it.

CHAPTER XXII

WHEN he heard of his grandfather's death,
Shelley hurried to Field Place. Not being
allowed to enter the house, he sat on the door-
step reading Milton while the will was being read
in the dining-room. Mary being unfit to travel,
Jane had come with him, not indeed as far as
the door-step, but to a house in the neighbourhood : a fact which may have had its bearings
on his exclusion. Referred to Sir Timothy's
solicitor, he returned to London.

The next few months were passed in various
London lodgings. Mary's first baby was born—
a seven months' child—and died after a few
days' life; but she herself made a fairly good
recovery. Fanny's desire to see the baby proved
stronger than her fear of Godwin; she came to
the Shelleys and spent the night with them.
Mrs. Godwin once more satisfied her curiosity
by peeping through the windows, and also despatched Charles Clairmont with a bundle of
baby linen. Charles, on his part, was very
anxious to share Shelley's good fortune; and
Shelley raised no objection. His purse, when
full, was always at the disposal of his friends;

and Trelawny declared, after his death, that he himself and Hogg were the only two of his friends who had never taken advantage of his generosity; whereas Peacock, Leigh Hunt, Charles Clairmont, Tom Medwin, and the others had all plundered him to the best of their ability.

Hogg, at this time, became a constant visitor. "Hogg comes in the evening" is, for many weeks, almost a daily entry in the Diary. Or else it is: "Hogg stays all day with us . . ." . . . "Hogg sleeps here." Hogg also read Gibbon to Mary; Shelley evidently remaining convinced that his old suspicions of Hogg had been unfounded; and Hogg, on his part, evidently realizing that Mary was no barmaidenly maiden, and that the casual manner which he had adopted with Harriet must not be assumed with her. So she could net a purse for him without fear that he would misunderstand her motives; and for the rest, there was a great deal of reading, and a certain amount of sightseeing. Shelley was absorbed in Seneca, while Mary wrestled with Ovid; Hogg sometimes helping her in Shelley's absence. Beyond this, we read of visits to the British Museum and walks in Kensington Gardens. It is said that Shelley sailed a paper boat made of a £10 note on the Round Pond: a story which deserves to be true.

Mary, however, while struggling with the classics, was also struggling with a personal problem: how best, and most speedily, to get rid of Jane. If she had needed Jane's moral support at the time of the elopement, she was getting very tired of Jane's society now—the more tired of it, no doubt, because Shelley and Jane got on so well together. The reconciliation of the claims of friendship with the monopoly of love is always difficult when one is young; and Shelley, to the end of his life, never mastered it. His manners, in friendship, were apt to resemble those of a lover. It was first his instinct and afterwards his avowed policy to love all lovable women, looking to each to help him, in her special way, to self-development, self-realization, self-expression. Jane said as much to Trelawny, when they exchanged their recollections of Shelley in their old age; and Trelawny replied brutally that all men were like that in the 'twenties. He certainly was so himself—and not only in the 'twenties; but there is no reason why that reflection should detain us.

Mary, at any rate, did not see things quite as Shelley saw them. Possibly it was a disappointment to her that Shelley's attitude towards Jane was not like his attitude towards Miss Hitchener; certainly she was not pleased to see Shelley perpetually taking Jane for walks, teaching her Italian, and sitting up late with her. She thought that, if Jane could not, or would not, return to the Godwins, she had better seek a situation as a lady companion. She was bitterly disappointed that a Mrs. Knapp would not receive Jane, though Jane described Mrs. Knapp as " a forward, impertinent, and superficial woman." We also, on March 14, come upon this cry of pain :—

"Shelley and I go upstairs and talk of Clara's [1] going; the prospect appears to me more dismal than ever; not the least hope. This is, indeed, hard to bear."

Followed, about two months later, by this cry of joy :—

"Clara goes; Shelley walks with her. . . . I begin a new journal with our regeneration."

Jane, in fact, had drawn a prize in a lottery, and had been despatched to a solitary lodging at Lynmouth. One does not know whether the prize was large enough to pay for her trip; but it is more probable that Shelley paid for it. It cannot actually be proved that she was hustled off to Devonshire because she had shown herself too fond of Shelley; but there are striking indications to that effect—and still more striking indications that she herself took that view of her exile, though it was a pleasant exile of which, at first at all events, she did not complain.

Our first hint is in a letter which she wrote, immediately on her arrival at Lynmouth, to Fanny :—

"After so much discontent, such violent

[1] Jane, at this stage, assumed the more romantic name of Clara. Afterwards she called herself Claire, and sometimes Constantia.

250

scenes, such a turmoil of passion and hatred, you will hardly believe how enraptured I am with this dear little quiet spot. . . . It is in solitude that the powers concentre round the soul, and teach it the calm determined path of virtue and wisdom."

That indicates, as clearly as anything can, that there has been unpleasantness with Mary. It might also, if it stood alone, seem to indicate unpleasantness with Shelley; but it does not stand alone. Our second hint is contained in one of Mary's letters to Shelley. She writes, on July 27, from Clifton, where Shelley has left her while he goes house-hunting in South Devon, begging him to make haste and return to her. This house-hunting, she complains, "is a very, *very* long job, too long for one love to undertake in the absence of the other"—especially as his and her birthdays are both close at hand. She is "quite sick of passing day after day in this hopeless way"; she would very much prefer "a delightful excursion to Tintern Abbey;" and then she asks a significant question :—

"Pray, is Clare with you? for I have inquired several times and no letters; but, seriously, it would not in the least surprise me, if you have written to her from London, and let her know that you are without me, that she should have taken some such freak."

That establishes the fact of Mary's jealousy,

though it does not prove that there was any reason for it. Shelley, indeed, seems to have attracted all the girls in the Godwin household—Jane no less than Mary, and Fanny no less than Jane. Fanny was a girl who guarded her own secret; but Jane was at little pains to guard hers :—

" Have you never loved, madame ? " I asked.
" A delicate blush suffused the cheeks, and this time she made no reply, gazing on the ground.
" ' Shelley ? ' I murmured.
" ' With all my heart and soul,' she replied, without moving her eyes from the ground."

That is the confession of her old age, reported by Mr. William Graham in his *Last Links with Byron, Shelley, and Keats.* It has not been taken seriously. Either the lady's or the interviewer's memory has been commonly assumed to have been at fault ; but there is a remarkable contemporary confirmation, which biographers have overlooked, in one of Jane's letters to Byron.

We shall come to the story of Jane's relations with Byron almost immediately ; but we may anticipate. Mrs. Marshall saw Jane's letters to Byron when she was preparing her *Life of Mrs. Shelley,* but was not allowed to print them. The only inference which she draws from them is that Jane was not very deeply in love with

Byron; but there was another inference which she might have drawn if she had read them more carefully. Shelley's name appears in them several times. Jane quotes Shelley for, as it were, a testimonial to her charms. He had told her, she says, that she was " the most engaging of human creatures; " and she continues :—

" I do not report this through vanity; I know Shelley is too fond of me not to be indulgent, yet I think it is an honourable testimony to that part of my character you have accused, that the man whom I have loved, and for whom I have suffered much, should report this of me."

If this does not mean that love for Shelley—not carefully hidden like Fanny's love for him—was the cause of Jane's precipitate banishment to Lynmouth, then one does not know what it means. The proof seems clear that Jane was in love with Shelley, though not that Shelley was in love with Jane. His view of love, indeed, so far as one can define it, seems to have been that it was an infinite emotion, and that the metaphysics and mathematics of infinity applied to it : that the love which he gave to one woman, left the sum-total of the love which he could give to other women unaffected.

Mary, however, would not be expected to take that view; and no woman will blame her for not taking it. Even George Sand could not persuade herself to take it where Chopin was concerned, though she had expected Alfred de Musset and Dr. Pagello to take it when her own affections were in a state of flux. What Mary wanted was, naturally, to have Shelley to herself; and for about a year, she got her way. He travelled with her, after their departure from the London lodgings, in South Devon; and after the sojourn at Clifton, they settled down, in a furnished house, at Bishopgate, near Windsor Park, some time in August, 1815. " No events, as you know," Shelley wrote thence to Hogg, " disturb our tranquillity."

No notable events happened, indeed, except the birth of Mary's boy William. The exchange of visits with Hogg, who was in London, and Peacock who was at Marlow; an excursion with Peacock and Charles Clairmont up the river as far as Lechlade; negotiations with Sir Timothy about the settlement of the estate; correspondence with Godwin, who wanted Shelley to pay further debts, but was too proud and punctilious to take a cheque from him drawn to his own order :—those are the details, and it is not worth while to dwell on them. Nor is it of much moment that Peacock, at this period, induced Shelley, vegetarian though he professed to be, to eat " mutton chops well peppered," or that the example of Hogg's hunger gave him a taste for bacon. The sojourn is chiefly to be remembered for the composition of *Alastor*.

That, of course, marked an epoch. Before *Alastor* Shelley was mainly a dialectician,

254

persuaded that the human race was perfectible, and might be made perfect by mob orators speaking the language of pure reason. With the writing of *Alastor*, the dialectician was lost in the poet, who, without renouncing—probably without doubting—any of the old principles, found that the task which lay nearest to him was, not propagandism, but self-realization and self-expression. Mary was restful—especially restful when Jane was out of the way—and he could wander in the woods and remember emotion in tranquillity for the first time in his tempestuous life.

Perhaps—for he always expected the temporary to be permanent—he imagined that Jane would remain in her Lynmouth lodging for ever. Perhaps Mary too, being so young and inexperienced, cherished the same delusion. It was the sort of thing that might happen at the end of a fairy tale. But no one in real life ever stays for ever in a Lynmouth lodging-house; and Jane was a very real person. *Frasques* were impossible at Lynmouth; and *frasques* were necessary to her. Exactly when and how she got away from Lynmouth—exactly where she went when she did get away—no one appears to know. Apparently she quartered herself for a time upon her brother Charles, and then proposed herself once more as Mary's guest. Apparently she had established herself as Mary's guest at the time when she burst into the house with the memorable exclamation :—

THE ROMANTIC LIFE OF SHELLEY

" Percy ! Mary ! What do you think ? The great Lord Byron loves me ! "

That brings us to the most daring of all Jane's *frasques ;* and it will be worth while to get at the exact truth about it. That exact truth certainly is not to be found in Professor Dowden's *Life of Shelley,* or in Mrs. Marshall's *Life of Mrs. Shelley ;* nor did Cordy Jeaffreson present it in either *The Real Shelley* or *The Real Byron ;* nor did Jane herself tell it, when Mr. William Graham interviewed her at Florence. But, if we check Mr. Graham's interview with Jane's letters, printed in Mr. Prothero's edition of Byron's works, we shall find that, while much which has been said can be contradicted, very little need, in the end, be left doubtful.

CHAPTER XXIII

JANE CLAIRMONT'S RELATIONS WITH BYRON

THE generally accepted version of the Byron-Jane Clairmont story is as follows :—

Jane took it into her head to seek a career on the stage. She called on Byron in his capacity of member of the Committee of Management of Drury Lane. Byron, as Professor Dowden puts it, " was skilled in the dangers which beset a woman's heart," and took advantage of that skill—for, still to quote Professor Dowden, " why should a man of genius set bounds to his appetite for delighted sensations ? " Jane, on her part, " eagerly desired to keep the great event of her life a secret," told neither Shelley nor Mary what had happened, but arranged, without confiding in them, either that they should go to Geneva to meet Byron, or else that Byron should go to Geneva to meet them. Cordy Jeaffreson added the conjecture—which Jane endorsed in conversation with Mr. Graham—that the intrigue was the real cause of the Byron separation.

The real causes of the Byron separation are now known; and it is established that Jane Clairmont had nothing whatever to do with them. Her name does not appear in the presentation of Lady Byron's case in *Astarte*. That error is the first to put aside; and the next mistake is best presented in Jane's own story, reported by Mr. Graham :—

"I called . . . on Byron in his capacity of manager, and he promised to do what he could to help me as regards the stage. The result you know. I am too old now to play with any mock repentance. I was young, and vain, and poor. He was famous beyond all precedent, so famous that people, and especially young people, hardly considered him as a man at all, but rather as a god. His beauty was as haunting as his fame, and he was all-powerful in the direction in which my ambition turned. It seemed to me, almost needless to say, that the attentions of a man like this, with all London at his feet, very quickly completely turned the head of a girl in my position; and when you recollect that I was brought up to consider marriage not only as a useless but as an absolutely sinful custom, that only bigotry made necessary, you will scarcely wonder at the result which you know."

It is very plausible. The story hangs together; but—*litera scripta manet*. Documents in Jane's handwriting—to say nothing of documents in Byron's handwriting—contradict most of the statements; and others of them can be contradicted from other sources.

It was not true that Jane had been brought up in the doctrines of Free Love. Her mother

had never held those doctrines, and her step-
father had abandoned them before he married
her mother; while both father and mother had
quarrelled with Mary and Shelley for putting
them in practice. Nor is it true that Jane introduced herself to Byron with a view to obtaining
a theatrical engagement; or that Byron took
the initiative in the matter of " attentions."
What really happened was that Jane wrote to
Byron under an assumed name from an accom-
modation address, making no mention whatsoever
of theatrical ambitions, but laying her heart at
his feet :—

" An utter stranger takes the liberty of addressing you. . . . It is not charity I demand,
for of that I stand in no need. . . . I tremble
with fear at the fate of this letter. I cannot
blame if it shall be received by you as an impudent imposture. . . . It may seem a strange
assertion, but it is not the less true that I place
my happiness in your hands. . . . If a woman
whose reputation has yet remained unstained,
if, without either guardian or husband to control,
she should throw herself upon your mercy, if
with a beating heart she should confess the love
she has borne you many years, if she should
secure to you secrecy and safety, if she should
return your kindness with fond affection and
unbounded devotion, could you betray her, or
could you be silent as the grave ? . . . I must
entreat your answer without delay. . . . Address

me as E. Trefusis, 21, Noley Place, Mary le Bonne."

That letter removes all question as to who began the love-making. Byron seems not to have answered it; so we find Jane returning to the charge under another *nom de guerre* :—

" Lord Byron is requested to state whether seven o'clock this evening will be convenient to him to receive a lady to communicate with him on business of peculiar importance. She desires to be admitted alone, and with the utmost privacy."

That letter is signed " G. C. B." Byron replied by making an appointment which he does not appear to have kept; for we next find Jane writing : " I have called twice on you; but your servants declare you to be out of town." This time she drops pseudonyms, and signs her own name; and this is the first letter in which the theatre appears. Jane asks not for help, but for advice : " Is it absolutely necessary to go through the intolerable and disgusting drudgery of the provincial theatres before commencing on the boards of a metropolis ? "

Byron, in answer, referred Jane to his colleague in management, Douglas Kinnaird; but Jane did not go to Douglas Kinnaird : a fact which may be taken as giving the measure of the sincerity of her theatrical aspirations. In

260

the next letter there is a change of front. Jane's ambitions are no longer theatrical, but literary. She has written "half of a novel or tale," and wants Byron to criticize it. She is afraid he may think her "intruding and troublesome," but —she also feels that she knows him well enough to invite his sympathy by remarks about that married state which, as all the world knows, he has found so unsatisfactory :—

"Do you remember his (Dante's) inscription over the gate of hell—

Lasciate ogni speranza voi ch' entrate.

I think it is a most admirable description of marriage. The subject makes me prolix. I can never resist the temptation of throwing a pebble at it as I pass by."

Still Byron remained unmoved. One gathers as much from Jane's complaint that "there is little in your lordship's stern silence to embolden me;" but Jane was one of those women with whom a little emboldening goes a very long way. "You bade me believe," she protests, "that it was a fancy which made me cherish an attachment to you." She adds that "it cannot be a fancy since you have been for the last year the object upon which every solitary moment led me to muse." And then she makes her final plunge, sending her note by hand to Piccadilly Terrace, and waiting in Hamilton Place for the answer :—

" I may appear to you imprudent, vicious
. . . but one thing at least time shall show you,
that I love gently and with affection, that I am
incapable of anything approaching to the feeling
of revenge or malice : I do assure you your
future will, shall be mine. . . .

" Have you then any objection to the following plan ? On Thursday evening we may go
out of town together by some stage or mail
about the distance of ten or twelve miles. There
we shall be free and unknown; we can return
early the following morning. I have arranged
everything here so that the slightest suspicion
may not be excited. . . .

" Will you admit me for two moments to
settle with you *where ?* Indeed, I will not stay
an instant after you tell me to go. . . . Do
what you will, or go where you will, refuse to see
me, and behave unkindly, I shall never forget
you. I shall ever remember the gentleness of
your manners and the wild originality of your
eountenance."

And so on, and so forth. No one who has
analysed that correspondence will ever again
believe that Byron took advantage of the innocence of a young woman who appealed to him
to exert " influence " in favour of her professional career on the stage. On the contrary,
it is as clear as daylight that the young woman
in question only pretended that she wanted to
be an actress in order to obtain admission to

Byron's house, and then left him no peace until he consented to make her his mistress. His own version of the matter, reported to his sister Augusta when he and Jane met again at Geneva, is evidently the true one :—

" Now, dearest, I do most truly tell thee that I could not help this, that I did all I could to prevent it, and have at last put an end to it. I was not in love, nor have any love left for any; but I could not exactly play the Stoic with a woman who had scrambled eight hundred miles to unphilosophise me."

That letter seems to dispose of the view that Byron went to Geneva to meet Jane. The meeting can hardly have been accidental; and the conclusion follows that Jane went there to meet Byron. The question remains : Did she get Shelley to take her there by persuading him and Mary that Geneva was a place they really ought to see ? Or did she arrange the meeting with their help and connivance ? That is a point on which there is a direct conflict of testimony between Jane, and Shelley's and Mrs. Shelley's biographers.

Perhaps the least plausible of the theories is that set forth by Mrs. Marshall. Shelley and Mary, she says, were " ignorant and unsuspecting of the intrigue " between Byron and Jane; but they nevertheless went to Geneva with the idea of meeting Byron, of whose movements Jane had informed them. In reply to that it suffices to say that Shelley and Mary must have been very unsuspecting indeed if they had accepted Jane's knowledge of Byron's itinerary as a matter of course and asked no questions about it. Professor Dowden at all events avoids that pitfall.

" That Shelley," he writes, " had decided to leave England independently of Clara's solicitations we know for certain; it is not improbable, however, that her desire to visit Geneva may have hastened his departure, and may have helped to determine his destination."

Professor Dowden adds that Mary, at that date, can be proved by letters which he has seen, not even to have known that Byron and Miss Clairmont were acquainted. One would like to see his evidence; and, while awaiting it, one notes that he guards himself against making the statement that Shelley shared Mary's ignorance. Jane's own statements, however, if correctly reported, are equally at variance with those of both biographers. She says that she took Byron down to Marlow to meet Shelley; that she and Byron and Shelley and Mary lunched together at the Marlow inn; and finally that " early in the following year all was arranged for the meeting at Geneva." And when Mr. Graham asked her whether Shelley and Mary approved of the intimacy :—

" Most certainly," she replied briefly. " I
264

have already told you—what you know, of course,
already—what the Shelleys' opinions on these
matters were, or what Shelley's were, because
Mary docilely followed his lead in these things;
and in a lasting union, as he hoped it would be,
between his sister-in-law, as he always called me,
and a man whom he at that time considered
almost as a god, he saw nothing but what should
ardently be desired. He thought that I would
be to Byron what Mary was to him. Alas! alas!
little did any one of us understand what Byron
really was then."

Thus Jane. But Jane, as we have just seen,
was a very inaccurate person. Nothing that
Jane says can be believed simply because Jane
says it. Jane's story of the Marlow trip does not
accord with the evidence of Jane's letters. Her
relations with Byron, if they had begun, certainly did not mature until after Shelley had come
to London; so that, if any meeting between the
two poets did take place, London was almost
certainly the scene of it. Mrs. Marshall, in fact,
speaks of a meeting between Byron and Mary,
though without naming her authority; but that
is a detail. The essential question is: Did
Mary and Shelley know? Did they, as Jane
says, approve?

No positive answer to these questions is possible; but, when we come to balance con-
jectures:—

1. There is no iota of suggestion anywhere in

the published correspondence that their subsequent discovery of what had happened shocked, or even surprised, them.

2. A motive is badly wanted—and their knowledge and approval would supply one—for Mary's willingness to accept Jane as the companion of her journey.

Mary, as we have seen, was so tired of Jane that she moved heaven and earth to get her out of the house. Jane, on her own showing, was an incorrigible flirt. "It was not my fault that men fell in love with me," she said to Mr. Graham, when he suggested that her presence in Shelley's house must have been disconcerting to Mary. We have already seen reasons—and we shall see others—for believing that Mary was jealous; and, if Mary was jealous, nothing would have been more natural than that she should rejoice to see Jane's affections diverted into another channel.

She could not have been shocked; for what Jane was proposing to do was only what she herself had done. On no conceivable grounds could she hold that Byron and Jane were bound to obey conventions which she and Shelley were free to break. At the most she could only fear that Jane might find it easier to get into trouble than to extricate herself from it—as indeed proved to be the case. But that was Jane's affair; and if she had to choose between seeing Jane make love to Byron and seeing her make love to Shelley, she would have been more than human if she had not encouraged Jane in her capricious fancy for throwing herself into Byron's arms. Nothing, too, is more natural than that she should afterwards, in the light of all that happened, prefer to forget that she had done so.

On the whole, therefore (though nothing is certain), it is with Jane's version of the story that the balance of probability lies. That point made clear, we may once more return to Shelley, and follow him on his Swiss excursion.

CHAPTER XXIV

AT GENEVA AND GREAT MARLOW—SHELLEY'S SECOND MARRIAGE

THE Genevan episode, belonging as it does to Byron's life as well as Shelley's, has been much written about and may be passed over briefly. How the two parties left their hotel for suburban villas; how Byron and Shelley, sailing together on the Lake, narrowly escaped shipwreck on the rocks at Meillerie; how the telling of ghost stories led to the writing of them —and especially to the writing of Mary's *Frankenstein ;* how Shelley took Mary to Chamonix, and made a memorable entry in a visitor's book [1] —all these things are well known, and there is nothing to be added. Still, if we are to get things in their true perspective, one point must be made.

It was Byron who drew attention to Shelley, who, but for Byron, would almost have escaped observation. Nobody, in fact, took any notice of Shelley until Byron joined him. The boarders at Dejeante's hotel may or may not have known that he had been expelled from Oxford, had left his wife, and had eloped with his friend's daughter; they certainly did not let their minds dwell upon the matter to the exclusion of other

---

[1] Εἰμὶ φιλάνθρωπος δημοκράτικός τ' ἄθεός τε.

interests; they had no opportunity of refusing him their society, for he did not seek it. It was not till Byron arrived with his coach and his retinue, and ignored all the boarders except Shelley and his party, that they began to stare.

When once they had begun to stare, however, nothing could stop them from staring. They stared from morn till eve. They stared at the party when they went out, and they stared at them when they came home. They gathered on the hotel steps to stare, much as idle women gather on the pavement outside a church when a wedding is in progress within; they gathered with similar curiosity on the Lake landing-stages. In the end they stared the party out of the hotel; and they continued to stare at them after they had left it for their suburban villas. It seemed to them they might thus at once satisfy their curiosity and prove their moral worth.

A queer contrast truly! The immoral people in the villas absolutely indifferent to the proceedings of the moral people in the hotel; the moral people in the hotel so inquisitive about the " goings-on " of the immoral people in the villas that they persuaded the landlord to rig up a telescope at some point of vantage in order that they might take it in turns to peep at them. One can imagine their self-complacent conversations — the self-complacent conversations of the women in particular—while they waited for their turns. No doubt they thanked God that they were not as other women were—

269

even as Mary and Jane—unless, as is quite as likely, they took the credit to themselves; and we may be quite sure that they never suspected that thoughts and conversation were, just then, moving on a higher plane in immoral than in moral circles. Happily, or unhappily, as one prefers to put it, life does, from time to time, present such ironies.

It was in one of the immoral villas, for example, that "Monk" Lewis, after a conversation on the iniquities of the slave-trade, signed the famous codicil to his will, forbidding the sale and securing the good treatment of the negroes on his West Indian plantation; and no action so creditable as that is recorded of any of the boarders at the moral hotel. It was at the villas, too, that Shelley brought Byron under the new influence of Wordsworth, with results which may be clearly traced in the Third Canto of *Childe Harold*. And, of course, there was "talk about virtue" and diligent study of the best authors, even at the time when the "inquisitive moralists" with the telescope discerned, as Hobhouse told Mrs. Leigh, "certain robes and flounces on his lordship's balcony."

Scandal, of course, was busy. Scandal said that Byron and Shelley were living in promiscuity with Jane and Mary. Southey, as a virtuous man, thought it a virtuous act to repeat the calumny. One cannot be sure whether Shelley heard the scandal at the time or not—there are, at any rate, no indications that it troubled him. And so the days passed until it was time for him to go home, and—to take Jane with him.

Jane did not want to go—that point is clear from Byron's letter to Augusta :—

" I found her here—and I have had all the plague possible to persuade her to go back again; but at last she went. Now, dearest, I do most truly tell thee that I did all I could to prevent it, and have at last put an end to it. . . . I was fain to take a little love (if pressed particularly) by way of novelty. And now you know all that I know of the matter, and it's over."

For Jane had dreamt the dream of which she has told us; and the dream had been as brief as it was bright. She had dreamt it on her own responsibility, without encouragement from Byron, and—what are the precise obligations of a man towards a young woman with whom he has entered into intimate relations when separated from a wife who will not allow him to return to her ?

Shelley, at any rate, did not censure Byron— possibly because he knew Jane too well to do so. He took with him, on his return, not only Byron's mistress, but also his manuscripts; and we find him correcting the proofs of the latter while providing a home for the former. And not merely providing a home for her, but guarding her secret from her mother and step-father, **who** seemed likely to renounce her if it became

271

known to them. It must have been a great nuisance to Mary, whose hopes of getting rid of Jane were thus nipped in the bud, and who might well ask herself whether Jane was to be quartered on her for ever. The cry is quickly heard in a letter which she wrote to Shelley when he was once more house-hunting :—

" A house with a lawn, a river or lake, noble trees, and divine mountains, that should be our little mouse-hole to retire to. But never mind this; give me a garden, and *absentia* Claire, and I will thank my love for many favours."

That was written from Bath, where Shelley had his headquarters until he took a house at Great Marlow. Before it was written, a tragedy had happened. Fanny Godwin had been found dead in an inn at Swansea with a bottle of laudanum by her side. It was in connection with her death that Shelley wrote the well-known lines :—

> *Her voice did quiver as we parted ;*
> *Yet knew I not that heart was broken*
> *From whence it came, and I departed*
> *Heeding not the words then spoken.*
> *Misery—O Misery,*
> *This world is all too wide for thee !*

He evidently wrote the lines in the belief that Fanny had died of unrequited love for him. Whether it was so or not we have no certain means of knowing. Mrs. Gisborne said

272

that Mrs. Godwin told her so; but Mrs. Godwin had a lively imagination, and may have wished to make it clear that it was not her fault that Fanny had been unhappy at home. Jane also said so, in later years; but Jane's imagination was even livelier than Mrs. Godwin's. There is no evidence there; and from other sources we can only gather hints.

Shelley, as we know, began to correspond with Fanny before he fell in love with Mary; there may be a clue in that fact, though a faint one. Possibly, again, there is a clue in the reverential affection for Shelley—coupled with the complaint that Shelley laughs at her—contained in some of Fanny's letters to Mary. It might be thought that Fanny showed more than a stranger's or mere acquaintance's interest alike in Shelley's health and in his poems :—

" I am angry with Shelley for not giving me an account of his health. All that I saw of him gave me great uneasiness about him, and as I see him but seldom, I am much more alarmed perhaps than you, who are constantly with him. . . . Beg the favour of Shelley to copy for me his poem on the scenes at the foot of Mont Blanc, and tell him or remind him of a letter which you said he had written on these scenes; you cannot think what a treasure they would be to me."

The fact may seem strange, too, that Fanny, on that last journey, got as near to Bath as

Bristol, and then passed on (though there was no need for hurry) without turning aside to visit Shelley and Mary. Seeing her come to their neighbourhood without any visible motive, and then, also without visible motive, avoid them, one is tempted to guess pretty much what Jane guessed. In short, one can build up a case if one cares to try; but one cannot be sure.

Fanny was a good, plain, sensitive, and morbid girl : a Cinderella who needed a fairy godmother, but never found one. She had never known either her father or her mother. She had been born into a world in which there was no proper place for her—in which she failed to make herself a place. She was the drudge of a gloomy, impecunious household; and the circumstances of her birth made the hope of escape from it by marriage faint. Escape from it into the calling of a school-mistress would have been better than nothing; and even that escape failed her. Her aunt, Everina Wollstonecraft—a stern worshipper at the shrine of appearances—refused in the end to have her in her Seminary. All her letters are despondent letters. She speaks to Mary of " the dreadful state of mind I generally labour under, and which I in vain endeavour to get rid of." Unreciprocated love, if it indeed troubled her, can only have been one of many troubles; and, in any case, if she had a secret to guard, she guarded it,—giving no hint of it even in the farewell letter found beside the poison bottle : " Perhaps to hear of my death may give you

pain, but you will soon have the blessing of forgetting that such a creature ever existed as . . ."

It was over; and there was no more to be
said, and nothing to do except to hush the
matter up. That, in response to Godwin's
appeal, was done; and a verdict of death by
misadventure was secured. But the shock—
which was none the less a shock, however
little Shelley knew or suspected—was quickly
followed by another. It was only two months
after Fanny's death that the body identified as
Harriet's was found in the Serpentine; and after
that ensued the Chancery suit, the judgment in
which was delivered on March 27, 1817.

That, at least, set Shelley free to marry
Mary, and he married her at once. He believed,
wrongly as it proved, that his haste to regularize
an irregular situation would influence the Court
in his favour; and it did, at any rate, reconcile
Godwin. That philosopher now proceeded to
sponge on the poet directly instead of doing so
through the medium of solicitors—showing his
independence the while by telling the poet that
he did not think much of his poetry. That,
broadly speaking, was the position of things
when Shelley settled at Marlow, taking his house
on a twenty-one years lease, with the declared
intention of remaining there, if not " for ever,"
at least until his father died.

The realities of life were never more real for
him than then. The months of poverty in London lodgings had tried and aged him; but there

had been compensations,—the thrill of a new romance—the exciting sense of adventure. He had been able to face his troubles with Bohemian lightness of heart, cheered by the moral certainty that a way out of them would, before long, be found. There was no reason why he should not look back on them in the spirit of the prosperous French sage who cried regretfully : *O les beaux jours, les beaux jours de ma jeunesse, quand j'étais si malheureux !*

All that was over, and Shelley was as prosperous as a man with simple tastes need wish to be. He had no need to hide from creditors or besiege money-lenders with his importunities. He was free to dream his dreams in his boat in the Thames back-waters; and that was how he passed the summer of 1817. *Laon and Cythna* is the tangible outcome of the dreams. Yet his melancholy deepened as his social life expanded.

Viewed from without, the period is one of great sociability. Shelley had dropped out of the circle in which he had shone in the later days of his union with Harriet—the Boinvilles, the Newtons, and the Turners saw no more of him; but he was forming a new circle in place of it. He became intimate with Leigh Hunt [1] and Horace Smith; he continued to be intimate with Hogg and Peacock; he met Keats and Charles Lamb. With most of his friends he exchanged hospi-

---

[1] He had already written to Leigh Hunt, to express sympathy with his opinions, when an undergraduate.

talities. A country gentleman, the casual observer would have said, who was rather fond of running up to town, and enjoying himself in good company when he got there. But—there are a good many buts.

Perhaps we may sum them up by saying that Shelley was discovering the truths about life which some men never discover at all, and few men discover until they are middle-aged. The game of life, in which he had engaged in such utter ignorance of the rules, had been one partly of chance, partly of skill. He had played without skill, and the luck had been against him. The consequences of his first defeat pursued him in his second experiment. He had learnt that, in life, it is not intention but action which carries consequences. His case was that of a man who, setting out to take his part in a pastoral idyll, finds himself involved in an uncontcmplated tragedy; and he was not framed to sustain a tragic rôle, but was of an extreme sensibility— quick to perceive the difference between life as it might have been and life as it turned out to be : easily oppressed by the sense of death and doom, and of the nets of calamity closing round him.

It had to be so. On no other condition could he have become the poet whom we know. One searches literary history in vain for a poet of his mark who has not learnt in suffering what he has taught in song. The garish contrast between the dream and the business besieges all of them in greater or less degree. They cannot live as they dream even if the world would let them; and the world will not let them. They cannot separate the business from the dream; but each disturbs the other. Ideal causes produce material effects, and entail material responsibilities. So with Shelley.

He had meant well—no bishop on the bench could have meant better. It had seemed to him that he really had a " call," as the religious say, to spread the light, to redress wrong, to pursue romance in disregard of the warnings of the purse-proud and the worldly-wise. It had seemed to him, further, that it would be an act of treason to love if he hid a love he felt or affected a love which he had ceased to feel. No one who reads his letters can question his absolute sincerity in all these matters. He was quite as conscientious an idealist, quite as zealous for the amelioration of the world, as his Oxford contemporaries, John Keble and Thomas Arnold, when they embarked on their respective enterprises for the reform of the church and the schools; but whereas they were in a fair way to be canonised, he was in a fair way to become a Pariah, enduring, as the result of his conscientious candour, a persecution which a hypocrite and a libertine would have escaped.

Repudiated by his family, held to blame for his wife's suicide, deprived of his children by the Courts,—he had paid a heavy price for his precocious experiments with life, and would never again be able to face life in the old fearless spirit. The new friends whom he had found were hardly friends who could help him to do that; for those of them who professed most affection fastened themselves on him like leeches to suck his blood. Godwin demanded loans with as much insistence as if he had been demanding the payment of a debt. Leigh Hunt borrowed large sums from him, while his wife borrowed small sums from Mary. Peacock wanted £100 a year, and got it. Charles Clairmont, who had found his way to the Pyrenees, asked for such an allowance as would enable him to marry and settle down there.

Perhaps Shelley did not mind; but Mary most certainly minded. One begins, at this date, to detect a certain plaintive peevishness in her letters: the tone of a woman who loves her husband, indeed, but has her own opinion about her husband's friends. She is never, or hardly ever, violent; but she says something disagreeable—or something to arouse suspicion—about each of them in turn. The solicitor, Longdill, for instance, " makes out long bills and does nothing." Peacock " dines here every day, *uninvited*, to drink his bottle." Claire " is for ever wearying with her idle and childish complaints."

Of what Claire complained one does not know; but Mary certainly had something to complain of in connection with her. It may or may not have aggrieved her that Shelley wrote verses

279

to Claire as well as to herself. The lines " To Constantia singing," which belong to this date, do certainly read as if they rendered something more than mere admiration of the trained art of the vocalist; and it is also certain that Shelley, at this date, made the will in which he bequeathed Claire £12,000. Far worse than that, however, was the fact that gossip asserted Shelley to be the father of Claire's child : a cruel reward truly for Mary's kindness in giving Claire a home before, during, and after her confinement.

That we may take it was the deciding circumstance which made Mary—and Shelley himself, in a less degree—anxious, once more, to go abroad. Shelley's health was the reason given to those who were in a position to ask for reasons; and no doubt he did believe himself to be in danger of pulmonary consumption. But there undoubtedly were other reasons also; and the desire to put an end to scandal by placing Allegra in the hands of her actual father—if not also to induce Allegra's father to take charge of Allegra's mother—may be supposed to have been the most potent of them.

CHAPTER XXV

THE mood and motive—the inwardness and the psychology—of Shelley's last departure for the Continent differed widely from those of the preceding journeys. The first trip had been a frolic, conceived in the spirit of irresponsible frivolity. The second (in spite of the complications which it originated) had been a very ordinary holiday excursion. The third (whatever the immediate occasion of it) must be classed with the endeavours of baffled men to " escape from life."

Not, of course, that Shelley was hounded out of the country as Byron had been. In spite of the Chancery suit—in spite of the wild utterances of *Laon and Cythna*—he was far too inconspicuous to receive such treatment. His name was hardly ever in the papers; hardly any one read what he wrote; hardly any one knew who he was. But he had lost his way in life, and knew it; his illusions were falling like the autumn leaves. It was not merely that, having set out buoyantly to fight the battle of " enthusiasm " against " prejudice," he had found prejudice too strongly entrenched for enthusiasm to make any impression on it. He had also got

281

himself so entangled in a net of circumstance that it was only of the inward life that he could, in the future, hope to make anything.

That was how he differed from those brilliant Oxford contemporaries with whom we have contrasted him. John Keble and Thomas Arnold were no more his moral than his intellectual superiors. Their advantage over him (in the view of those who assign them advantage) lay in their comparative lack of originality. They marched a little ahead of the mob, but not too far ahead to get out of sight. They saw visions—but only such visions as the multitude could understand. The gospels which they respectively preached were gospels which the world was ready to receive. They did not shock—or not to any great extent; they were not difficult to understand; they did not use any but the approved machinery for their propagandism. Above all, they had no troublesome impulses driving them to hasty action. Consequently they reaped their reward in their lifetime; and, whether they were in sympathy with commonplace people or not, it was easy for commonplace people to be in sympathy with them.

Shelley, on the contrary, had had emotions, and had been betrayed by them. When he wanted to do a thing, and saw no obvious reason for not doing it, he jumped to the conclusion that he ought to do it, and did it at once. Alike in eloping with Harriet, and in separating from her, and in eloping with Mary, he had been trying, according to his lights, to discharge the duty which seemed to lie nearest to him. He had always said what he thought, and done what he felt impelled to do, without regard to the tender feelings of the weaker brethren; and the weaker brethren are not so weak as they seem to be, but can be terrible when roused. Shelley had roused them, and they had turned on him, exclaiming, as is their wont, that the strong man is the man who swims with the tide, and the virtuous man he who shouts with the crowd. That was his punishment for not being like other people; and he felt it keenly, and was already in the mood to write, as he wrote later :—

" *I fall upon the thorns of life ; I bleed.*"

It is the tradition that the man in such a mood should travel. It is also the tradition that he should go south or east, rather than north or west. Life, it seems to him, will be less troublesome among strangers, and in the sunshine. He will be able to dream out his dream there, unimpeded by the business. His melancholy, though there may be no escape from it, will take a softer tone; discomfort will be eliminated; self-realization will console. Thus he reflects, and packs; thus we may picture Shelley reflecting while he packed.

It was not his destiny—perhaps it is no man's destiny—quite to realize his dream. A certain shining halo of false impressions has gradually formed about the records of his life in Italy.

One has come to imagine him and Mary, lovers always—lovers as devoted at the end as at the beginning—counting the world well lost for love, yet winning back as much of the world as was worth winning by the spectacle of genius and beauty in accord; sufficing for each other, and on that account envied by all who were privileged to behold; comforting each other in sorrow, supporting each other in joy, and so building and embellishing a perfect romance, which the abhorred shears cut prematurely short.

Things were not quite like that, however; and the world is the gainer from the fact that they were not. If they had been, we should never have heard the " deep autumnal tone " sighing through the Ode to the West Wind, or the passionate appeal for " half the gladness " of the Skylark; the cry that " our sweetest songs are those which tell of saddest thought," or the longing for

> " *That content surpassing wealth*
> *The sage in meditation found,*
> *And walked with inward glory crowned.*"

Content of that kind was not for Shelley any more than the base content of those who only ask to be well-fed, well-clothed, and well-to-do. He could say, indeed, when the sun shone on the Bay of Naples, that

> " *Now despair itself is mild*
> *Even as the waves and waters are.*"

But the mildest despair is a different thing from either hope or joy.

It may be that Shelley asked more from life than life has to give. Most of us do that, in our several degrees, and in accordance with our several capacities for asking; but Shelley's capacity for asking—and for imagining the things to be asked for—exceeded that of other men. He resented the limitations which his thoughts transcended but his life could not transcend. His power of dreaming was such as no single dream could satisfy : his passion for romance too exacting for any single romance to fulfil all its needs. And so there were fluctuations between rapture and despondency, illusions followed by disillusions, notes of discord where there should have been harmony, an increasing pallor of the pale cast of his thoughts.

What all this means, when expressed in plain statements of fact, we shall see, more or less clearly, as we proceed. It means, in a general way, of course, that the escape from life was, as it always is, incomplete; that the business pursued the dreamer even into the world of dreams; that the dreams caused embarrassment, and that there were awakenings from them. It means, in particular, that Shelley's aspirations after universal love made trouble; that Mary's soul was sometimes vexed; that Mary and Shelley sometimes had opposing ambitions; that Emilia Viviani, and Jane Williams, and Jane

Clairmont ruffled the calm current of his life in ways to be related.

Shelley's first task, on reaching Italy, was to deliver Allegra to Byron, whom he visited at Venice, and who refused either to see or to correspond with Allegra's mother. He has sometimes been censured for accepting Byron's friendship when Byron treated Allegra's mother so badly; but the rights and wrongs of the case are not so simple as such a censure would imply. We have already seen that Jane Clairmont threw herself at Byron's head; we also have her confession that she was not in love with Byron when she did so :—

" ' I suppose you are as crass as most men, and think that I loved Byron ? '

" I made no reply.

" ' My young friend, no doubt you will know a woman's heart better some day. I was dazzled; but that does not mean love. It might perhaps have grown into love; but it never did.' "

That is another scrap from Miss Clairmont's confessions to Mr. Graham. It immediately precedes the confession, previously quoted, that she loved Shelley—" with all my heart and soul." There follows Miss Clairmont's protest that Byron " told lies about Shelley "; and then come expressions of scepticism from Mr. Graham; and then we read :—

286

" ' You impertinent boy ! If you do not believe what I tell you, why traverse Europe to see me ? '

" ' There are things, madam,' I said, ' which it is the duty of every man to believe when told him by a lady, and I have conquered my scepticism. I remember you told me Shelley was a devoted student of Plato.'

" Two smart boxes on the ear were the only reply I received to this. A sorry return, indeed, for obedience and faith."

If that was Jane Clairmont's attitude, then Byron's attitude is intelligible; and one can readily believe that her language about Byron was not such as to make Shelley eager to press her suit on her behalf and quarrel with Byron for rejecting it. Nor is there any reason whatever to believe that Shelley regarded, or wished to regard, himself as Byron's successful rival. One feels throughout, in spite of the Lines to Constantia, in spite of the legacy, in spite of Mary's bitter outbreaks, in spite of everything, that there never was any question of a grand passion on Shelley's side—least of all at this particular epoch; and one suspects, also, that Jane, in retrospect, exaggerated the vehemence of her own feelings.

Still, Shelley did his best for Jane; and his best was far better than it would have been if he had approached Byron in the spirit of the indignant champion of innocence betrayed.

Byron lent him and his party his country villa at Este, and allowed Allegra to be received there on a visit; Mary, on her part, approving, and showing as little inclination as Shelley himself to force a mistress on a reluctant lover. No doubt she was disappointed; but the situation was one of those tangles in which either nobody is to blame for anything, or else everybody is to blame for everything. Attempts to unravel the tangle could only have tangled it the more; and there really was nothing for it except to behave as if nothing in particular had happened.

Nothing, at any rate, had happened perturbing to Mary's peace of mind. Her only trouble at this time was the death of her baby Clara[1] from a sudden fever : a cruel blow, but not, as she had another child, a grief to break her spirit. Nor is there anything in the outward events of the period under review which need detain us. The route of the wanderers was from Milan to Pisa, from Pisa to Leghorn, from Leghorn to Bagni di Lucca; thence to Florence, to Padua, and, as we have seen, to Venice and Este; thence, after some delay, to Rome. They read and wrote, of course, as always. Shelley, with a book or a pen in his hand, could always, even in the shadow of calamity, escape from the business to the dream. Mary tried to do so too— and sometimes did so—and, more often, thought that she did so; but in one of Mary's letters we come across a pathetic note, which is like a flash

[1] Born at Marlow.

of lightning revealing the secret thoughts in her mind. Her correspondent is Mrs. Gisborne :—[1]

" If all of you, or any of you would come and cheer my solitude, it would be exceedingly kind. . . . We know no one; we speak to one or two people at the Casino, and that is all."

That is our first hint of the social boycott, which meant far more to Mary than to Shelley, —as it always means more to a woman than to a man. It meant more to her than it would have meant to some women; for she was not a heroine designed by nature for the rôle which she sustained. Credible witnesses depose that she was the most conventional woman who ever let herself be lured, for once in her life, into unconventional courses. She desired gaiety—or, at least, society; balls, and grand receptions, if it might be—but at least, tea-parties, afternoon callers, a social position. Trelawny says that she " even affected the pious dodge," and attended church, in the hope of earning these privileges. She was to have some success in the end, but not much; and, in the meantime, she had none. That was the first cloud on the Italian sky.

Shelley was not sensible of it. It was neither at the receptions of Italian countesses, nor at

---

[1] A friend of Godwin's, formerly Mrs. Reveley. Godwin, when a widower, had proposed marriage to her; but she had preferred Mr. Gisborne, with whom she lived principally on the Continent.

the tea-tables of English trippers, that he sought his escape from life. The things which Mary would have liked to fly to were pretty much the things which he had fled from. Perhaps he never realized that these were the things which Mary really missed and wanted—certainly he realized nothing of the kind as yet. His letters breathe no doubt of Mary's adequacy to his happiness. But they do record something of a fight for happiness—an unexplained depression of spirits which the Italian skies alleviate, but do not remove :—

" We have now warm, sunny days, and soft winds, and a sky of deep azure, the most serene I ever saw. . . . My spirits and health sympathise in the change. Indeed, before I left London, my spirits were as feeble as my health, and I had demands on them which I found it difficult to supply."

" No sooner had we arrived at Italy than the loveliness of the earth and the serenity of the sky made the greatest difference in my sensations. I depend on these things for my life; for in the smoke of cities, and the tumult of humankind, and the chilling fogs and rain of our own country, I can hardly be said to live. . . . My health is improved already—and my spirits somewhat."

" I will endeavour to tell you something of these celebrated places in my next letter; but

I cannot promise much, for though my health is much improved, my spirits are unequal and seem to desert me when I attempt to write."

" My health is, I think, better, and, I imagine, continues to improve, but I still have busy thoughts and dispiriting cares, which I would shake off—and it is now summer."

And so forth; the same note being struck in the very last letter written, in October, 1818, before the start for Rome and Naples : " I will write again, from Rome and Florence—in better spirits, and to more agreeable purpose, I hope."

There are, of course, many other things in the letters : accounts of literary projects, descriptions of scenery and sights, criticisms of Italian manners, complaints of English tourists, denunciations of Wordsworth as " a beastly and pitiful wretch,"—an apostate, that is to say, false to the faith of the French Revolution. There are passages eloquently commemorative of moments when the sunshine seems about to triumph,—notably the well-known passage in which Shelley, at Bagni di Lucca, pictures himself bathing " in a pool or fountain, formed in the middle of the forests by a torrent " :—

" My custom is to undress and sit on the rocks, reading Herodotus, until the perspiration has subsided, and then to leap from the edge of the rock into this fountain—a practice in the hot weather excessively refreshing. This torrent is composed, as it were, of a succession of pools and waterfalls, up which I sometimes amuse myself by climbing when I bathe, and receiving the spray all over my body, whilst I clamber up the moist crags with difficulty."

The sunshine, it would seem, triumphed for the moment then,—but only for the moment. It nearly triumphed, yet again, when Shelley lay on his back in a gondola in the lagoons of Venice —but the triumph was never complete or lasting. *Coelum non animum mutant qui trans mare currunt*,—one is always brought to think of that hackneyed phrase as one reads on; and *Quisque suos patimur Manes* comes to the mind together with it. The picture from which one cannot escape is that of Shelley dreeing a weird— haunted by the vague shape of his own shadow— realizing himself, indeed, but realizing also the pain of the gestation. One is irresistibly reminded of the rendering of the mood by another poet, widely different from Shelley in most ways, but a traveller who saw the same scenes :—

> *A Pise, au pied de l'Apennin ;*
> *A Cologne, en face du Rhin ;*
> *A Nice, au penchant des vallées ;*
> *A Florence, au fond des palais ;*
> *A Brigues, dans les vieux chalets ;*
> *Au sein des Alpes désolées ;*

THE SOCIAL BOYCOTT

A Gênes, sous les citronniers ;
A Vevay, sous les verts pommiers ;
Au Hâvre devant l'Atlantique ;
A Venise, à l'affreux Lido,
Où vient sur l'herbe d'un tombeau
Mourir la pâle Adriatique ;

Partout où j'ai voulu dormir,
Partout où j'ai voulu mourir,
Partout où j'ai touché la terre,
Sur ma route est venu s'asseoir
Un malheureux vêtu de noir,
Qui me ressemblait comme un frère :

" Le ciel m'a confié ton cœur.
Quand tu seras dans la douleur,
Viens à moi sans inquiétude ;
Je te suivrai sur le chemin,
Mais je ne puis toucher ta main.
Ami, je suis la Solitude."

Thus Alfred de Musset, who had none of Shelley's fine enthusiasms, and in whose life gaslight and limelight played the part which sunlight played in Shelley's; but who is made kin with him by the discovery that he who would travel far must travel alone—and that he who travels alone cannot travel gleefully.

And so to Rome and Naples.

293

CHAPTER XXVI

SHELLEY, with Mary and Jane, spent a week
at Rome, and three months at Naples, and then
returned to Rome, where he remained until the
middle of June, 1819, when his boy William
died after a brief illness.

The story of the sojourn at Naples holds a
puzzle—one puzzle at least, and perhaps more—
for the biographer. The gloom which we have
already seen besieging Shelley deepened there;
and it was there, so far as one knows, that Mary
began to notice it :—

" Though he observed the appearance of cheerfulness, and often greatly enjoyed our wanderings
in the environs of Naples, and our excursions
on its sunny sea, yet many hours were passed
when his thoughts, shadowed by illness, were
gloomy; and then he escaped to solitude, and
in verses which he hid from fear of wounding me,
poured forth morbid, but too natural, bursts of
discontent and sadness. One looks back with
unspeakable regret and gnawing remorse to such
periods; fancying that had we been more alive
to the nature of his feelings, and more attentive

to soothe them, such would not have existed.
And yet, enjoying as he appeared to do, every
sight or influence of earth or sky, it was difficult
to imagine that any melancholy he showed was
aught but the effect of the constant pain to
which he was a martyr."

An Italian physician, in fact, treated him, at
this time, with applications of caustic, for a
disease of the liver from which he was not
suffering. There are complaints of the effect of
the counter-irritant in his letters; and there is
no doubt that he was, and for some time had been,
suffering from some inflammation,[1] which, at
intervals, caused him acute pain. Yet, even so,
no one will believe that physical pain, and
nothing else, inspired the Stanzas written in
Dejection :—

> *I see the Deep's untrampled floor*
> *With green and purple sea-weeds strown ;*
> *I see the waves upon the shore*
> *Like light dissolved in star-showers, thrown.*
> *I sit upon the sands alone.*
> *The lightning of the noontide ocean*
> *Is flashing round me, and a tone*
> *Arises from its measured motion.*
> *How sweet! Did any heart now share in my*
> *emotion!*

[1] Shelley's symptoms are not described with sufficient
precision to permit of a confident diagnosis of the case.
His own view—that he was suffering from nephritis—is
improbable. His pains may, very possibly, only have been
rheumatic in origin.

THE ROMANTIC LIFE OF SHELLEY

Alas! I have nor hope nor health,
Nor peace within, nor calm around,
Nor that content surpassing wealth
The sage in meditation found,
And walked with inward glory crowned,—
Nor fame, nor power, nor love, nor leisure.
Others I see whom these surround—
Smiling they live and call life pleasure ;
To me that cup has been dealt in another measure.

Decidedly there is more there than distress caused by a pain in the side; and Mary herself begins a second paragraph with a second explanation :—

" We lived in utter solitude. And such is not often the nurse of cheerfulness; for then, at least with those who have been exposed to adversity, the mind broods over its sorrows too intently; while the society of the enlightened, the witty, and the wise, enables us to forget ourselves by making us the sharers of the thoughts of others, which is a portion of the philosophy of happiness. . . . Had not a wall of prejudice been raised, at this time, between him and his countrymen, how many would have sought the acquaintance of one whom to know was to love and to revere ! How many of the more enlightened of his contemporaries have since regretted that they did not seek him ! how very few knew his worth while he lived ! and of those few several were withheld by timidity or envy from declaring their sense of it."

With which compare a letter of Shelley's, written from Rome, but equally applicable—probably even more applicable—to his circumstances at Naples :—

" We see no English society here ; it is not probable that we would if we desired it, and I am certain that we should find it unsupportable. The manners of the rich English are wholly unsupportable, and they assume pretensions which they would not venture upon in their own country."

And, of course, there were reasons why admission to English society—whether they would have found it insupportable or not—was difficult for them ; and those reasons were not exactly—at all events not solely—the reasons which Mary gives. She herself must have been the chief obstacle ; for social prejudices are stronger than religious prejudices ; and if Shelley had offended the latter, she had offended the former. He, from the point of view of the travelling English of those days, was only the *brebis égaré*—and society has a tenderness for such ; whereas Mary had never belonged to the exclusive flock. She was, from the point of view of that same society, a tradesman's daughter, who had been her husband's mistress before he married her : a woman, therefore, who could not be called upon.

But a woman very anxious to be called upon : one for whom the society from which she was excluded had all the fascination of the unattainable. She was the Peri at the gate of Paradise, —not merely disconsolate, but peevish; and one feels that Shelley's depression must have been, in a large measure, a reflection of hers. A man is never sadder than when the sight of a woman's discontent awakens him from dreams of a life which shall be like a fairy tale.

Medwin, however, adds another explanation of the gloom :—

" The night before his departure from London, in 1814, he received a visit from a married lady, young, handsome, and of noble connections, and whose disappearance from the world of fashion in which she moved, may furnish, to those curious in such iniquities, a clue to her identity."

The visitor had read *Queen Mab*, had fallen in love with the author of *Queen Mab*, and had come to declare her passion on the very eve of his elopement. She had renounced her husband, her name, her family, her friends; and she was " resolved after mature deliberation " to lay her fortune at Shelley's feet, and follow him through the world. He was moved—but of course it could not be. She acquiesced, but begged him to pity a heart torn by his indifference. She spoke of " blighted hopes, a life of loneliness, withered affections; " he replied that her image would never cease to be associated in his mind with " all that is noble, pure, generous, and lovely." They parted; and Medwin continues :—

" This meeting, instead of extinguishing, only seemed to fan the flame in the bosom of the *Incognita*. This infatuated lady followed him to the Continent. He had given her a clue to his place of destination, Geneva. She traced him to Sécheron—used to watch him with her glass in his water parties on the lake. On his return to England, he thought she had long forgotten him; but her constancy was untired. During his journey to Rome and Naples, she once lodged with him at the same hotel, *en route,* and finally arrived at the latter city the same day as himself.

" He must have been more or less than man to have been unmoved by the devotedness of this unfortunate and infatuated lady. At Naples, he told me that they met, and when he learnt from her all those particulars of her wanderings, of which he had been previously ignorant; and at Naples—she died."

The story has sometimes been waved on one side as a figment of Shelley's luxuriant imagi-nation; and that it is true in the exact form in which Medwin reports it is, indeed, improbable. But Mr. Rossetti says that he got a partial con-firmation of it from Miss Clairmont, who declared that she had seen the lady in question, and even knew her name; and one inclines to think that

Medwin's elaborate fiction must have been, in some undiscoverable way, based upon a fact. Mary's peevishness at the social boycott would have made Shelley more, rather than less, sensible to a fresh sentimental attraction. The passion of a stranger who was not peevish—who professed eagerness to face the social boycott, with her eyes open, for his sake—may well have filled his mind, for a little while, with the thought that things might have been, and ought to have been, other than they were. And if the dream ended suddenly—and tragically—then the Stanzas written in Dejection would be more plausibly explained than by Mary's suggestion that they were due to an application of caustic for an imaginary disorder.

Medwin believed the tragedy to have inspired these other lines :—

> *Hasten to the bridal bed!*
> *Underneath the grave 'tis spread!*
> *In darkness may our love be hid,*
> *Oblivion be our coverlid!*
> *We may rest, and none forbid,*
>
> *Kiss me! Oh! my lips are cold!*
> *Round my neck thine arms enfold.*
> *They are soft—yet chill and dead,*
> *And thy tears upon my heart*
> *Burn like points of frozen lead.*

But that is only Medwin's conjecture—whether

true or false one cannot say. One does not even know whether the mystery is related to another mystery which belongs to the same period, and ultimately made a ringing scandal through the talk of Mary's Swiss maid and Shelley's Italian valet, Paolo.

Paolo was pressed by the Shelleys to marry Elise—to " make her an honest woman "; and he was also dismissed from the Shelleys' service for dishonesty. He submitted to marriage with a tranquil mind; but he resented his dismissal, and vowed to be avenged, or, if not to be avenged, then to extort blackmail. A letter from Shelley to the Gisbornes, who had gone to London, gives us our first glimpse of Paolo at work, and our first hint of the circumstances which furnished him with a handle :—

" My poor little Neapolitan, I hear, has a severe attack of dentition. I suppose she will die and leave another memory to those which already torture me. . . . Domestic peace I might have—I may have—if I see you I shall have—but have not, for Mary suffers dreadfully about the state of Godwin's circumstances. I am very nervous, but better in general health. We have had a most infernal business with Paolo, whom, however, we have succeeded in crushing. . . .

" I have later news of my Neapolitan. I have taken every possible precaution for her, and hope that they will succeed. She is to come to us as soon as she recovers. . . .

" My Neapolitan charge is dead. It seems as if the destruction that is consuming me were as an atmosphere which wrapt and *infected* everything connected with me. That rascal Paolo has been taking advantage of my situation at Naples in December, 1818, to attempt to extort money by threatening to charge me with the most horrible crimes. He is connected with some English here (at Leghorn), who hate me with a fervour that almost does credit to their phlegmatic brains, and listen to and vent the most prodigious falsehoods."

It is very vague. All that appears is that Shelley has a particular interest in an infant, at the teething stage, at Naples—and that Mary knows all about it, and is prepared to receive the infant—and that something happened at Naples on which an uncharitable construction could be placed. Paolo seems to have been temporarily frightened into quiescence by a lawyer's letter; but he talked—or he induced Elise to talk. A year later, when visiting Byron at Ravenna, Shelley heard what he, or Elise on his behalf, had said. The Hoppners, who had been very kind to them at Venice, had announced their intention of having nothing more to do with them on account of " a story so monstrous and incredible that they must have been prone to believe any evil to have believed such assertions upon such evidence " :—

" Elise says that Claire was my mistress; that is all very well, and so far there is nothing new; all the world has heard so much, and people may believe or believe not as they think good. She then proceeds to say that Claire was with child by me; that I gave her the most violent medicine to produce abortion; that, this not succeeding, she was brought to bed, and that I immediately tore the child from her and sent it to the Foundling Hospital. . . . In addition, she says that both I and Claire treated you in the most shameful manner, that I neglected and beat you, and that Claire never let a day pass without offering you insults of the most violent kind, in which she was abetted by me."

That is the form in which Shelley reported the scandal to Mary,—the probability is strong that his heated imagination had heightened its colour. Mary, at Shelley's instance, wrote to Mrs. Hoppner, repudiating the calumnies with an equal indignation. Elise, charged with having uttered them, denied that she had done so, or that there was any basis for them. But, in Mary's letter to Shelley, covering the letter to Mrs. Hoppner, there are these significant sentences : " Do not think me imprudent in mentioning Claire's illness at Naples. It is well to meet facts." And the letter, as printed in the biographies, contains no reference whatever to any illness—as though Mary had changed her mind, and thought it better not to mention it after all.

What, then, are the facts which Mary first thought it " well to meet," but afterwards—if there has been no tampering with the text of her letter—decided to ignore ? Our only hint is contained in those *Chats with Jane Clairmont*, by Mr. Graham, from which so many quotations have already been taken. The conversation had turned on Byron's refusal to surrender Allegra :—

" ' Of course,' she went on, ' there was a reason that Byron used as an excuse for his vile conduct in thus robbing me of my child. That vile note at the foot of my letter to him, which he sent on to Hoppner, and which has since been unearthed, explains it. But it was a lie.'

"As I made no reply, she continued, ' I presume that you think there can be no smoke without fire ? Well, I will tell you the whole truth now, and you may judge for yourself.'

" Nothing more, however, shall be written by me on this subject, so highly distasteful to me, until 1909, and not even then, had not Miss Clairmont requested me to give what I know to the world after the lapse of time before mentioned."

There is a further note on the subject in Mr. Graham's Preface :—

JANE CLAIRMONT'S LOVE FOR SHELLEY

" Shelley's indignation, if you will kindly refer to his letter, was not caused by the suggestion that he might be on terms of greater intimacy with Miss Clairmont than is desirable in a well-regulated household, but by the suggestion that she had had a child by him which had been sent to the Florence Foundling, and this was quite a mistake, so far in any case as Shelley was concerned. The rights of the story are known to myself, and I do not intend to say anything further thereon until 1901, when, owing to the publication of the *Hobhouse Memoirs*, I shall be at liberty to deal with Clairmont matters in full, eight years earlier than my promise to the lady would otherwise have permitted me."

The *Hobhouse Memoirs* have appeared, and have revealed nothing. We are now in 1911; and the fresh light promised has not yet been thrown. The mystery remains mysterious. Whether Miss Clairmont had an adventure at Naples in which Shelley played no part except that of guarding her secret; whether the Neapolitan infant—supposed by Professor Dowden to have been the ward bequeathed to Shelley by his *Inconnue*—was in any way related to that adventure; whether Shelley knew more of that adventure than was known to Mary :—these things are riddles, and might still hold an element of doubt, even if we had Mr. Graham's report of Miss Clairmont's statement.

But two things are clear. Mary had no knowledge of any circumstance which could shake her faith in Shelley's loyalty to herself. Shelley still found it impossible to escape from the thorns of life to the peace of dreamland. Life pursued him, clutching at him, and clinging to him, and harassing him. He was not like other people; but he had to live in the same world as other people; and the same things happened to him as to other people,—and hurt him more than they hurt other people, because of his failure to realize the life about him until it disturbed him and forced itself on his attention.

CHAPTER XXVII

AT PISA—EMILIA VIVIANI

From Rome Shelley came north to Leghorn, arriving in June, and remaining until November, when he went to Florence, where he stayed until he moved to Pisa, in February, 1820. He took a villa in the outskirts of Leghorn, and, in a study which he contrived on the roof, wrote *The Cenci* and began *Prometheus*. His melancholy did not leave him, however, and his life continued to be solitary. Practically his only friends were the Gisbornes, whose friendship was not quite disinterested. Mrs. Gisborne's son, Henry Reveley, proposed to build a steamer to ply between Leghorn and Marseilles; and Shelley was asked to finance the adventure. Marine engineering appealed to him as a kind of poetry—a magical stretching of hands across the seas to promote the comity of nations; and he entered into the scheme with enthusiasm, though it came to nothing.

Another enterprise which brought him into contact with the hard facts of real life was his attempt to procure the production of *The Cenci* at Covent Garden, with Miss O'Neill in the principal part, and his letters on the subject illustrate his naive inability to realize actual

U 2

307

conditions. He considers the question whether incest " would be admitted on the stage," and concludes that " it will form no objection," because the story of *The Cenci* is true, and has been treated with " peculiar delicacy." Peacock was asked to submit those considerations to the Covent Garden Management; but of course he submitted them in vain. Mr. Harris of Covent Garden declared the subject of the piece so objectionable that he could not even let Miss O'Neill read it; whereupon Shelley protested that the theatre had " rejected it with expressions of the greatest insolence," that he regarded it as " singularly fitted for the stage," and that as for Mr. Harris's motives in declining it, he can imagine none unless it be that he " has guessed at the author."

At the same time an article in the *Quarterly* attacked his character as well as his poetry. He read it in a public reading-room at Florence, and was seen to burst into scoffing laughter over the bathos of the reviewer's peroration; but the laughter, as his letters show, was more bitter than merry. It led him into a correspondence, from which some quotations have been given, with Southey, whom he believed to be the author of the review, though it is now known to have been the work of his old schoolfellow and College contemporary, John Taylor Coleridge—a writer who afterwards employed his talents to better advantage by writing the Life of Keble.

His ill health, too, continued, and there was

intermittent discord between Mary and Jane, and the usual trouble with Godwin. The way of that needy philosopher was to ask for a large sum of money, and then, if he only received a part of the sum he asked for, to regard the remainder as the balance of an overdue account, and to dun for payment of it in the offensive style of a debt collector. Without even thanking Shelley for what he had already given, he clamoured for more, treating his benefactor as he might have treated a man who had lost to him at cards and would not pay. Nor was he content to address his reproaches to Shelley himself. He also complained to Mary of Shelley's selfishness; and Mary became more and more melancholy, and more and more peevish. He called Shelley " a disgraceful and flagrant person ;" and Shelley, writing to Leigh Hunt, commented bitterly :—

" I suspect my character, if measured with his, would sustain no diminution among those who know us both. I have bought bitter knowledge with £4,700. I wish it were all yours now."

Thus business unceasingly broke in upon the dream of self-realization in the sunshine; and cries, not merely of anger, but of anguish, found utterance in Shelley's letters,—especially those written to Peacock, with whom he discussed the prospects of his return to England :—

" I believe, my dear Peacock, that you wish us to come back to England. How is it possible ? Health, competence, tranquillity—all these Italy permits, and England takes away. I am regarded by all who know or hear of me, except, I think, on the whole, five individuals, as a rare prodigy of crime and pollution, whose look even might infect. This is a large computation, and I don't think I could mention more than three. Such is the spirit of the English abroad as well as at home.

" Few compensate, indeed, for all the rest, and if I were *alone*, I should laugh."

But how shall a man laugh at the social boycott, when a peevish woman, to whom it means much more than to him, is always beside him whining about it ? Shelley could not; and the regret for England and its social amenities soon reappears :—

" I most devoutly wish I were living near London. . . . Social enjoyment, in some form or other, is the alpha and omega of existence. All that I see in Italy—and from my tower windows I now see the magnificent peaks of the Apennines half enclosing the plain—is nothing; it dwindles into smoke in the mind, when I think of some familiar forms of scenery, little perhaps in themselves, over which old remembrances have thrown a delightful colour. How we prize what we despised when present! So the ghosts of our dead associations rise and haunt us, in revenge for our having let them starve, and abandoned them to perish."

There is no cheerfulness in that letter, written eighteen months after the arrival in Italy. Shelley, confronted perpetually by Mary's "depression of spirits," could see no hope of cheerfulness unless his few faithful English friends would come out to him. Leigh Hunt, Hogg, Peacock, and Horace Smith were all invited in vain; but life, nevertheless, brightened somewhat at Pisa. The birth of Percy Florence Shelley—the only one of Mary's three children who grew up—relieved her dejection in some, albeit only a slight, degree. A wise friend, Lady Mountcashell, discerning the lack of harmony in the household, persuaded Miss Clairmont to accept a post as governess in the family of a Florentine professor. Shelley's cousin, Tom Medwin, who had been in the army and in India, and was now home on a loose end, turned up.

Mary, it is true, did not like Medwin. At the time she called him a " bore "; and she accused him, in later years, of borrowing " crowns which we could ill spare "; but Mary's criticisms of her friends were rarely kind. Of the only lady who was polite to her, in spite of the social boycott, at Rome, she wrote that she was " very old, very miserly, and very mean "; and her judgments are, as a rule, to be discounted. The man who amiably borrows an occasional crown is, at any rate, a preferable companion to the man who surlily borrows £4,700; and Medwin, borrower or not, was a hero-worshipper. He had discovered his cousin's genius from a " remaindered " copy of *Laon and Cythna* which he had seen in India; and he now gave his cousin the companionship of a man of taste and culture, if not of great ability. That must have been helpful to Mary as well as Shelley; and Medwin's arrival coincides with the widening of the social circle.

It was not much of a circle. Matthew Arnold's famous exclamation : " What a set ! " is as applicable to it as to the set of which Godwin was the central luminary. Lady Mountcashell, in whose father's house Mary's mother had once been a governess, was separated from her husband, and was living conjugally with a Mr. Tighe, under the assumed name of Mason. Count Taaffe was an Irish poetaster whose claims to the title which he used are not very clear. Signor Sgricci was only an *improvisatore*. Signor Pacchiani, a friar who ought to have been unfrocked, lived in an equivocal fashion on his wits, and is pilloried by Mary, with her usual amiability, as having " disgusted Shelley by telling a dirty story." In fact, the only quite reputable member of the society seems to have been Prince Mavrocordato, who was presently to give his proofs in the Greek Revolution, and now taught Mary the Greek language, and inspired Shelly to write *Hellas*. And then there was Emilia Viviani, who will be for ever famous because she inspired *Epipsychidion*.

Emilia was the daughter by his first wife of

a Count Viviani who had married, *en secondes noces*, a lady of about his daughter's age. The wife, being jealous of the daughter's beauty, had sent her to a convent—half pension, half boarding-school. There she was to be detained—never allowed to walk farther than the convent garden, which was about the size of a modern lawn tennis court—until a suitor should be found willing to marry her without a dowry. But such suitors are rare in Italy, so that the quest was likely to be long, and Emilia herself to be an old maid before it ended.

Pacchiani told the Shelleys about her :—

" Poverina," he said with a deep sigh, " she pines like a bird in a cage—ardently longs to escape from her prison-house—pines with *ennui*, and wanders about the corridors like an unquiet spirit; she sees her young days glide on without an aim or purpose. She was made for love. Yesterday she was watering some flowers in her cell—she has nothing else to love but her flowers— ' Yes,' said she, addressing them, ' you are born to vegetate, but we thinking beings were made for action—not to be penned up in a corner or set at a window to blow and die.' "

That was enough for Shelley. Life had been very tedious of late, and here was real romance, —a real damsel in a real distress. Something must be done for her—and done at once. Pacchiani must introduce him. Medwin must also

313

be introduced. Mary must call on Emilia. Jane Clairmont must call. As many people as possible must call. And so they did, and found that Emilia was, indeed, as beautiful as she was unfortunate :—

" Her profuse black hair, tied in the most simple knot, after the manner of a Greek Muse in the Florence gallery, displayed to its full height her brow, fair as that of the marble of which I speak. She was also of about the same height as the antique. Her features possessed a rare faultlessness, and almost German (? Grecian) contour, the nose and forehead making a straight line,—a style of face so rare that I remember Bartolini's telling Byron that he had scarcely seen an instance of such in the numerous casts of busts which his studio contained. Her eyes had the sleepy voluptuousness, if not the colour, of Beatrice Cenci's. . . . Her cheek was pale, too, as marble, owing to her confinement and want of air, or perhaps to ' thought.' "

So Medwin, flowing on in his characteristic style : and Professor Dowden gravely sums up the matter thus :—

" Of a sudden three persons had fallen in love with Emilia—Mary, Claire, and Shelley. In Mary's regard there was, indeed, a moderating good sense which to Emilia at times appeared to have a touch of coldness in it. Yet Mary's

visits to the convent were frequent, and grew more
frequent as the weeks went by. "

Which is a ve.y charitable way of putting it,
but hardly a way which deals out even-handed
justice among the parties. Shelley and Mary
and Jane no doubt began the acquaintance with
a simultaneous outburst of sympathy for the
victim of Italian customs and parental tyranny;
but the few documents at our disposal show their
sentiments quickly diverging in three different
directions : Jane amused; Mary critical and
suspicious; Shelley under a spell which he finds
temporarily irresistibie.

Not that there was any " affair " in the common
sense of the word. The " convent's narrow
room " was much too narrow for that; and only
once, so far as is known, were Shelley and Emilia
alone together outside the convent. Nor can
one even say that Shelley found in Emilia merits
which he had failed to find in Mary. He fully
recognized that fact himself after the spell was
broken—fully recognized that Emilia was, in
vulgar parlance, " a fraud." But the spell, in
order to be broken, had first to exist. It never
existed for any one but him; but, while it did
exist, Emilia seemed to satisfy an ideal which
Mary failed to satisfy, and Shelley dreamed a
dream in which Mary only figured in a subsidiary
part. In *Epipsychidion*, where much is obscure,
it is at least clear that Mary figures as the Moon
—beautiful, but of an icy coldness; whereas :—

315

Soft as an Incarnation of the Sun,
When light is changed to love, this glorious One
Floated into the cavern where I lay,
And called my spirit, and the dreaming clay
Was lifted by the thing that dreamed below
As smoke by fire, and in her beauty's glow
I stood, and felt the dawn of my long night
Was penetrating me with living light :
I knew it was the vision veiled from me
So many years—that it was Emily.

And then the appeal which every lover of poetry knows by heart :—

Emily,
A ship is floating in the harbour now,
A wind is hovering o'er the mountains' brow ;
There is a path on the sea's azure floor,
No keel has ever ploughed that path before ;
The halcyons brood around the foamless isles ;
The treacherous Ocean has forsworn its wiles ;
The merry mariners are bold and free :
Say, my heart's sister, wilt thou sail with me ?

As a matter of sober prose, of course, there was no ship waiting in the harbour to take these particular passengers to any land where it would be always summer, or always afternoon,—where the dream would be everything and the business nothing. It does not appear that Emilia hoped for, or that Mary feared, any actual proposal to elope. But that Mary was " in love " with

Emilia, and was pleased, as Professor Dowden seems to think, that Emilia rather than herself moved Shelley to the worship of Abstract Beauty, and sublime thoughts of the Communion of Souls, is what one finds it very difficult to believe. Mary was very feminine, and even a little feline; and the situation was one to call out her feminine attributes. Four extracts from four letters may help us to read her mind a little more accurately than Professor Dowden read it :—

" Yesterday night," Emilia writes to Mary, " Claire related to me part of his history. His many misfortunes, his unjust persecutions, and his firm innate virtue in the midst of these terrible and unmerited sorrows, filled my heart with admiration and affection, and made me think, and perhaps not untruly, that he is not a human creature; he has only a human exterior, but the interior is all divine. The Being of all things has doubtless sent him to earth to accredit virtue and to give an exact image of himself."

" My conception of Emilia's talents," Shelley writes to Jane, " augments every day. Her moral nature is fine, but not above circumstances; yet I think her tender and true, which is always something. How many are only one of these things at a time ! "

" Mary does not write to me," Emilia complains to Shelley. " Is it possible that she loves me

less than the others do ? I should be very much
pained by that. I wish to flatter myself that it
is her only son and her occupations which cause
this. Is not this the case ? "

" You seem to me a little cold sometimes,"
Emilia protested to Mary, " and that causes an
uncomfortable feeling; but I know that your
husband said well when he said that your apparent
coldness is only *the ash which covers an affectionate
heart.*"

Those passages are the keys which unlock the
situation. Let any woman judge for herself
whether Mary is likely to have been pleased to
hear another woman, more beautiful than herself,
speak of her husband as the image of the divine
—whether she is likely to have felt a warmer
affection for Emilia than she displayed—whether
the frequency of her visits to Emilia in her convent
is likely to have been due to any other motive
than a desire to keep a close watch upon what
must have struck her as a flirtation fraught with
possibilities perilous to her peace.

She watched the danger till it passed; and it
passed quickly. The Emilia who had inspired
Epipsychidion was not the real Emilia but an
Emilia created by Shelley's imagination. The
real Emilia introduced business into the dream
by borrowing money. The real Emilia accepted
the husband provided for her, and, as Mary, with
her genius for saying unpleasant things, put it,

" led him a devil of a life." Shelley himself awoke from this dream, and admitted that his disillusion was complete :—

" The *Epipsychidion*," he wrote to Gisborne, " I cannot look at; the person whom it celebrates was a cloud instead of a Juno; and poor Ixion starts from the centaur that was the offspring of his own embrace. If you are curious, however, to hear what I am and have been, it will tell you something thereof. It is an idealised history of my life and feelings. I think one is always in love with something or other; the error—and I confess it is not easy for spirits cased in flesh and blood to avoid it—consists in seeking in a mortal image the likeness of what is, perhaps, eternal."

That is all; and perhaps the letter tells us more even of Shelley's life and feelings than the poem, being vastly easier to understand. He was " always in love with something or other." Perhaps he would have said that he could not have loved Mary so much, had he not loved Emilia more. The woman, it is to be feared, has not yet been born who would have been an ideal companion for him. The letter, more explicitly than *Epipsychidion*, sets forth that Mary was not such a one. He knew it, and she knew it also, and in the end she blamed herself. One is brought to that note at last, whether it properly arises out of the story of Emilia Viviani or not.

CHAPTER XXVIII

MARY'S CONFESSION OF FAILURE

MARY's confession of failure is contained in
the Poem which she wrote on Shelley's death :—

Oh, gentle Spirit, thou hast often sung
How fallen on evil days thy heart was wrung ;
Now fierce remorse and unreplying death
Waken a chord within my heart, whose breath,
Thrilling and keen, in accents audible,
A tale of unrequited love doth tell.
It was not anger,—while thy earthly dress
Encompassed still thy soul's rare loveliness,
All anger was atoned by many a kind
Caress or tear, that spoke the softened mind.—
It speaks of cold neglect, averted eyes,
That blindly crushed thy soul's fond sacrifice :—
My heart was all thine own,—but yet a shell
Closed in its core, which seemed impenetrable,
Till sharp-toothed misery tore the husk in twain,
Which gaping lies, nor may unite again.
Forgive me !

That is as formal as one can expect a confession in verse to be. It is a new rendering of the
old lament : *Mea culpa ! Mea culpa ! Peccavi.*
Benedicite ! Mary had sulked and been peevish;
320

she owned it and repented. If only she had foreseen ! That is the plain prose of the cry over the body which the pitiless sea washed up. There is an entry in Mary's Journal, dated on Shelley's last birthday, which should be read in connection with it :—

" Seven years are now gone; what changes ! what a life ! We now appear tranquil, yet who knows what wind—but I will not prognosticate evil; we have had enough of it. When Shelley came to Italy I said, all is well if it were permanent; it was more passing than an Italian twilight. I now say the same. May it be a polar day, yet that, too, has an end."

And, for further light, we may turn to a letter of Shelley's—one of the last letters which he wrote :—

" Italy is more and more delightful to me. . . . I only feel the want of those who can feel and understand me. Whether from proximity and the continuity of domestic intercourse, Mary cannot. . . . It is the curse of Tantalus that a person possessing such excellent powers and so pure a mind as hers should not excite the sympathy indispensable to their application to domestic life."

The three passages fit together like the pieces of a Chinese puzzle. One could easily find other passages which would complicate the puzzle in

x   321

appearance, without really altering it. The resulting picture, in any case, is of a marriage which husband and wife independently admit to have brought them less happiness than they had hoped for. The admission is clear; and it only remains to consider how much or how little we will make of it.

Something we must make; and no doubt Trelawny, though personally disposed to make too much of it, gives us our clue. He shows us a Shelley who dwelt in the clouds, and a Mary who was of the earth, earthy; a Mary who was at heart a Martha, but an incompetent Martha, —a Martha whose house-keeping was of a Bohemian amateurishness; a Mary whose love of poetry and philosophy was as nothing beside her passion for being received in good society; a Mary who even "affected the pious dodge" and attended the ministrations of the English chaplain—a chaplain who seized the opportunity to preach against her husband—in the hope of inducing society to open its arms to her.

If we start with that, and then discount it liberally—remembering that Trelawny was an impetuous partisan who did not weigh his words —we shall probably have a fair presentation of the case from Shelley's point of view. The "pious dodge," at any rate, is no figment of Trelawny's imagination. Mary, taxed with it, admitted it, albeit with a plea of extenuating circumstances : she had only tried it once a month, not once a week as had been alleged, and even so only " for good neighbourhood's sake," and because the chaplain had politely expressed the hope that he would see her at his services. A small offence truly : very small indeed when we set it side by side with the offence which Shelley committed when, on his return from bathing, he crossed his wife's dining-room, on his way to his bed-room, without even a bathing-dress to cover him, regardless that his wife was giving a dinner-party at the time, and, instead of vanishing, when he discovered the presence of guests, stood still to offer explanations and excuses.

The two stories should certainly be read to-gether, for extremes meet in them. They not merely illustrate, but typify, a clashing conflict of ideals; and the majority of unbiassed readers will probably agree that Shelley's rebellion against the conventions was at least as exaggerated as Mary's subservience to them. Even those who lay most stress upon the title of genius to its eccentricities will realize that there were obstacles to the maintenance of perfect harmony between a husband so careless of decorum and a wife who served God and Mammon simultaneously in her Sunday silks. That the lute should be quite without rifts in such a case is almost unimaginable.

As matter of fact, it certainly had more rifts than one. As Shelley had outgrown Harriet, so also had he outgrown Mary,—intellectually, emotionally, and morally. Even when she

studied Greek—even when she studied mathematics—she was anxious and troubled about
many things : anxious for comfort, and well-
cut gowns, and becoming bonnets; anxious for
the removal of the social boycott, and for tea-
parties, and the common lot of esteemed matrons
of the respectable middle-classes. Let it be
granted that these are good things and desirable.
The fact nevertheless remains that, when a poet
idealizes a woman, he does so in the belief that
she looks above and beyond them,—and that,
when he knows that she does not look above and
beyond them, he ceases to idealize her, and is
apt to idealize other women whom he does not
know so well.

That is how Shelley came to idealize Emilia
Viviani—whom he found out; that is how he
came to idealize Jane Williams—whom he did
not live to find out. Mary, no doubt, saw what
was happening, and behaved in the way for
which she afterwards expressed remorse. But
there was no actual estrangement—only a cool-
ing of ardour and an occasional misunderstanding. A few of Shelley's phrases reported
by Trelawny seem to give us the measure of the
trouble :—

" Poor Mary ! hers is a sad fate. Come along;
she can't bear solitude nor I society—the quick
coupled with the dead."

And then, again, when Trelawny pointed out

a jealous wife, who excused her jealousy on the ground of " excess of love " :—

" Shelley answered :—
" ' Love is not akin to jealousy; love does not seek its own pleasures, but the happiness of another. Jealousy is gross selfishness; it looks upon every one who approaches as an enemy : it is the idolatry of self, and, like canine madness, incurable.'
" His eyes flashed as he spoke. I did not then know that the green-eyed monster haunted his own house."

No more than that—and perhaps not even quite so much. For years after Shelley's death, Mary lived on terms of close intimacy with Jane Williams. She did not quarrel with her until Jane, then married to Hogg, made the foolish and unworthy boast that Shelley had loved her better than he loved Mary; and that would hardly have happened if the green-eyed monster had appeared in any very formidable shape. And Shelley's letters to Mary remain affectionate until the last,—though it is true that he wrote affectionate letters to other women also. There was a moment, within a year of the end, when he faced the question whether he should take a still further flight from society, and live out the rest of his life absolutely alone with Mary. It was at the time of his visit to Byron at

Ravenna—a visit already mentioned in connection with the calumny spread about Shelley and Miss Clairmont. He had left Mary at Pisa; and their future movements were uncertain. Florence had been talked of; there were strong arguments in favour of Florence; but :—

" My greatest content would be utterly to desert all human society. I would retire with you and our child to a solitary island in the sea, and shut upon my retreat the flood-gates of the world. I would read no reviews and talk with no authors. If I dared trust my imagination, it would tell me that there are one or two chosen companions besides yourself whom I should desire. But to this I would not listen—where two or three are gathered together, the devil is among them. And good, far more than evil, impulses, love, far more than hatred, has been to me, except as you have been its object, the source of all sorts of mischief. So on this plan, I would be *alone*, and would devote, either to oblivion, or to future generations, the overflowings of a mind which, timely withdrawn from the contagion, should be kept for no baser object."

It is the reappearance of the dream of the escape from life—not coupled with any thought of an escape from Mary. Perhaps the thought came as a counsel of despair rather than of hope; but still it came. Most likely it was for Mary's
326

sake, even more than for his own, that Shelley
dismissed it. This is how he goes on :—

" The other side of the alternative (for a
medium ought not to be adopted) is to form for
ourselves a society of our own class, as much as
possible in intellect or in feelings; and to connect
ourselves with the interests of that society. Our
roots never struck so deeply as at Pisa, and the
transplanted tree flourishes not. People who
lead the lives which we led until last winter are
like a family of Wahabee Arabs, pitching their
tent in the midst of London. We must do one
thing or the other—for yourself, for our child,
for our existence. The calumnies, the source of
which are probably deeper than we perceive,
have ultimately for object the depriving us of
the means of security and subsistence. You will
easily perceive the gradations by which calumny
proceeds to pretext, pretext to persecution, and
persecution to the ban of fire and water. It is
for this, and not because this or that fool, or the
whole court of fools curse and rail, that calumny
is worth refuting or chastising."

Which means that Byron is coming to Pisa
with the Guiccioli, and that there will be a set
of a sort in which Mary as well as Shelley will be
able to have a recognized social status. It will
not mean exactly the removal of the social boycott; but it will, at least, mean the creation of
circumstances in which the social boycott will

no longer matter much,—will perhaps matter no more than it mattered in that happy summer when the respectable people in the Geneva hotel spied on the outlaws in the villas through the telescope which their landlord had set up for them.

And so, most naturally, the vote was cast for Pisa; and Shelley engaged a better lodging there, and entered upon the most tranquil time of his tameless and swift career.

CHAPTER XXIX

THE pillar of the Pisa set was, of course, Byron. He was the only one of them whose name was widely known; he was rich, and he lived, as he had travelled *en grand seigneur*. He lived cleanly now, and not as at Venice. His house was a palace. He kept horses; he entertained; he was in touch with England. Travelling Englishmen, if they passed through Pisa, esteemed it a privilege to be received by him. It was he, in short, and he alone, who drew the eyes of Europe to Pisa. But for him, nobody would have had any curiosity to know what was happening at Pisa. He figured before the world as the central sun of a lurid system, shedding a reflected glory on the satellites. Some of the satellites took notes of his table-talk with a view to future publication. They all, from time to time, and more or less regularly, rode with him, practised pistol shooting with him, played billiards with him, dined with him. Shelley and Mary had never lived so socially since their marriage. At first, at any rate, the change suited them :—

" Lord Byron," Shelley wrote to Peacock, " is

established here, and we are constant companions. No small relief this after the dreary solitude of the understanding and the imagination in which we passed the first years of our expatriation, yoked to all sorts of miseries and discomforts. . . . We live, as usual, tranquilly. I get up, or at least wake, early; read and write till two; dine; go to Lord B.'s, and ride, or play at billiards, as the weather permits. . . . My health is better—my cares are lighter."

" Our party at Pisa," he writes to Horace Smith, " is the same as when I wrote last. Lord Byron unites us at a weekly dinner, when my nerves are generally shaken to pieces by sitting up contemplating the rest making themselves vats of claret, etc., till three o'clock in the morning."

Mary, at the same time, had more society than ever before. " Ride with La Guiccioli " is an entry in her Journal several times repeated; and she was accepted by persons whose social position was less equivocal than La Guiccioli's. " I have been once," Shelley writes to Miss Clairmont, " to Mrs. Beauclerc's, who did me the favour to caress me exceedingly. Unless she calls on Mary I shall not repeat my visit." But Mrs. Beauclerc did call, and even sent an invitation, for we read presently in Mary's Diary : " Walk with Jane and to the opera with her in the evening. With E. Trelawny afterwards to

Mrs. Beauclerc's ball." It was an indication
that doors were opening and might open wider
if Mary played her cards well. It was then
that the " pious dodge " was tried. We read:
" A note to, and a visit from, Dr. Nott. Go to
church."

It was at this period that Byron formed his
final estimate of Shelley's character, expressed
in letters written after Shelley's death :—

" There is another man gone, about whom the
world was ill-naturedly, and ignorantly, and
brutally mistaken. It will, perhaps, do him
justice *now*, when he can be no better for it."

" You were all mistaken about Shelley, who
was without exception the best and least selfish
man I ever knew."

" You are all mistaken about Shelley; you do
not know how mild, how tolerant, how good he
was."

A striking answer truly to the people who used
to stop Horace Smith in the street and ask him
whether it was really true that Shelley was such
a wicked man, guilty of such enormities; and
the tribute is the more remarkable because
Shelley and Byron did not, in the end, get on
very well together. In part, no doubt, Jane
Clairmont's constant lamentations over her
wrongs made trouble between them; but there
were also deeper incompatibilities with which

those wrongs had nothing to do. Byron posed, and Shelley protested that " the canker of aristocracy " needed to be cut out of him. He had brought too many of the traditions of the Dandies of the Regency to Pisa to please Shelley, and was too proud of his literary success. Shelley came to find his personality overpowering and distasteful. It overbore him and sterilized him. " It is of vital importance," we find him writing, " that I should put a period to my intimacy with Lord Byron." And again, when the question of going from Pisa to the sea arises : " I shall certainly take our house *far* from Lord Byron's, although it may be impossible suddenly to put an end to his detested intimacy." And then—to Leigh Hunt :—

" Certain it is that Lord Byron has made me bitterly feel the inferiority which the world has presumed to place between us and which subsists nowhere in reality but in our own talents, which are not our own but Nature's—or in our rank—which is not our own but Fortune's."

How much of that estrangement was due to Jane Clairmont's affairs, and how much to divergence of ideals, is matter of conjecture. Jane Clairmont's affairs may have been the occasion without being the cause—she had a wild plan for kidnapping Allegra, and wanted Shelley to help her to execute it. The fact of the estrangement, at any rate, is well attested ; and Shelley's relations with Byron were, at best, those of a minor with a major potentate. There was admiration—and a little envy—but no affection. Shelley's affection was reserved for Medwin, Trelawny, and Captain and Mrs. Williams; and they returned it. No man has ever written of Byron with the ardour of personal devotion which they showed to Shelley.

They were not, like him, it must be remembered, social Pariahs. If Trelawny was a Bohemian, the others were not. Medwin and Williams were officers on half-pay, eligible for membership of exclusive Service Clubs, if such then existed, qualified by birth and breeding to be pillars of that respectable middle-class society in which the name of Shelley continued to be *anathema maranatha*. Mrs. Williams— there was no Mrs. Medwin—could perfectly well have taken the line that Mrs. Shelley was not the sort of person whom one could call upon. But Anglo-Saxon and Anglo-Indian prejudices melted in the genial warmth of the Italian sun. Captain and Mrs. Williams preferred Shelley (and Mary also) to the most respectable people of their acquaintance. They came presently to live in a flat in the same house with the Shelleys; they met them daily, and made the sunshine of the last months of Shelley's life. And Shelley, on his part, wove a spell about them which none of their respectable acquaintances would have been capable of weaving. To quote Trelawny :—

" Shelley's mental activity was infectious; he kept your brain in constant action. Its effect on his comrade was very striking. Williams gave up all his accustomed sport for books, and the bettering of his mind; he had excellent natural ability; and the Poet delighted to see the seeds he had sown germinating. Shelley said he was the sparrow educating the young of the cuckoo. After a protracted labour, Ned was delivered of a five-act tragedy. Shelley was sanguine that his pupil would succeed as a dramatic writer."

That the play, though finished and offered to a London theatre, remains to this day unproduced is no great matter for surprise. The wonder is rather that the communicative warmth of a poet's enthusiasm should thus have altered the tastes and diverted the activities of an Anglo-Indian officer who had come to Italy to shoot in the Maremma; and the spell which Shelley threw at once over Trelawny—a spell which never lifted to the end of Trelawny's immensely long life—is an equal marvel.

Trelawny was, on the face of it, the last man whom one would have expected to seek, or retain, the friendship of one who was at once scholar, poet, and idealist. He was, like Shelley, of the county, yet in revolt against it; but he cannot be said to have resembled Shelley in any other way. It is customary to liken him to the Norwegian vikings, and to suspect that he had been a pirate in his time. He looked, at any rate, picturesque enough for the part of pirate in either comic opera or melodrama,—with a wife in every port; he had gone to sea at an age at which other lads go to Eton; he had had wild adventures in the Malay archipelago, and was presently to cap them by still more desperate doings as the lieutenant of Odysseus, the Greek revolutionist, in his cave in Attica. His constitution, too, was of cast-iron; and, after enduring hardships which would have made most men prematurely old at forty, he was to live to be the hardiest of hardy octogenarians, rejoicing in his cold bath in the dead of winter, and facing the March winds on the Sussex Downs with sublime disdain for overcoats and underclothing.

An absolutely uneducated man. One cannot even say that his education had been neglected, for he had had no education. But he had genius, —or, at least, the temperament which instinctively recognizes genius and responds to it. Shelley's genius conquered him from the first day of their acquaintance. He felt—and never ceased to feel—the beauty of Shelley's character. He constituted himself Shelley's prophet, and took his part against the world—sacrificing the reputations of Byron, and even of Mary, on the altar at which he worshipped. His recently published Letters complete the revelation of his loyalty. No man was ever more faithful to the memory of a mistress than he to Shelley's. Few things in literature are more touching than his

enthusiastic exchange of recollections with Jane
Clairmont, then a picturesque old woman, living
alone at Florence, of those golden months of
their romantic youth.

It was a story more than half a century old
which he then recalled; and it was all as fresh
in his memory—and in Jane's memory too—as
if it had been a matter of the day before yesterday. It may be that neither memory was literally accurate. We have caught Jane tripping;
and Byron once said that Trelawny was con-
stitutionally incapable of telling the truth. That
does not matter. Literal truth is of less value
than artistic truth; and facts are often more
misleading than impressions. For the radiant
period at Pisa, Trelawny is, after all, our best
witness : —

" Swiftly gliding in, blushing like a girl, a tall,
thin stripling held out both his hands; and although I could hardly believe as I looked at his
flushed, feminine, and artless face, that it could be
the Poet, I returned his warm pressure. After the
ordinary greetings and courtesies, he sat down
and listened. I was silent from astonishment :
was it possible this mild-looking, beardless boy
could be the veritable monster at war with all
the world ?—excommunicated by the fathers of
the Church, deprived of his civil rights by the
fiat of a grim Lord Chancellor, discarded by every
member of his family, and denounced by the
rival sages of our literature as the founder of a

Satanic school ? I could not believe it; it must
be a hoax."

That is the picture of the presentation in the
Williams' apartment. Then, when Shelley had
talked, warming to his subject :—

" After this touch of his quality I no longer
doubted his identity; a dead silence ensued;
looking up, I asked,
" ' Where is he ? '
" Mrs. Williams said, ' Who ? Shelley ? Oh,
he comes and goes like a spirit, no one knows
when or where.' "

After that Trelawny saw Shelley almost daily,
either in the Williams' flat or in his own. Here
is another vignette with a touch of character in
it. It was on the day on which Williams read
that five-act drama which the London managers
did not see their way to produce :—

" Shelley stood before us with a most woeful
expression.
" Mrs. Williams started up, exclaiming,
' What's the matter, Percy ? '
" ' Mary has threatened me.'
" ' Threatened you with what ? '
" He looked mysterious and too agitated to
reply.
" Mrs. Williams repeated, ' With what ? to
box your ears ? '
" ' Oh, much worse than that; Mary says she

will have a party; there are English singers here, the Sinclairs, and she will ask them, and every one she or you know—oh, the horror!'

" We all burst into a laugh except his friend Ned.

"' It will kill me.'

"' Music kill you!' said Mrs. Williams. 'Why, you have told me, you flatterer, that you loved music.'

"' So I do. It's the company terrifies me. For pity, go to Mary and intercede for me; I will submit to any other species of torture than that of being bored to death by idle ladies and gentlemen.'"

This picture also claims to be presented :—

" I called on him one morning at ten; he was in his study with a German folio open, resting on the broad marble mantelpiece over an old-fashioned fire-place, and with a dictionary in his hand. He always read standing if possible. He had promised overnight to go with me, but now begged me to let him off. I then rode to Leghorn, eleven or twelve miles distant, and passed the day there; on returning at six in the evening to dine with Mrs. Shelley and the Williamses, as I had engaged to do, I went into the Poet's room and found him exactly in the position in which I had left him in the morning, but looking pale and exhausted.

"' Well,' I said, ' have you found it?'

" Shutting the book and going to the window,

he replied, ' No, I have lost it '; with a deep
sigh : ' I have lost a day.'
" ' Cheer up, my lad, and come to dinner.'
" Putting his long fingers through his wild
masses of wild tangled hair, he answered faintly,
' You go, I have dined—late eating don't do for
me.'
" ' What is this ? ' I asked as I was going out
of the room, pointing to one of his bookshelves
with a plate containing bread and cold meat on it.
" ' That '—colouring—' why, that must be my
dinner. It's very foolish; I thought I had eaten
it.' "

Which leads up to remarks on Shelley's frugal
habits, and Mary's haphazard house-keeping—
" the cupboards of literary ladies are like Mother
Hubbard's, bare "—and to another anecdote
which ends with another criticism, implied rather
than expressed, of Mary :—

" An Italian who knew his way of life, not
believing it possible that any human being
would live as Shelley did, unless compelled by
poverty, was astonished when told the amount
of his income, and thought he was defrauded or
grossly ignorant of the value of money. He,
therefore, made a proposition which greatly
amused the Poet, that he, the friendly Italian,
would undertake, for ten thousand crowns a
year, to keep Shelley like a grand Seigneur, to
provide his table with luxuries, his house with

attendants, a carriage and opera-box for my lady, besides adorning his person after the most approved Parisian style. Mrs. Shelley's toilette was not included in the wily Italian's estimate."

And then there is the story of Mary discovering Shelley in the wood, to which he had fled to compose his poetry in peace. The words which Trelawny puts into her mouth shows us very clearly the picture which Trelawny had formed of her :—

" What a wild goose you are, Percy ! If my thoughts have strayed from my book, it was to the opera, and my new dress from Florence— and especially the ivy wreath so much admired for my hair, and not to you, you silly fellow ! When I left home, my satin slippers had not arrived. These are serious matters to gentle- women, enough to ruffle the serenest tempered. As to you and your ungallant companion, I had forgotten that such things are ; but as it is the ridiculous custom to have men at balls and operas, I must take you with me, though, from your uncouth ways, you will be taken for Valen- tine and he for Orson."

And the story, already given, of Shelley's denun- ciation of jealousy ; and then the story of Shelley bringing home a bag of scudi from the bank :—

" Standing up, he turned out the bag on to the hearthrug, and the glittering coins bespangled the floor. It was amusing to see him scraping them together with the shovel out of the fire-place; having adroitly got them into a lump, he pressed them as flat as he could with his feet, then skilfully with the shovel divided them as nearly as possible into two equal portions; one of the halves he divided again into two equal portions by guess-work, saying to Mary,

" 'That half will feed the house and pay the rent,' then pointing to the smaller portion he said, ' that will do for you. This is my portion.'

" Then he spoke lower to her that I might not hear, but she told me that he said,

" ' I will give this to poor Tom Medwin, who wants to go to Naples and has no money.'

" I said to Mary as we were dining,

" ' Why, he has left nothing for himself.'

" She said,

" ' No, if he wants anything he tells me to get it, and if he wants a scudo to give any one perhaps I lend it him ' (smiling), ' but he can't be trusted with money, and he won't have it.' "

And the story of the Scottish lady, who met Shelley, but was not told who he was, lest she should be shocked, and her exclamation :—

" Shocked !—why, I would have knelt to him in penitence for having wronged him even in my thoughts. If he is not pure and good, then there is no truth and goodness in this world. His looks reminded me of my own blessed baby —so innocent—so full of love and sweetness."

And so on, and so forth; for Trelawny is a hero-worshipper with a sense of humour, and one never tires of quoting such. His impressions may be rather truer than his stories; but the stories enshrine and give shape to his impressions, and therefore they also may be treated as artistically true. In them, as in Hogg's stories, far more than in any of the stately and exhaustive biographies which weigh evidence and balance pros and cons, the actual and convincing Shelley appears. If they overlook the melancholy which now and again flashes out in a letter, we must remember that Shelley's last months were, after all, the most serene of his career. The jealousy which, Trelawny says, embittered some of his moments was not visible to him at the time, though he heard a good deal about it afterwards.

Even then, it would seem, he attached very little importance to it. He had himself loved many women both successively and simultaneously; and he considered—so he confided to Miss Clairmont, whom he had loved among the rest, in his old age—that all young men were apt to do the same. It seemed to him as natural that a poet should have a mistress for every poem as that a sailor should have a wife in every port. One need not argue with him, but may reasonably leave the general question to take care of itself. In its particular aspects, however, it still concerns us a little. It remains to be seen whether we can make as light of it as Trelawny did. In any case, it always faces us in connection with Jane Clairmont; and it crops up for the last time in connection with Jane Williams.

CHAPTER XXX

JANE WILLIAMS

As regards Miss Clairmont, a rhyme composed by one of the party tells us that,

> *The Claire and the Ma*
> *Find something to fight about every day.*

We need not jump to the conclusion that they fought about Shelley, for there were other causes of friction. Miss Clairmont's position as an unmarried matron may well have seemed as compromising to Mary as it was uncomfortable to herself. That reason might, without any other, explain Mary's desire for her removal to a distance. She went to Florence, as has been mentioned, and she talked of going to Vienna, where her brother Charles, no longer dependent on Shelley's bounty, was at last establishing himself as a teacher of languages. It would doubtless have been a relief to Mary if she had gone.

She did not go, and affection for Shelley may have been one of her reasons for not going. That inference from her confession that she loved Shelley with all her heart and soul, gets some support from the difference in tone between Shelley's and Mary's letters to her. In Mary's letters there is always a certain assumption of superiority, as of one who addresses an unfortunate but erring sister to whom she wishes to do her duty, though she is not fond of her. Shelley's manner is far more intimate. He invites Jane to return—as she presently did—to his home. He anticipates modernity to the point of calling her " my best girl." He goes out of his way to assure her that Mary does not see either his letters or hers, and signs himself " yours most tenderly." He also goes out of his way to protest to her that he is not in love with Emilia Viviani. When sending her money, he writes : " Pardon me, my dearest, for mentioning scudi, and do not love me less because they are a portion of the inevitable dross of life which clings to our friendship."

Still that may have been nothing more than an example of Shelley's caressing way with women. He was a Romantic; and it is the characteristic of the Romantics to substitute the language of sentiment for that of gallantry, and then, at times, to be carried away by their own eloquence. Two things, at any rate, are certain about Shelley. When women attracted him, he could with difficulty refrain—and did not, indeed, try to refrain—from talking, and perhaps behaving, as if he were in love with them; but he never, in his Italian period, felt the *coup de foudre* which impels men to do mad and desperate things. On the whole he was, towards the end, far more in love with love than with any particular woman.

Jealousy, as we know, was in his view an

abominable emotion. One does not know for
certain whether he had any need to live up to
the doctrine, or any difficulty in doing so. He
laughed when the ludicrous Taaffe sent Mary two
guinea-pigs as a present, with the note : " O, that
I were one of those guinea-pigs, that I might see
you, this morning ! " But Prince Mavrocordato
had also been very attentive, visiting Mary regularly, to give her lessons in Greek; and this is
how Shelley announces his departure :—

" A vessel has arrived to take the Greek Prince
and his suite to join the army in Morea. He is
a great loss to Mary and *therefore* to me . . . but
not otherwise."

One wonders; but one can get no further than
wondering. The situation—the existence of
jealousy and the distribution of it—is much
clearer in the passage in Mr. Graham's interview
relating to the days when Shelley, Mary, the
Williamses, and Miss Clairmont were all living in
the same house at Lerici :—

" What did she (Mary) think," Mr. Graham
asked, " of that poem beginning (and to whom did
it allude)—

' *The serpent is shut out from Paradise,*
The wounded deer must seek the herb no more
In which its heart-cure lies ? '

" Miss Clairmont did not appear altogether
to care for this allusion to a *tendresse* for another

345

Jane, and I directed my conversation to a more personal channel.

" ' Poor Mary,' I replied. ' Fancy such a disturbing element in the house ! It cannot be altogether bliss to have a lovely sister and an arch-charmeuse under the same roof with a husband who speaks the language of the gods, whose ' food is love and fame.'

" ' Well, it was not my fault that men fell in love with me,' she replied, with that strange half-shy, tantalizing smile which irradiated her face with a flood of youth, and put it out of one's power to realize that this was a woman of eighty."

There is jealousy there : two women jealous, even if the third is not; the third being of course Jane Williams. Her portrait in the Bodleian attests her beauty; and we have a cloud of witnesses to her charm. The same witnesses, it is true, depose that she was shallow; but whereas a woman's charm leaps to the eyes, her shallowness, supposing her to be shallow, may long remain hidden; and when it is discovered, her charm may be held to excuse it.

Jane Williams was vain; and no woman would call her " nice." The circumstances of her second marriage, to Thomas Jefferson Hogg, irradiate her portrait rather unpleasingly. Her acceptance of his proposal was conditional,— he must " qualify " by a nine months' tour on the Continent. When he had qualified, and

Jane Williams
from the painting by Clint in the Bodleian Library

been rewarded, she regaled him with talk about
Shelley which, fond as he had been of Shelley,
cannot have been quite to his taste,—boasting
of her "conquest," and declaring that Shelley
had, in his last months, neglected Mary to make
love to her. Her boasts reached Mary's ears,
and there was a quarrel. One does not like
the sort of woman who does that sort of thing,
even if one feels sure that she is more silly than
vicious.

Yet Jane was very charming until she was
found out; and she was clever, for all her silli-
ness; and she would probably have said—fully
persuaded that she spoke the truth—that she
had neither meant any harm nor done any. Her
husband never doubted her. "I am proud,
dear girl, beyond words to express," he wrote
in his very last letter to her, "in the conviction
that *wherever* we may be together, you could be
cheerful and contented;" and he added : "This
is our longest separation, and seems a year to
me." He was sure, that is to say—the context
implies it—that his wife's attachment to him
was of a different quality from Mary's attachment to Shelley, who had made certain confessions, to him as well as to Jane, of his domestic
discontents.

Nor is there any reason whatever to suppose
that he was mistaken. Jane was quite loyal,—
silly, that is to say, but not vicious,—innocent
in thought as well as deed, and not in the least
in love with Shelley. But she was vain, and

capable, like the other Jane, of the vain woman's argument that it is not her fault if men fall in love with her. She liked admiration,—perhaps it made her feel a better woman. She liked a poet—especially if he were a handsome poet with soulful eyes—to sit at her feet, and delight in her singing, and tell her that he found his best inspiration in communing with her. She trusted herself; she knew where to draw the line; she was quite sure of her power to check her admirer's ill-timed impetuosity if the need arose. As for Mary—one imagines that Jane was, in a mild, kind way, rather sorry for her, though sorrier for Shelley. One can imagine the pitying, sympathetic smile with which she would have read the lines which Shelley sent to her :—

When I return to my cold home, you ask
  Why I am not as I have lately been.
You spoil me for the task
  Of acting a forced part on life's dull scene,—
Of wearing on my brow the idle mask
  Of author, great or mean,
  In the world's carnival, I sought
Peace thus, and but in you I found it not.

Or these :—

  Though thou art ever fair and kind,
    And forests ever green,
  Less oft is peace in Shelley's mind
    Than calm in water seen.

JANE WILLIAMS

Or the famous lyric :—

One word is too often profaned
For me to profane it :
One feeling too falsely disdained
For thee to disdain it.
One hope is too like despair
For prudence to smother ;
And pity from thee more dear
Than that from another.
I can give not what men call love :
But wilt thou accept not
The homage the heart lifts above,
And the Heavens reject not :
The desire of the moth for the star,
Of the night for the morrow,
The devotion to something afar
From the sphere of our sorrow.

Lyric after lyric, written in that tone of
sorrowful aspiration, was laid at Jane Williams'
feet in those last months. Nothing else inspired Shelley at that period. The inference is
irresistible that he was vastly more in love with
her than she with him ; but even so one need
infer no passion of the kind which threatens the
breaking up of homes. Shelley was once more,
as he put it in the case of Emilia, " seeking in
mortal image the likeness of what is perhaps
eternal." As he had failed to find that likeness
in Emilia, so he would, in the end, have failed
to find it in Jane. One knows Jane well enough

to feel quite sure of that. But the quest appealed to him, even though he only followed it in a spirit of elaborate make-believe. It was his one way of escape from the melancholy which seemed to grow upon him as the years were heaped upon his head, and the illusions of his boyhood burst like bubbles.

Of one thing, however, we may be certain. If Jane Williams showed little tact when she recalled Shelley's homage in the alcove with Hogg, she must have shown great tact and discretion at the time when she accepted it. Her husband looked on and approved, regarding Shelley with a devotion greater than her own, and feeling proud of a wife who thus inspired a poet's flights to the empyrean. Mary, if conscious of a barrier growing up between her soul and Shelley's, never charged—and it would almost seem never suspected—Jane Williams of building it. Jane remained her friend until the day when she blurted out her vain-glorious boasts to Hogg; and, in the meantime, they were on such cordial terms that they could agree to share a seaside villa for the summer.

And so to Casa Magni, at Lerici, on the Bay of Spezia.

CHAPTER XXXI

CASA MAGNI

CASA MAGNI stood at the water's edge,—the ground floor almost in the sea, unpaved and used as a store-room. Dark woods rose behind the villa; its situation was beautiful, but desolate. The Williamses had one room; the Shelleys two. Jane Clairmont came, and went, and came again. It was a case of close packing when she was there; but still neither the men nor the women quarrelled to any extent which those who knew them have thought it worth while to mention; and that fact is eloquent. It may, or may not, prove that Mary was long-suffering. It certainly proves that Jane Williams was tactful, and that Shelley's love-making was more ethereal than passionate.

It was at Casa Magni that the news of Allegra's death in her convent school was broken to Jane Clairmont. Her first passionate sorrow died away and left her calmer,—relieved, as it were, to be released from the wearing and unequal struggle with Allegra's father. The sorrow which puts an end to strife is sometimes, in that sense, restful and almost grateful. Mary, at the same time, had a serious illness,—a miscarriage and its consequences giving grounds for real

351

anxiety. She recovered her health—more or less—but not her spirits. Her nerves were shaken. She was in the mood in which little troubles seem great, and great troubles terrible. We have her own account of her complaints, and it would be easy to say that they were exaggerated complaints of trifling inconveniences.

" Such a place as this ! The poverty of the people is beyond anything, yet they do not appear unhappy, but go on in dirty content, or contented dirt, while we find it hard work to purvey miles around for a few eatables. We were in wretched discomfort at first, but now are in a kind of disorderly order, living from day to day as we can. . . . As only one house was to be found habitable in this gulf, the Williamses have taken up their abode with us, and their servants and mine quarrel like cats and dogs ; and besides, you may imagine how ill a large family agrees with my laziness, when accounts and domestic concerns come to be talked of."

So Mary wrote at the time to Mrs. Gisborne, and she wrote similarly at a later date :—

" I was not well in body or mind. My nerves were wound up to the utmost irritation, and the sense of misfortune hung over my spirits. No words can tell you how I hated our house and the country about it. Shelley reproached me for this. His health was good, and the place was quite after his own heart. What could I answer ? That the people were wild and hateful; that though the country was beautiful, yet I liked a more *countrified* place, and that there was great difficulty in living; that all our Tuscans would leave us, and that the very jargon of those *Genovese* was disgusting. That was all I had to say, but no words could describe my feelings; the beauty of the woods made we weep and shudder."

The same lamentation occurs in the Note on the Poems written in 1822 :—

" The natives were wilder than the place. Our near neighbours of San Terenzo were more like savages than any people I ever before lived among . . . . We could get no provisions nearer than Sarzana, at a distance of three miles and a half off, with the torrent of the Magra between; and even there the supply was very deficient. Had we been wrecked on an island of the South Seas, we could scarcely have felt ourselves further from civilisation and comfort; but where the sun shines the latter becomes an unnecessary luxury, and we had enough society among ourselves. Yet I confess housekeeping became rather a toilsome task, especially as I was suffering in my health, and could not exert myself actively."

Small matters truly, if one could be sure that

z

they formed the sum-total of the trouble; but
that, of course, is what one cannot be sure of.
Causes are generally veiled behind occasions;
and occasions are easier to expound than causes.
Worry with the servants and the tradespeople—
joints which did not turn up in time—difficulties
of converse in an unaccustomed dialect with an
uncouth peasantry : these things, in other moods,
would have been trifles, to be dismissed with a
shrug of the shoulders. But if Mary felt that
she was a failure—that things were drifting
whither she would not—that she had not the
power to check the drift—the case was different.

On two conditions she could have been happy :
if everything had continued to be as in the days
of the honeymoon, when Shelley had signed his
letters to her " Your Elfin Knight," and had laid
Laon and Cythna at her feet with the dedication :—

"*So now my summer task is ended, Mary,*
And I return to thee, mine own heart's home ;
As to his Queen some victor Knight of Faery,
Earning bright spoils for her enchanted dome."

On that condition, or if marriage had had its
ordinary sequel, and she had been able to
settle down, at peace with the world, making
a fixed home, striking root, sharing the common
lot.

But neither of these conditions had been
fulfilled. She had been a wanderer for years,—

and not only a wanderer, but a Pariah,—she who assuredly was not born to be anything of the kind, but was a British Matron at heart, forbidden to live as a British Matron because of the *coup de tête* of her seventeenth year. At the same time she knew—what even a stupid woman could not have failed to know—that she was no longer all that she once had been to Shelley. He was still affectionate; but he dreamed dreams in which she did not figure; he looked to other women—however Platonically—for inspiration. Hence the sense of failure, springing up in a morbid mind, in circumstances in which women tend to harbour morbid thoughts. Hence also the sense that things were drifting—as no doubt they were.

How far they would have drifted, if Fate had let them drift, one can but guess. Not, probably, to any immediate catastrophe; Jane Williams being passionless and tactful, and Shelley no longer the creature of impulse which he once had been. Yet it is just as unlikely that they would have drifted to any calm and happy haven. A man's heart at Shelley's age is far more ready to travel forward than to travel back; and mere drifting, though to no definite disaster, is itself catastrophe. It is anti-climax, which is a sadder thing even than tragedy. If one may choose, then better than anti-climax is a sudden and poignantly heart-rending end.

So Shelley seems to have felt. One may not, indeed, draw the inference from his proposal to

Jane Williams that he should upset the boat in which he was rowing her, in order that they might "together solve the great mystery." That, though it frightened Jane Williams, may have been mere playfulness; but one finds no playfulness in this letter to Trelawny :—

"Should you meet with any scientific person capable of preparing the *Prussic Acid, or essential oil of bitter almonds,* I should regard it as a great kindness if you could procure me a small quantity. It requires the greatest caution in preparation, and ought to be highly concentrated; I would give any price for this medicine. You remember we talked of it the other night, and we both expressed a wish to possess it; my wish was serious, and sprung from the desire of avoiding needless suffering. I need not tell you I have no intention of suicide at present, but I confess it would be a comfort to me to hold in my possession that golden key to the chamber of perpetual rest."

That the suffering from which Shelley wished to be able to escape at will was merely physical suffering one does not easily believe. His health, just then, was better than it had been for a long time; his spirits, on the whole, were higher. But things were drifting—visibly drifting, though he knew not whither. He may have feared the consequences if he let them drift much further—but meantime it was pleasant

enough to let them drift. He enjoyed the heat
and the shadow, and the sea and the woods,
even when he found Mary fretful. Jane
Williams helped him to enjoy, singing to him
on the balcony, to the accompaniment of the
guitar which he had given her, accepting the
homage of his verse in the spirit in which
a Queen accepts the flattery of courtiers,—re-
warding it with smiles, though not deeply moved
by it. Afterwards, no doubt,—but there was to
be no afterwards.

The day came when Leigh Hunt and his wife
and family arrived at Leghorn. He had been
invited to Italy to associate himself with Byron
and Shelley in the editing of a periodical publication—the ill-fated *Liberal ;* and an apartment
had been furnished for him in Byron's palace.
It was an unfortunate expedition ; but the story
of the misunderstandings attending it belongs
to another book than this. Shelley had nothing,
or at any rate very little, to do with them. The
end was to come before that trouble reached
its culmination. Meanwhile he hurried off to
Leghorn to greet Hunt, and see him comfortably
settled in his new home. Thornton Hunt, then
a small boy, remembered the enthusiasm of
his welcome, and his cry : " I am inexpressibly
delighted ; you cannot think how inexpressibly
happy it makes me."

There was much to be done : sights to be seen,
calls to be paid, purchases to be made, a physician
to be consulted about Mrs. Hunt's health, a

misunderstanding with Byron to be smoothed
over. Hunt, too, had to be supplied with money;
for he had landed practically penniless, depending
on his friends, according to his habit, for the
necessaries as well as the luxuries of life. But
that mattered little to Shelley, though Byron
resented the presumption. Gold was dross to
Shelley when the friends who asked him for it
were amiable; and Hunt's amiability was irresistible. He would have been remembered as
one of the most lovable men of his age, if it had
not been for the imperious necessity which
compelled him to be for ever dipping into the
pockets of those who loved him. Trelawny
says that he was not only Shelley's " dearest "
but also his " most costly " friend; but Shelley
himself drew no such distinction.

He had looked forward to Hunt's coming—
he gladly paid the price; and a week passed
happily. " We talked of a thousand things,"
says Hunt. " We anticipated a thousand
pleasures,"—pleasures which, as we know, were
never to be realized. Yet, even so, one suspects
that the anticipations were keener in Hunt's
mind than in Shelley's. Hunt admitted that
he found an undertone of melancholy in Shelley's
talk. The sanguine enthusiasm which he remembered seemed to him to have taken a more sober
hue. He guessed at no reason for the change.
The fact that Shelley was growing older—though,
in truth, he was not yet twenty-nine—and that
the world still refused a hearing to his message

may well have seemed reason enough to him. Melancholy, at any rate, whatever the reason for it, is the note of his last letters. This is what he wrote to Jane Williams on the eve of his return :—

" I fear you are solitary and melancholy at Villa Magni, and, in the intervals of the greater and more serious distress in which I am compelled to sympathize here, I figure to myself the countenance which had been the source of such consolation to me, shadowed by a veil of sorrow. How soon those hours passed, and how slowly they return to pass so soon again, perhaps for ever, in which we have lived together so intimately, so happily ! Adieu, my dearest friend ! I only write these lines for the pleasure of writing what will meet your eyes."

A letter to Mary went by the same post. It dealt chiefly with Hunt's troubles and embarrassments. The only personal words are these :—

" How are you, my best Mary ? Write especially how is your health and how your spirits are, and whether you are not more reconciled to staying at Lerici, at least during the summer. You have no idea how I am hurried and occupied ; I have not a moment's leisure, but will write by next post."

The letter was hardly written when he started

—he and Williams together—to sail back to their house on the bay of Spezzia. Trelawny was to have borne them company, a part of the way, in Byron's yacht; but his papers were not in order, and the Public Health Authorities of the Port stopped him. He returned, and cast anchor, and watched the smaller boat through his telescope, conversing with the mate. The boat, said the mate, was carrying too much sail. It was standing too much in shore. The dirty clouds in the south-west betokened danger. The devil was brewing mischief. There would be a squall.

He had hardly spoken when a sea fog descended and the boat was lost from view. When the storm broke, and scattered the mist, the boat was no more to be seen. The sea change had been suffered,—no one quite knew how; and there followed several awful days of suspense, until at last the mangled bodies were thrown up on the beach, and Trelawny spurred his horse that he might break the news, before any rude stranger had time to blurt it out, to the women who waited weeping, in their home.

THE SEQUEL

MARY SHELLEY'S SUITORS

SHELLEY's biographer is under no obligation
to look for a sequel to his story in the subsequent
events of Mary Shelley's life; and it has always
been the assumption even of Mary Shelley's own
biographers that there was no sequel worth pursuing. For the rest of her days, it has been
commonly supposed, she merely mourned her
loss, devoted herself to the education of her son,
and earned her living by literary work of no
particular importance, regarding the emotional
chapter of her life as closed for ever. But that
is not quite the case. There is still something to
be added : something which it was impossible
for previous biographers to add.

One fact, of course, some previous biographers
have added : that Mary received a proposal of
marriage from Trelawny. He was sufficiently a
creature of impulse to propose marriage to any
woman—and also to regret having done so; but,
in this instance, the evidence that Mary declined
the proposal is stronger than the evidence that
Trelawny made it. Let us have the passages
from the letters on which the story rests before
us :—

Trelawny to Mary :—

" Do not you, dear Mary, abandon me by
following the evil example of my other ladies.
I should not wonder if fate, without our choice,
united us; and who can control his fate ? I
blindly follow his decrees, dear Mary."

Mary to Trelawny :—

" Do you think that I shall ever marry ?
Never—neither you nor anybody else. Mary
Shelley shall be written on my tomb—and why ?
I cannot tell, except that it is so pretty a name
that, though I were to preach to myself for years,
I never should have the heart to get rid of it."

Trelawny to Mary :—

" I was more delighted with your resolve not
to change your name than with any other portion
of your letter. Trelawny, too, is a good name,
and sounds as well as Shelley; it fills the mouth
as well, and will as soon raise a spirit."

Mary Shelley to Trelawny,—saying the last
word in the matter :—

" My name will never be Trelawny. I am not
so young as I was when you first knew me, but
I am as proud. I must have the entire affection,
devotion, and, above all, the solicitous protection
of one who would win me. You belong to women-
kind in general, and Mary Shelley will *never* be
yours."

E. J. Trelawny

MARY SHELLEY'S SUITORS

That is all. It is an extraordinary situation, made the more extraordinary by the revelation, in Trelawny's letters, that, at the time of Shelley's death, Trelawny was making violent protestations of love to Jane Clairmont—to whom, as we have already seen, he was to confide in his old age that he regarded Mary as "devoid of imagination and Poetry," "the weakest of her sex," and "the most conventional slave I ever knew,"—one who "even affected the pious dodge, such was her yearning for society."

Truly it is a queer tangle; and it increases in queerness when we read Miss Clairmont's remarks about Trelawny in her letters to Mary : "There is a certain want of sympathy between us which makes writing to him extremely disagreeable to me. . . . He is full of fine feelings and has no principles, I am full of fine principles but never had a feeling; he receives all his impressions through his heart, I through my head. *Que voulez-vous? Le moyen de se rencontrer* when one is bound for the North Pole and the other for the South?" One can make little of it all except that Trelawny was a violent, variable, and terrifying suitor, and that both Mary and Claire felt apprehension, not unnaturally, mingled with their genuine and high regard for him. An article on Mary Shelley's suitors would be quickly finished if Trelawny had been the only one.

But he was not; and this preface brings us to a curious three-cornered love affair in which the three names involved are those of Mary Shelley, John Howard Payne, the author of " Home, Sweet Home," and—Washington Irving. That story is new as well as strange. There is no word about it in the Lives of any of the three actors in the drama. Mrs. Shelley's name is not even mentioned in the Lives of Washington Irving and Payne. Payne's and Washington Irving's names are not even mentioned in any of the Lives of Mrs. Shelley. Payne was the only one of the three to whom the things which happened mattered; and he did not speak about it. The record of them, however, was among his papers, which passed through the hands of autograph collectors for a long time before their significance was recognized; and from those papers the story can be reconstructed.

A word to begin with about John Howard Payne.

Born in 1791, Payne was the son of a New York school-master, and began life as a clerk in a mercantile house. Inspired by the fame of Betty, the Young Roscius, he went on the stage and became known as the Young Roscius of America. Cooke, who met him during his American tour, wrote that he thought him " a polite sensible youth, and the reverse of our Young Roscius." He came to England in 1813, with good introductions, and presently abandoned acting for theatrical management and dramatic authorship. He was in Paris during the " hundred days," sharing an apartment there with Washington Irving; and Byron's friend Hobhouse gave him, just as he gave Jane Clairmont, an introduction to Douglas Kinnaird, who commissioned him to look out for French plays which could be adapted for the English stage. He was, for some time, in partnership with Washington Irving for this purpose; and he also wrote original theatrical pieces—notably *Clari the Maid of Milan*, which had " Home, Sweet Home " for one of its lyrics.

Of " Home, Sweet Home " one hundred thousand copies were sold in the first year, at a profit of 2,000 guineas; but the profit was not for the author. Payne was always poor; and an unsuccessful venture in management as lessee of Sadler's Wells first brought him to a debtor's prison, and then compelled him to retire to the Continent in order to avoid his creditors. He returned to America in 1835, and, after engaging for some time in journalism, received from President Tyler, in 1842, the appointment of United States Consul in Tunis. He was the Consul to whom the Bey of Tunis exclaimed : " America ! America ! Where is it ? I do not know of any such country." Recalled in 1845, he was reinstated in 1851, but died, at the Consulate, in the following year—unmarried.

" It was," writes a subsequent Consul, Amos Perry, " a sad issue and a cruel lot. He was in a foreign land, deprived of the pleasures of the sweet home about which he had sung, and of the

365

presence of long-cherished friends. Yet he was cared for. Sweet charity from Christians, Mussulmans, and Jews failed him not. He was tenderly and lovingly nursed till his spirit departed from the clayey tabernacle."

He died in debt, though his obligations amounted to no more than 700 dollars; so Amos Perry continues :—

" For the want of this amount of money, after due notice had been given to Mr. Payne's relatives in America, his library, household furniture, pictures, sword of office, and numerous manuscripts and works of art, were appraised and sold at auction. His personal apparel, an extensive collection of manuscripts, mostly in bound volumes, an autograph-album of distinguished contemporary authors, and numerous choice keepsakes were not appraised or sold. What became of them is rather a matter of conjecture than of proof. They were unquestionably taken away by unauthorized persons and were effectually scattered and lost. The autograph-album referred to has, I am assured, been offered for sale in New York at a price sufficient to have paid all Mr. Payne's debts."

Not all the wanderings of the letters thus lost can be traced; but some of them, removed from Tunis by Mr. M. P. Chandler, who succeeded Payne as Consul there, have been recovered. They were bought by Mr. William K. Bixby, and have quite recently been printed, for private circulation, by the Boston Bibliophile Society. They include letters from Mary Shelley to Payne; letters from Payne to Mary Shelley; letters from Payne to Washington Irving. They tell a story, and show us why Payne never married.

His biographer, of course, has a theory on that subject, which is the usual theory. This is how he puts it :—

" A heavy shadow was cast over his eventful life by the unhappy termination of a romance of his early manhood when he became devotedly attached to a lady of Boston, whose rare beauty and mental accomplishments made her the idol of the social circle in which she moved. The affection of the gifted lover was warmly reciprocated, and a marriage would have completed the happiness of both but for parental interference."

That story, however, even if true, is by no means the whole truth. Payne can hardly have been more than twenty at the time of that disappointment; and the heart of man is too elastic an organ to have all the spring taken out of it by the sentimental mishaps of early youth; and it was with Payne as with others. He loved again at the age of thirty-four. He loved Mary Shelley—who used him as her stalking-horse for the pursuit of Washington Irving—whose heart was not to be captured by her.

The acquaintance was made, apparently at the Hotel Nelson, in Paris. Mary Shelley stayed there on her melancholy way home from Italy in 1823, and Payne was then in Paris, evading his English creditors, and writing plays in collaboration with Irving. In the early months of 1824, Payne was once more in London—on what precise terms with his creditors one does not know; and our first letter shows Mary Shelley addressing him as a comparative stranger, but inviting him to tea. She begins " My dear Sir," and says :—

" Mrs. Harwood called on me to-day, and, expressing a great desire to find some opportunity of conversing with you about your American friend, I thought that I might venture to say that I would ask you to meet her here, and fixed with her Sunday evening, *i.e.* at six p.m. Will you come and over a cup of hyson drink to the better delivering of embassies, and that all messengers do not set amicable powers by the ears ? "

Mrs. Harwood has nothing to do with the story. The sequel will show that it was not by her but by Mary Shelley that the interest in the "American friend" was principally felt. Payne, however, misread the letter, called on Monday by mistake, and found Mrs. Shelley out. He apologized, and Mrs. Shelley, in return, apologized for her " ill-formed pothooks," and asked Payne to " tempt fortune again." He did so, and once more missed her, with the result that he received a third invitation, accompanied by specific directions as to the means of travelling from Arundel Street, Strand, to Kentish Town, where Mrs. Shelley was then living :—

" Will you drink tea with me to-morrow ? as a cold of Percy's will detain me at home from my expected engagement.

" If you are in the Strand, you will find stages in James Street, Covent Garden, every hour; if in Lancaster Street, attain the turnpike at Battle Bridge at ten minutes exactly after any hour being struck, and soon one of our vehicles will pass, which, on being directed, will set you down at my door.

" You see how diligently I try to repair an inconsequence which must not make you think me unpunctual, which I am not."

That was the beginning; and a letter from Mrs. Shelley to Miss Curran shows what was the manner of her life at the time. She saw few people " so far from the centre of bustling London." Her principal companion was Jane Williams, with whom she had not yet quarrelled. She could not " dream of society," because she could not afford to give dinner-parties; and " as to theatres, etc., how can a ' lone woman ' think of such things ? "

She could, however, and did, think of such things a good deal, when her acquaintance with Payne developed into friendship. Payne, though a poor man, was a power at the box-offices; and his pockets were always full of complimentary tickets. He could give Mrs. Shelley " orders," and he could lend her books. We presently find him lending her Cooper's *Lionel Lincoln*, and making that work a text for the defence of

A A   369

American manners. Americans, he says, " having no privileged class to keep them in mind of high manners, become habitually careless and abrupt "; but he protests : " We have refined feelings . . . and these are no bad substitutes after all." The reason why he is anxious that Mrs. Shelley should believe in the " refined feelings " of his countrymen appears in the same letter :—

" Do not think that I, like Miss Fanny Holcroft, am in a patronising mood, if I say that your yesterday's conversations filled my mind so full of yourself that my poor pillow had but a small portion of its due. A heroine in love and friend-ship and duty to a parent,—and to the two former almost a martyr, is to me a being so beyond all others that, even though her qualities are certainly ' images ' of what is promised in ' heaven above,' I can kneel down and worship them without dreading the visitation upon idolatry. The union of superior intellectual en-dowments with simplicity, fervour, and elevation and purity of character, is so rare that, where it does exist, there can be no high treason against forms in welcoming so delightful a family with some enthusiasm. To any ordinary woman I should not dare to say this. It would certainly be interpreted to my disadvantage. But I think you would never have entered upon what related to yourself with me had you been utterly in-different to my opinion, and where we resist the world, there is some satisfaction in knowing that

370

our motives are appreciated by those for whom we have any, even the humblest, value. Be certain I feel the limit I am bound to set to the compliment of your unreserve, and that I am incapable of presuming upon it even in the wildest dreams. This would be the most despicable vanity, and though, in talking to you for talking's sake, you have often found me falling into vapid egotism, I can assure you I am only just vain enough to think I have no vanity— certainly none on these points. May I not, then, praise you, and like you, and more, much more than like you, without a box on the ear, or frowns, or wonder that I should presume to do so, or be so impertinent as to tell you I do ? I can only be convinced I may by your commands, whenever there is anything in the world I can at any time or in any way do to show with how much truth I am

" Yours, J. H. P."

Payne, it is clear, had already gone a good way towards falling in love when he wrote that; but the answer which he received was only moderately encouraging. " You must not make me vain," wrote Mrs. Shelley in reply; and she continued : " You are good and kind, and deserve, therefore, nothing but kindness. But we must tread lightly on the mosaic of circumstance; for, if we press too hard, the beauty and charm is defaced." A non-committal letter, but one accompanied by " commands " such as Payne had solicited. Mrs. Shelley would like to see *Virginius*, and " a box would be preferable, wherever it might be, if it could be obtained."

Of course, she received the tickets—of course, with an offer of Payne's escort : " If you like to have me with you, let me know by three o'clock on the appointed day; if more convenient to make up the party without me, do so." One perceives Payne here still very much afraid of presuming. He hopes that he does not intrude, —he promises not to intrude; but the grounds on which he bases his promise almost amount to a declaration of love :—

" I can have your company without oppressing you with mine. You are perpetually in my presence, and if I close my eyes you are still there, and if I cross my arms over them and try to wave you away, still you will not be gone. This madness of my imagination flatters itself with a forlorn hope of a delightful vagueness in part of your note. . . . If the *fata morgana* WILL fling these pretty pictures over the heart, are we to shut our eyes and not rejoice in them ? They are as beautiful as reality while they last, and when reality itself fades, what becomes of the difference ? I would not have you check my delusion. If in looking above my path at the sweet paradise of vapour, I am doomed to fall into a pit, I must scramble out again as well as I can, and say, ' it will all be the same a hundred years hence. . . .'

" . . . For all your smiling I know very well what that part of your letter means which I pretended just now not to understand. If you tread lightly on the beautiful mosaic of my day dreams, still you do tread on it, and only leave me liberty to be grateful for the pressure—and I am grateful—and care nothing about myself so I may care for you, and tell you so without your being angry."

The writer's reward was to be addressed no longer as " My dear Sir," but as " My dear Payne." One feels that it was time for some such concession. " We depend upon you as our escort," Mrs. Shelley writes; and one feels that that also was due. She adds, however, the request : " Do not, I entreat you, frighten me by any more interpretations; " and Payne seems to have been abashed. He now ventures to write to Mrs. Shelley as " My excellent friend "; but he says :—

" I was frightened at myself after I had sent that last letter, for though all true, yet it might have been as well to have kept it to myself. It is considerate in you to take it in such good part, and more than considerate to think of reducing my extravagance by a diet of friendship. I hope I may some time or other be enabled to show I am not unworthy of the distinction."

He endeavoured to prove his worthiness by keeping up a regular supply of complimentary tickets for both Covent Garden and Drury Lane. Pasta was in London that season; and Mrs. Shelley was enabled to see her in *Faustus*, *Otello*,

William Tell, and other operas. She often had as many as six tickets for a single performance; and Payne continued not to press his company, though he always offered it :—

" Do not imagine I can be weary of anything you may require of me. I only wish you not to think yourself bound by politeness to ask me to be your escort, if you can supply my place more agreeably to yourself and others; and I say this honestly and without affectation."

There was some question at this time of Payne having committed what he calls a " *fatuité.*" Mrs. Shelley says that she could not possibly accuse him of anything bordering on *fatuité ;* but adds :—

" Your note looks as if you remembered all the nonsense I talked usually with Jane and you and the silent man in Lamb's garden; but, do you know ? I am rather given to talk nonsense —and then only half of it was nonsense—a veil, a make-believe, which means everything and nothing,—if this is intelligible."

It is only moderately intelligible. Payne, in his reply, professed not to understand it at all, saying, " I am determined never to remember anything about you which may not be remembered with pleasure," and also, " I shall always be confident you mean as kindly towards me as you can, and more, too, than I have any right to claim." Yet one divines that something has happened—something which Payne does not

374

altogether like. Was the "silent man" in Lamb's garden Washington Irving? Had he and Mrs. Shelley . . . ? It is impossible to say; but Washington Irving does figure in this story as a silent man, spoken of but never speaking, and we are nearing the moment when his figure must appear in the background.

His initials appear in two sentences, which may mean anything or nothing : " Thank you for W. I.," and also, " I am still faithful to W. I." This synchronizes with the perception by Payne of a certain coolness towards himself; and we find him asking : " Has any careless act or expression offended or vexed you ? " He was informed that no offence had been taken, and was invited to dine with Mrs. Shelley at Godwin's house, and to see her home afterwards. He accepted with protestations of delight; but a passage in the letter of acceptance shows that jealousy was tormenting him :—

" I am glad you return to Irving, for it is tantalizing to have one's heart in a state of miscellany. What I myself might have thought on Saturday could I have presumed so far as to feel a personal interest in your fidelity ! Is *ice* a non-conductor? But, if it is, how do you convey impressions ? "

Mrs. Shelley, however, was quite capable of conveying impressions; and she conveyed them while walking home with Payne after the party. A memorandum of the conversation was one of

375

the documents which Payne laid before Irving. It plainly marks a crisis :—

" She attempted fully but delicately to explain herself. . . . She said she felt herself so placed with the world that she never could expect its distinctions; and that the high feeling she entertained for the memory of her husband forbade the hope of any future connection which should make the world indifferent to her—or, rather, the *English* world. Therefore she was desirous of getting to Italy, and there passing the rest of her life. . . . The conversation then turned upon you. She said you had interested her more than any one she had seen since she left Italy; that you were gentle and cordial, and that she longed for friendship with you. I rallied her a little upon the declaration, and at first she fired at my mentioning that she talked as if she were in love. Upon her reply I answered : ' What ! would you make me a plaything of Mr. I. ? ' And then the chat sank into mere commonplace. The scope of her remarks was that, whenever she formed any alliance, it must be with some one whose high character and mind should be worthy of him who had drawn her from obscurity, and that her selection must not dishonour his choice."

This memorandum was accompanied by a letter in which Payne was still more explicit. " It was some time," he wrote, " before I discovered that I was only sought as a source of an introduction to you—and I think you will, on reading the papers, feel that I might have mistaken the nature of my acquaintance with the writer without any gratuitous vanity."

The Court of opinion is likely to be with him there, and may also admire the unselfishness of his endeavour to make his friends happy when he saw that happiness was not for him. He proceeds to praise Mrs. Shelley as " a woman of the highest and most amiable qualities, and one whose wish for friendship it would be doing yourself injustice not to meet; " and he begs Irving to " see and know Mrs. S. whenever you go to London." He effaces himself, saying : " I am not in the least dissatisfied with the way in which she considers me, however difficult an affair so little flattering to one's pride and affections is to endure at first; " and he even goes so far as to plead for Mrs. Shelley, and to beg that Irving will excuse her for having made advances which may seem temerarious in one of her sex :—

" No doubt it will cost you some reflection fully to appreciate the trouble I am taking to make you well acquainted with one I have known so well—to transfer an intimacy of which any one ought to be proud. I do not ask you to fall in love—but I should even feel a little proud of myself if you thought the lady worthy of that distinction, and very possibly you would have fallen in love with her, had you met her casually —but she is too much out of society to enable you to do so—and sentiments stronger than friendship seldom result from this sort of previous earnestness for intimacy when it comes from the wrong side."

That letter is not dated; so one does not know precisely at what stage of the proceedings it was dispatched. There seems, however, to have been an interval between Mrs. Shelley's admission that Payne was only her stalking-horse for the pursuit of Irving and Payne's formal withdrawal from the field. Mrs. Shelley still wanted orders for the theatres, and Payne continued to provide them in abundance. Mrs. Shelley wanted a practical opinion on a play which Mrs. Williams had written, and Payne gave one. It was unfavourable, but there are some interesting sentences in it: " The play would not succeed if acted. . . . Whatever merit it has is literary. . . . If English plays are not understood by English galleries, the boxes are never permitted to hear them. . . . Stage heroes are not expected to account for the ways in which they raise money. Mr. Rothschild would make but a sorry figure in a play about the Battle of Waterloo." Payne further offered to help Mrs. Williams in reconstructing her piece, but that offer was rejected with scorn. " Mrs. Williams has no idea of making the *radical* alterations that you suggest." Finally Mrs. Shelley wished Payne to show her one of Washington Irving's letters.

What she expected to find in the letter one can only guess without any confidence that one guesses right. Payne hesitated to send it because of some references which it contained to his own private affairs, but ultimately sent it "lest circumstances should give a false colouring to its being withheld." His own covering letter is a very long one, and contains his definite resignation of his pretensions. He tells Mrs. Shelley in it how he came to fall in love with her : " A flash, as it were, and that at a time and place of which you can form no idea, gave me a thorough impression of all which I have since found confirmed of the beauty of your heart and intellect." That was before meeting her ; but then :—

" I met you afterwards, and left you witn a thorough determination not to trust myself to the danger of your acquaintance, with a wish, if you can understand such a wish, to pay you the same homage as I would the memory of one whom I had loved, but whose form, were it to appear, would only perplex me."

And then :—

" I *did* meet you again, and presumed too much on my courage, forgetting that, the rein once given to feelings between the sexes, they are apt involuntarily to spurn the curb and gallop over the prescribed boundary. The error was perfectly gratuitous. I told you I knew my danger and could laugh at it. I am afraid now the laugh is not on my side."

Payne adds that he has " given way to an absurdity," and has only himself to blame. He

acquits Mrs. Shelley of unkindness, saying : " I
have never yet met an instance of so much frankness and honest determination, the moment the
truth became obvious, not to commit the feelings
of the one party or the integrity of the other."
But the pain is great, and the wound must be
allowed time to heal : " It is therefore better I
should not meet you till this strange fever is
over." And finally :—

" To return to the point at which our conversations began and have ended—Washington Irving
—be assured I will act the hero in this business;
and shall feel quite reconciled to the penalty to
which my folly has condemned me, and which, I
hope, I have firmness enough to make a light one,
if my friendship should prove the stepping-stone
to one so much more gratifying and desirable."

Whereto Mrs. Shelley replies with good advice,
exhorting Payne to " awaken to laudable ambition and exhilarating industry," expressing regret
that Payne's letter seems " to place a barrier to
any future meeting," and especially deploring the
fact that " it is ever one's hard fate either to be
deserted and neglected, or, which turns out the
same thing, to be liked too well and so avoided."
And then she goes on to ask for six complimentary tickets for a performance at Sadler's
Wells.

Truly it was a strange game of cross purposes;
but there was a further surprise to follow—
perhaps not a very great surprise to Payne, but
certainly a great surprise to Mrs. Shelley. Payne
380

was so much in Irving's confidence that he probably knew—what Mrs. Shelley evidently did not know—that Washington Irving was himself, at this time, suffering the pangs of unrequited love. He had quite lately, while on a visit to Dresden, proposed to, and been refused by, Miss Emily Foster, afterwards Mrs. Fuller; and a passage quoted by his biographer from a journal kept by Miss Emily Foster's sister shows how deeply his feelings were engaged :—

" He has written. He has confessed to my mother, as to a true and dear friend, his love for E . . . . , and his conviction of its utter hopelessness. He feels himself unable to combat it. He thinks he must try, by absence, to bring more peace to his mind. Yet he cannot bear to give up our friendship—an intercourse become so dear to him, and so necessary to his daily happiness. Poor Irving ! "

And, one may add : Poor Mary Shelley ! For Payne had abdicated in Washington Irving's favour in vain. Washington Irving, for the reason which the last extract indicates, showed no symptoms of any desire to assume the honours of the kingdom prepared for him. Mrs. Shelley confesses as much to Payne in a letter from which it seems a fair inference that marriage, and not mere friendship, was indeed her objective :—

" As for my favourite I., methinks our acquaintance proceeds at the rate of the Antediluvians who, I have somewhere read, thought nothing of an interval of a year or two between a visit. Alack ! I fear that, at this rate, if ever the church should make us one, it would be announced in the consoling phrase that the Bride and Bridegroom's joint ages amounted to the discreet number of 145 and three months."

The next letter is in reply to Payne's announcement that he is going to Paris (where Washington Irving was then living in the Rue Richelieu), and that he would like to see Mrs. Shelley again before he goes, but feels that the pleasure would be fraught with pain for him. We may ignore the demands for complimentary tickets, and only quote what is pertinent—Mrs. Shelley's admission of her fear that she has made herself ridiculous :—

" I trust that I shall see you because I do not see why the visit should be so painful as you suppose, and truly hope that you will soon return to this country.

" Now, my dear Payne, tho' I am a little fool, do not make me appear so in the Rue Richelieu by repeating tales out of school—nor mention the Antediluvians. But I am not afraid; I am sure you love me well enough not to be accessory in making me appear ridiculous to one whom I like and esteem, though I am sure that the time and space between us will never be shortened. Perhaps it is that very certainty that makes me, female Quixote as I am, pay such homage to the unattainable Dulcinea in the Cueva de Montesinos, *i.e.* Rue Richelieu.

" But again be not a tell-tale. So God bless you! Give my love, of course Platonic, to I——."

There is a note of bitterness in Payne's answer, mingled, as it seems to one, with a note of exultation over the failure of the pursuit to which he had been sacrificed :—

" My dearest Friend,—I shall be on my way to Paris when you get this; I ought to have been so before, but annoyances detained me. I need not tell you how deep is my regret at leaving a place so much dearer to you than the one to which I am going, and then to know at the same time that I must be quite forgotten in your ' favourite,' and only stray upon your memory now and then to supply a supernumerary laugh when you and your excellent friend have exhausted the review of your acquaintances, making the people below stairs at No. 6 Mortimer Terrace wonder what two lone, disconsolate ladies can find to be so merry about ? Who will be your favoured escort now ? Who will go with you to see plays and keep your patience from rusting from want of use ? Who will love you with all his heart, and not quarrel with you or with himself when you tempt him to encourage a great disposition in you to love somebody else ?

383

THE ROMANTIC LIFE OF SHELLEY

" The admissions you desired are enclosed. I tried, but without success, to get the Lyceum ones undated, but it could not be. The opera, I fear, is impracticable. All the orders there are crowded out by money."

So the curtain falls; and one is left wondering whether, if Payne had returned to the attack, after Washington Irving had bowed himself out, he might not, after all, have triumphed. It is impossible to say; for he had either too little courage, or too much pride, to try; and though he continued occasionally to exchange letters with Mrs. Shelley for several years, the subsequent letters only deal with the subject of free admission to the theatre.

" I am," writes Mrs. Shelley, in the last letter of all, dated 1831, " an enthusiastic admirer of Paganini, and wish excessively to hear him; but the *tariff* they put on the boxes renders this impossible " . . . , etc., etc., etc.; which seems to show that the passion for going to places of public entertainment without paying was at least as strong in Mrs. Shelley as the passion for romance.

INDEX

385

INDEX

INDEX